ROOTS OF WISDOM

Other books by Claus Westermann
from Westminster John Knox Press

*Prophetic Oracles of Salvation in the
Old Testament*

Basic Forms of Prophetic Speech

Praise and Lament in the Psalms

Isaiah 40–66, A Commentary
(The Old Testament Library)

ROOTS OF WISDOM

The Oldest Proverbs of
Israel and Other Peoples

CLAUS WESTERMANN

 Westminster John Knox Press
Louisville, Kentucky

Translated from *Wurzeln der Weisheit*, © 1990 Vandenhoeck & Ruprecht, Göttingen

English translation © 1995 Westminster John Knox Press

Translated by J. Daryl Charles

Book design by Drew Stevens
Cover design by Susan E. Jackson

First edition

Published by Westminster John Knox Press
Louisville, Kentucky

This book is printed on acid-free paper that meets the American National Standards Institute Z39.48 standard. ∞

PRINTED IN THE UNITED STATES OF AMERICA

95 96 97 98 99 00 01 02 03 04 — 10 9 8 7 6 5 4 3 2 1

Library of Congress Cataloging-in-Publication Data

Westermann, Claus, date.
[Wurzeln der Weisheit. English]
Roots of wisdom : the oldest proverbs of Israel and other peoples, Claus Westermann : translated by J. Daryl Charles.—1st ed.
p. cm.
Includes bibliographic references.
ISBN (invalid) 0-664-25559-0 (alk. paper)
1. Bible. O.T. Proverbs—Criticism, interpretation, etc. 2. Wisdom literature—Criticism, interpretation, etc. I. Title.
BS1465.W4513 1995
223'.06—dc20
94-33664

CONTENTS

INTRODUCTION

I. THE EARLY PROVERBIAL WISDOM OF ISRAEL

Wisdom is a capacity that is inherent in human beings as persons. It is a human trait, an element of our createdness. Although people are not wise by virtue of being created, they are created with the potential of thinking, speaking, and acting wisely. This capacity cannot be denied anyone; in fact, it was once even said that animals could behave wisely (Prov. 30:24–28).

A distinctly worldly concept, wisdom—or a similar idea—is found among all peoples. Wisdom is something that unites people, rather than dividing them. Religious wars persist to this day, yet wars have never been conducted for the sake of wisdom and never will be. Wherever there is any discussion of wisdom, its value is recognized.

Wisdom is therefore also something that unites the Old and New Testaments. Jesus' expressions show that wisdom was a component of his language and proclamation, for many of his preserved sayings are wisdom sayings (see below).

That wisdom, a secular concept, should become a component of both Testaments of the Bible is due to the fact that it is inherent in creation—more specifically, human creation. The Creator bestowed on the human being the capability of finding his own way through life and of understanding himself (thus W. Zimmerli), of distinguishing between that which is good or evil, beneficial or destructive.[1] Because this capacity is bestowed on all, it is part of the universal narrative about human beings found in the Genesis 1—11 primeval history, taken as a whole, but appears also in the Psalms, the book of Job, Deutero-Isaiah, and many other passages that deal with the human journey from birth to death. Wisdom is related to God's actions of blessing, and so it can grow as it accompanies and dwells within a person. For this reason, it is

1

especially acknowledged among older persons, those "ripe in years." However, this is not to say that an older person, as such, is already wise or must necessarily be wise.

Inasmuch as this book deals specifically with the early wisdom of Israel, it does so with a particular purpose. It has become the custom to broaden the notion of wisdom considerably. Wisdom (here meaning not a human capacity but rather wisdom literature) has been said to encompass both parts of the book of Proverbs[1a]—chapters 1—9 and 10—31 (which are very different)—in addition to quite diverse writings such as Job, Qohelet, Sirach, and the Wisdom of Solomon, along with the Near Eastern wisdom writings. Furthermore, still other parts of the Old Testament are characterized as wisdom as well. One cannot arrive at a precise definition of wisdom if all these different works are included.[2]

A sure point of departure for identifying helpful, solid criteria is the fact that the collections of sayings in Proverbs 10:1–22:16 and 25—29 are generally recognized to be the earliest compilations and that the short sayings contained therein have a governing significance. We may proceed from the basic premise that the early wisdom of Israel has the form of short sayings. This concise one- or two-line form not only occurs here but is spread widely around the world in the proverbs of many peoples. These have had and continue to have their greatest importance among nonliterate peoples and tribes in many places. Among such groups, proverbs have the significance of a preliterary "literature" in an early stage. This stands to reason, inasmuch as these smallest units were thought to be appropriate for transmission. They are easily grasped, retained, and passed on.

These sayings arose orally out of the situation in which they were spoken. A clever (wise) person discovered an apt linguistic expression that was accepted by those listening to him.[3] Such expressions lived on, for they would be employed again in similar situations. Out of this there developed an art of shedding light on a new situation with a saying that had been handed down and was familiar to all. The possibilities of application were diverse, and so from the very beginning the sayings had a wide range of meanings. They remained alive because they were applied in such diverse ways.

Proverbs flowered worldwide in the era when traditions were not yet written down. During this period they had definite and essential social functions, necessary for communal life; moreover, they were the bearers of its most important traditions.

It is important to differentiate between these short sayings and the longer texts of literary discourse, such as poems about wisdom or didactic poems, which have their own intellectual coherence, originated in written form, and were handed down in similar fashion.

Initially, as a result of the collecting and recording of proverbs that had originated orally in an earlier stage and were subsequently handed down by word of mouth, two speech forms deriving from different origins merged and were bound together: the collection of didactic poems in Proverbs 1—9 was joined to the beginning of the compilation of Proverbs 10—31. Wisdom literature emerged as a result of both these processes: the collecting and then recording of proverbs previously handed down orally, and their being joined together with didactic poems. To a large extent this meant the end of the oral transmission of proverbs, even as these were now becoming written literature. One can neither understand nor explain the book of Proverbs, originating as it did in this way, without reviewing this process. One must examine both parts of the book, taking into account the particular types found there, each with its own derivation and history of transmission.

It is not the case that the texts in Proverbs 10—31 and 1—9 are to be differentiated from each other merely on the basis of short sayings on the one hand and longer sayings on the other. Rather, it is a question of two different types of texts. It is not correct that "the wisdom of Israel" is a particular illustration of Near Eastern wisdom (so J. Fichtner); such a notion would be much more applicable to Proverbs 1—9 alone.

Consequently, it is of fundamental importance to distinguish the early wisdom of Israel, whose form was the short saying, from the later wisdom of the longer didactic poem, which developed in written form. Between these two lies the invention of writing.[4]

II. HISTORY OF RESEARCH

A recent, thorough history of research has been offered by R. E. Murphy in "Wisdom Theses and Hypotheses" (1978). I am grateful to him for many helpful insights. I am supplementing his work only with regard to the last several years.[5]

One of the main questions in previous research has been the matter of wisdom's origin: Did it grow out of oral folk wisdom or was it the work of wisdom teachers in schools? The former was presupposed at the beginning of the century, the latter in more recent research (e.g., G. von Rad and H. J. Hermisson). Countering the one-sided view that proverbs came from scholastic wisdom are H. W. Wolff, E. Gerstenberger, C. Westermann, and J. M. Thompson, the last of whom also emphasizes the universal character of proverbs.

Contra H. J. Hermisson (a student of Gerhard von Rad), whose one-sided view of proverbs as having originated in wisdom schools is linked to the rejection of any connection with folk wisdom, C. R. Fontaine (*Traditional Sayings in the Old Testament,* 1982) points to the use of proverbs in historical texts in the Old Testament and shows that at an early date (i.e., starting about the time of the Judges) they were circulated and well known, that they had a function in conversations about analogous situations, and that they were handed down orally. Her work agrees with that of O. Eissfeldt in *Der Maschal im Alten Testament* (1913).

Several recent works reflect this return to explaining proverbial wisdom of the Old Testament in terms of its connection with orally transmitted folk wisdom. C. Westermann, in "Weisheit im Sprichwort" (1971), argues the case that the genus of proverbs had its heyday in preliterary cultures. F. Golka (1983) concurs, making reference to the golden age of Near Eastern literary cultures and the lack of evidence that would clearly substantiate the existence of wisdom schools in preexilic Israel. He cites similarities in African royal proverbs as evidence for the view that the royal proverbs found in the Old Testament originated in folk culture. In *Menschenschöpfung und Weltschöpfung* (1985), P. Doll found that the creation of the world is referred to only in the later wisdom material of Proverbs 1—9, while mention of human creation is present only in the earlier proverbial wisdom, where it has a demonstrably social function. In his work *Those Who Ponder Proverbs* (1981), J. G. Williams starts with the assumption of oral transmission. Remaining opposed to this position is H. D. Preuss (*Einführung in die alttestamentliche Weisheit,* 1987), who holds to the view of von Rad and H. J. Hermisson.

This survey of the history of research reveals that, for the present, there is divergence concerning the question of the roots of wisdom. One strand of scholarship works from the premise that the wisdom texts of the Old Testament are to be seen as a special form of Near Eastern wisdom, such as one finds in the Egyptian and Mesopotamian wisdom writings. The other strand begins by insisting that there is such a thing as proverbial wisdom (or wisdom in proverbs), which is encountered not only in the Near East and, in a later stage of development, here in the Old Testament but also around the world—especially in cultures that are still preliterate.

Another distinction is closely related. The one stream of research proceeds on the basis of the literary form of wisdom, for it is seen as literature from the outset. The other stream assumes an early stage of development and transmission of sayings; hence, one must investigate the actual function of individual sayings in the oral phase of transmission, as well as ask about their application in the life of the community (so, in particular, C. R. Fontaine).

Many attempts have been made to identify definite points in the transmission of wisdom that reveal its trajectory, and two such fixed reference points have emerged. One is the recording during the time of Hezekiah of proverbs that had previously been passed down orally (Prov. 25:1). The second is the transition to literary composition of the didactic poem as found in Proverbs 1—9.

A difference in approach is also due to the fact that the scholars who presume Near Eastern wisdom literature are operating deductively on the basis of abstract, general conceptions, notably a classification taken directly from Egyptian wisdom literature (*ma'at*),[6] with wisdom understood in an abstract sense or as teaching. For those scholars, however, who assume an early oral stage for proverbs, an (inductive) explanation of individual sayings comes into play, whereby their function in the community and consequent classification according to groups is investigated.

The universal character of proverbs retains its significance by such investigation of the function of individual proverbs in the community. In this way, the proverbs of cultures that are still not literate can provide significant help for our understanding. However, this resource is overlooked when proverbs are seen only as literature.

Finally, it can be said that only when the universal character of proverbs is recognized can one see the close connection between what the proverbs say about God and the human being and what is said in the primeval history narrative in Genesis 1—11, which has the same universal character.

The differences in approach described above presuppose that only in the proverbs (which, at an early stage, were once orally transmitted) are the roots of the wisdom of ancient Israel to be found. The didactic poems of scholastic wisdom found in Proverbs 1—9, on the other hand, reflect a later stage in which Near Eastern wisdom literature exercised a notable influence.

1. PROVERBIAL STATEMENTS

I. PROVERBS OF OBSERVATION
AND EXPERIENCE

1. Observations about People

One of the two primary intentions of these approximately thirty proverbs is to convey the human drive for knowledge, for a person understanding himself in his world. "World" here is not to be interpreted as some abstract, general concept of the universe but strictly as the world of the person, insofar as it is accessible to his perception. In both realms—in his human existence and in the environment in which he lives—there is much that is puzzling. In both there is much for him to observe, to recognize, and to understand. However, this is not accomplished summarily, easily, or in a generalized way; rather, it occurs as he takes one groping step after another, for humanity is on a journey of learning, observing, and questioning.[7] Once something is observed, it is shaped into a sentence in proverbial form, enabling it to be preserved and passed on. Thus originate proverbs, each one embodying an observation about humanity. Hence, the scope of the observations encompasses both one's world and one's fellow creatures. Much can be expressed about these things through proverbs. Yet observation and discovery are always present, so that with regard to further subjects and areas, proverbs can be understood to be a deposit of observation or discovery—which is how they in fact arose. Proverbial statements as a whole, therefore, regardless of their subject matter, always involve this fundamental process of observation to a greater or lesser degree. They point to something that we do not otherwise encounter in the Old Testament: contemplative reflection on humanity and on the reality that surrounds it. This act of reflecting is a sort of precursor to philosophy, in which (as with Socrates) the results are less important than the questioning itself. Such questioning does

6

not remain fixed at what is known; rather, it seeks to move beyond it, into the realm of the new, which has not yet been uncovered. It perceives with amazement what is made accessible to the inquisitive mind: "The lamp of Yahweh is the breath of man; it searches out his innermost being" (20:27). "As water reflects a face, so our human heart reflects another" (27:19).

The first of these sayings is clearly recognizable as an observation of someone for whom the significance of human breath is not self-evident. This person takes note and asks himself, What, really, is breath? A comparison aids his reflection, in much the same way that it helps children in their observations: "Oh, that's like. . . ." Breath is compared with a light that shines in a dark chamber. This comparison enables him to express what has been discovered by observing breath: namely, that through its rhythms breath streams through the unknown, innermost parts of the body. The comparison indicates the discovery of the circulation inherent to breathing. Initially occurring in conversation, this statement strikes those hearing it as pertinent. The comparison resonates with the listeners' experience; thus they preserve it and pass it on to others.

The proverb in 27:19 is closely related to that in 20:27. This one discovery, which was the product of someone's observation, may have resulted from a sudden and unique experience, or it may have resulted from a longer series of observations. It dawned on someone that no human face is exactly the same as another—not even in the case of twins. Out of this observation a conclusion is to be drawn: this is valid not only for faces but for the whole person: "In the same way people's hearts are different." It is a discovery of the uniqueness that belongs to and distinguishes every person. This individuality, which no one can remove, for God has created people in this way, is a fact reflected by the diversity of human faces!

In these two proverbs, we encounter a kind of speech about being a creature that is quite different from what we are accustomed to in our Christian tradition. The question of how God created human beings or how human creation happened is totally foreign here. Humankind is simply present; man is beginning to understand himself as a creature and notice how wonderful it is to be human. Does the fact that an individual becomes aware of himself not bestow on the person a unique worth? This discovery must proceed in and of itself. In fact, even the person who encounters me and whom I speak to and have to do with on a daily basis—this person is unique. Should I then not see that person as such? Talk about human worth and respecting human worth is serious when it is one's own discovery, when it is not merely some worn-out expression on other people's lips. In the same way, one's relationship to one's own body necessarily changes when we speak in this manner about human breath and ponder it as it occurs here.

Proverbs are not words that I take cognizance of and then store away in a drawer as knowledge that I now happen to possess. If one does not reflect at length on a proverb, it remains inaccessible.

To these observations about humanity can be added still others. Nevertheless, through these two it becomes very apparent why the book of Proverbs has been included in the canon.

The Creator has entrusted his creature, the human, with this gift because he reckons him capable of finding his way through the world, using the special endowment given to him of understanding his own humanness. Proverbs ascribe the importance to the human intellect that it is due. They express an autonomy that is rooted in creatureliness,[8] in contradistinction to a conception that places too great an emphasis on education and instruction. Already in these proverbs we see that they have a different conception of wisdom than is found in the later wisdom, where full stress is laid on instruction. Identifying wisdom with teaching here would be a fundamental error.

The manner of human self-understanding here, albeit not expressly stated (designating breath as the "lamp of the Lord" has this ring), resembles that in Psalm 139, which, even though it is a prayer, is spoken in the face of God.[9] When the one praying here says, "I thank you that I am so wonderfully made" (v. 14) and "When I was made in the secret place, woven together in the depths of the earth" (v. 15), it presumes the same observant meditation as is expressed in the proverbs: "It is too wonderful and incomprehensible for me" (v. 6). The inquisitive and astonishing awareness of creatureliness links the psalm to the proverbs of observation (cf. also Ps. 94:9).

To this can be added a number of proverbs that arose from human observation—for example, 27:20: "As Hades and the abyss are never satisfied, neither are the eyes of man."

Here is an observation about humanity that is immediately intelligible to us without any difficulty. One initially marvels that such a "worldly" appearing statement is found in the Bible, that is, that at one time, early on, such a thought was conceived by an Israelite and then admitted to the canon by a later editor. We can only conclude that these people thought and spoke in a much worldlier fashion than it appears to the interpreters and readers of the Old Testament. It is a bold comparison that is being ventured here—"Hades and the abyss"—truly insatiable when we consider the huge number of those who are deceased! It appears severe when one compares with that the insatiability of our eyes, which never get enough. The correspondence of this saying to one of the numerical proverbs—"There are three things that are never satisfied, four that never say enough" (30:15–16)—reveals that reflecting on insatiability must have occupied others and on various levels. Even more conspicuous in both cases is the seeming absence of any indication of condemnation that might appear in the Christian ethic of many; rather, this phenomenon is viewed as something that is inherently human, whether one perceives it as good or not. Such an observation applies to all the proverbial statements, especially those about humanity. They intend to express, not condemn, the nature of being human.

"The purposes of a man's heart are deep waters, but a man of understanding draws them out" (20:5). This is one of those sayings about which it is difficult to tell whether the second verse originally belonged to the saying or was added on subsequently to create a parallelism. Thus, the interpretation can proceed along different lines. Verse 5a could be an independent saying, since it contains both sides of a comparison. Moreover, this saying expresses an observation. The person who uttered it has observed how someone else over time has concealed an intention, a purpose, or a plan; no one perceived what he intended. But when the intention is executed, it becomes apparent that it indeed was planned over time. Without any words of explanation, the proverb shows the difference between a person who continually lives merely from hand to mouth, whatever might come, and a person who is capable of laying hold of a purpose, calmly and quietly moving toward his goal. What the addition in v. 5b means is not certain; perhaps the wise person is one who has intuited what was to come and prepared himself accordingly. The proverb, however, has a more pointed effect without the addition. Once again, it is a thoroughly "worldly" phenomenon that for the author has value; it is this mystery of human creatureliness that is important to him. An African proverb is very similar: "The heart of a man is a sea" (see the Appendix). This parallel is evidence that Prov. 20:5a was at one time an independent saying.[9a]

"As a bird that strays from its nest, so is the man who strays from his home" (27:8). This is another saying that one would not expect in the Old Testament scriptures. It sounds much more like the songs found among various peoples that have the theme of yearning for home, much the same way that 27:20 (". . . neither are the eyes of man satisfied") is reminiscent of Gottfried Keller's "Abendlied": "Eyes, my dear little windows, take in what the eyelashes can keep of the world's golden plenty." Thus we encounter once more the purely secular orientation of the proverbs, just as they occur in songs and poems of our own time. In both cases, the sayings possess a poetic or near-poetic character. Similarly, in both it is creation that is involved in the comparisons: the observation of a bird leads to further reflection on being human.[10]

Reflection on humanity, based on a collection of observations, also sheds light on a saying in Jeremiah that corresponds to this group of proverbs: "The heart is a deceitful and corrupt thing. Who can fathom it?" (Jer. 17:9).[11] Here also is the amazing perception of the unfathomable nature of being human.

"The crucible for silver and the furnace for gold, but man is tested by his praise" (27:21). The furnace and crucible affect the production of a metal's genuineness and purity. Refinement is attained by means of the fire. This is the meaning of the second line of the proverb, though it is implicit. The comparison clearly shows that behind the good reputation stands the refining fire.

This saying affords insight into its function or *Sitz im Leben*. It is addressed to a relatively small circle of people in which everyone knows everyone else. In this context, one obtains a good reputation not through riches, not through connections, and not even through exceptional individual acheivements. A good reputation is possessed by that individual who has had his share of experiences and who has shown himself as having withstood the test, so that he stands steadfast before people with whom he lives. Job, for example, is depicted in this way. This proverb could have such a man in mind.

"As iron sharpens iron, so one man sharpens another" (27:17). The observation and experience out of which this proverb grew are obvious. One should not, however, read into it a universal condition or truth. Rather, out of the experience of the speaker comes this saying: namely, that through sloppiness, indulgence, and a lack of rigor trouble is caused and the corporate life of a community is endangered. The saying intends to call the weak and the indulgent to reflection. It is an expressly critical saying, though in the form not of a warning but of a reference to reality that should be heeded.[11a]

Let us take note of something at this point. In many proverbs, creaturely self-understanding is based on the Creator's gift of critical thought. This thinking does not allow itself to be deluded by superficial behavior; rather, it practices a sharp and critical discernment where it is necessary. We see this when the prophets of judgment confront the prophets of salvation. A disposition that is only benevolent and always pleasant to one's neighbor can, under certain conditions, do much harm; "iron is sharpened by iron."

There are many other proverbs that, though placed in other categories due to other characteristics, are based on observations about humanity. Here belongs a small group of paradoxes:[12] "Even in laughter the heart may ache" (14:13). "Each heart knows its own bitterness, and no one else can share its joy" (14:10). "He who oppresses the poor to increase his own wealth and he who gives gifts to the rich—both come to poverty" (22:16). "Perfume and incense bring joy to the heart, but the soul is torn by trouble" (27:9).

Many individual proverbs in other groupings belong to this category as well; for example, "'It's bad, it's bad!' says the buyer, then off he goes and boasts about his purchase" (20:14). "A worker's appetite works for him, for his hunger drives him on" (16:26).

Many others are similar, including 12:18; 13:12; 15:30; 17:22; and perhaps 20:9: "Who can say, 'I have kept my heart pure; I am clean and without sin'?" This last proverb, however, sounds a bit strange surrounded by the other observations about people. Strictly speaking, this is not an observation, rather a critical question. It is possible that this is a corrective gloss on 20:7: "The righteous man leads a blameless life; blessed are his children after him."

Even a few proverbs on instruction belong to this group: 17:10; 20:11; 22:6; 18:19.

"Anger is cruel and wrath is overwhelming, but who can stand before jealousy?" (27:4).[13] This proverb is no comparison; rather, it contains an intensification similar to the proverbs of valuation. Yet it expresses an observation that can, in certain instances, be essential for the community. Wrath and anger are outbursts that in most cases are overt. Jealousy, on the other hand, must conceal itself. As a result, its manifestation can be much more devastating.

We would describe this, whether rightly or not, as a psychological observation. The issue here, however, is psychology not in the sense of dogma or theory but rather as a practical and tested observation. While this is not valid in all situations, in a community of people such as a small town there is a need to draw attention to a particular complex of behaviors in order to prevent something dreadful from happening. The speaker does not necessarily seek agreement with his views. He does hope, however, that his listeners will be moved to reflection and consequently to cooperation, so that this danger is confronted.

A human observation containing no comparison is also found in 20:11: "Even a child is known by his actions, whether his conduct is pure and right."

This category of proverbs makes it especially clear that every single proverb calls for specific reflection—something that J. G. Williams expresses in the title of his book *Those Who Ponder Proverbs* (1981).

2. Contrasts

Joy and Sorrow

Of the ten proverbs that allude to joy and sorrow, only one speaks of joy alone. In the rest, joy and sorrow stand in polarity to each other. It should be noted that the form coheres with the subject here as well.[14] In addition, there are numerous other polarities. A particularly significant feature of proverbs is on display here—one that is characteristic of the anthropology of the Old Testament. A human being is never determined by an unchanging mode of existence; he is always moving in a force field, as it were, between two poles. The createdness of humanity is the reason for this. Being a creature means moving from birth to death. From birth on, the power of blessing is at work, a life force in the creature that awakens joy. Death, on the other hand, brings a life-stopping force to bear on one's existence. Precisely how the power that causes sorrow and that which causes joy take effect is impossible to establish. Hence, there are innumerable possibilities and situations in which joy and sorrow are related to each other. This abundance of possibilities is observed and described in the proverbs: "An anxious heart weighs a man down, but a kind word cheers him up" (12:25). "A happy heart makes the face cheerful, but heartache crushes the spirit" (15:13). "A cheerful heart is good medicine, but a crushed spirit dries up the bones" (17:22). "All the days of the oppressed are wretched, but the cheerful heart has a continual feast" (15:15).

One might consider these sayings to be simple, indeed banal; but to understand them, it is necessary to ask about their purpose. These are observations that are designed to call attention to the fact that, on the one hand, joy and suffering touch the whole person in body and soul and that, on the other hand, they define human life. The preacher in Qohelet 3 says it well: "a time to laugh and a time to weep." This alternation of joy and sorrow, given the nature of human existence, is appropriate; neither of these should constitute a permanent condition without the other. To those who would have said or heard these words, it would have seemed meaningless and foolish if someone was to exhort others to constant joy or to idealize joy ("Joy, that beautiful sparkle of the gods"), thereby drowning out the rhythm of joy and sorrow. The use of polar opposites in Qohelet 3—joy and sorrow, poor and rich, hunger and satiation, and so forth—is framed as a poem. Here the relationship of poetry to proverbs is illustrated quite well. The proverb in each case says something about an actual situation to which it is related; for example, 12:25: anxiety in the heart—a kind word. In Qohelet 3, the polarity as such becomes the actual theme: diversity is fashioned into a whole. Thus, both the derivation of the poem from proverbs and the transition from individual proverb to a reflective poem (the wisdom poem) are conspicuous. The poem is wisdom in a way other than the proverb from which it stems. The proverbs developed orally; the poems, literarily.[15]

Moreover, this group of proverbs shares a common understanding of humanity with the Psalms. In the Psalter, the pairing of psalms of lament with psalms of praise parallels the duality of joy and sorrow in Proverbs; praise is the language of joy, and lament is the language of sorrow.[16]

In one group of proverbs, there is indication not only that joy and sorrow succeed each other in a temporal sense but that they can also stand in tension with each other: "Even in laughter the heart may ache, and joy may end in grief" (14:13). "A man's spirit may sustain him in sickness, but a crushed spirit—who can bear it?" (18:14). "Each heart knows its own bitterness, and no one else can share its joy" (14:10). "Perfume and incense bring joy to the heart, but the soul is torn by trouble" (27:9).

Here are preserved two observations that point to substrata beneath the surface of a feigned joy. Tragic conflicts are suggested in both, where sorrow as well as joy lies concealed deep within: "Even in laughter the heart may ache"; "Each heart knows its own bitterness." When, in the process of pondering these words, one instinctively inquires into the situations in which such words could have been spoken and heard, he has hit on the proximity of these and similar proverbs to narratives. Indeed, a story has been condensed and concentrated in a proverb. It is true that one cannot reconstruct these narratives; however, the motif of the proverb suffices to represent the underlying story.[17]

If we find reminiscences of folk songs in other groups of proverbs and we encounter here what would seem to be narratives, then we have established— or at the very least, made likely—the close proximity between certain prover-bial statements and what we have come to call poetry. Songs and stories were integral to people's lives in ancient Israel and among other peoples, in the same way that they are a part of our lives—namely, secular songs and stories, which unquestionably were orally received among nonliterate peoples. The very fact that they existed is evidenced by certain proverbs that contain reminiscences of stories and songs.[18] This, too, illustrates the orientation of the proverbs to-ward the world.

"A cheerful look brings joy to the heart; good news refreshes the bones" (15:30). This is the lone proverb in which joy and sorrow do not stand in polarity, although this contrast does stand in the background and helps convey the sense of the saying. This saying, too, has grown out of an observation, probably out of a frequently occurring observation that finally came to be ex-pressed in this saying. It had struck the formulator of this proverb how sudden and astonishing a change had taken place within the sad, sorrowful person— a change effected merely by a cheerful look or good news. Yet with this alone, the proverb is not yet really intelligible; as to the form of the saying, this would be too little. The observation of the speaker encompasses the other side as well: he has observed frequently that a cheerful look and a good word that might have made the day of one who was suffering were left undone. Thus we may assume that the proverb is intended for those who need to be reminded of what a cheerful look or good news in and of itself can accomplish in the case of a depressed person. One notable refinement is contained in the two-fold parallelism—heart–body, look–word—indicating that 15:30 arose as a double-verse saying, whereas that cannot be said with certainty about 15:13. This latter saying needs to be heard together with the group of proverbs that advocate compassion for the lowly. Human awareness is a part of doing good.[19]

"Hope deferred makes the heart sick, but a longing fulfilled is a tree of life" (13:12). "A cheerful heart is good medicine, but a crushed spirit dries up the bones" (17:22). Both of these proverbs are examples of how profound this re-flection on joy and sorrow can be, as well as how thoroughly penetrating one's observation of their relationship to each other can become. On the positive side, we note the importance of the unity of body and soul: a cheerful heart has the power to heal. On the negative side, if a person looks forward to something too much, then the "hope deferred" is capable of "capsizing" that person in sorrow. What was mentioned earlier concerning the close proximity of proverb and narrative can be applied to both of the above proverbs: both are quite capable of expressing the core element of stories.

Hunger and Satiation

"The one who is full loathes honey; to the one who is hungry, even what is bitter tastes sweet" (27:7; cf. Ahiqar 188, *ANET,* 430: "Hunger makes bitterness sweet").

Not only do polar opposites speaking of joy and sorrow surface, but those relating to hunger and thirst arise as well. Proverbs 27:7 is a good example of how one's orientation to eating and drinking is dependent on one's experience; they are a part of one's history. To be hungry or full is not merely a state that one can determine or secure. As experiences of a human life, hunger and satiation are determined by heights and depths. "Food gained by deceit is sweet to a man, but afterward his mouth will be full of gravel" (20:17).

This sounds like a scene out of a humorous tale that elicits laughter from the listeners—a scene in which a rascal's prank has gone amiss. Humor is an important element in this particular contrast.[19a]

Each example of this sort of contrast can be numbered as well with those in the category of human observations.

The Good and the Evil Word

Proverbs of speech are very capable of demonstrating that in the Old Testament, speech is foremost an event. Not merely the content of what is being said but the actual occurrence transpiring between speaker and hearer,[20] rooted in a given situation, has primacy: "a word aptly spoken" (25:11; also 12:14; 25:12–20 on untimeliness; 26:2; 27:14). In all of the proverbs, speech is conceived as something that is an oral event befalling people. What is assessed as prudent in these sayings is speech that in a particular situation is good, fitting, and helpful (e.g., 12:25), not speech that is consciously thought out and subsequently written down, having significance due to its content alone. Such an understanding of speech stands in fundamental contrast to the notion that it is foremost the expression of a thought or idea. This Greek conceptualization of speech is foreign to Proverbs.[21]

Without exception, these proverbs concern themselves with transactions between persons—persons who live in one another's midst. The wisdom being signified here is that capacity which allows the one speaking to utter the appropriate word at the appropriate moment or, when necessary, to be still. A maxim is never a trite form of speech; rather, it is always pertinent. There exists, then, a correlation between this group of proverbs that observes a good word spoken at the right time and the function of proverbs in general. This category of proverbs alone is evidence that the majority of proverbs arose orally.[22] One considers as well the frequent occurrence of metaphors such as mouth, lips, and tongue. These metaphors are intended to assess not the mere content of what is being said, rather the transaction of speaking itself. Hence, the entire group of proverbs about speech is indirectly related to human observations. Even those comparisons that are taken from daily life are directed at the speech event. They demonstrate the purity and success of speech that is likened to "apples of gold in settings of silver"; they demonstrate as well the artificiality of speech that is "as earthenware coated with silver glaze": "A word aptly spoken is like apples of gold in settings of silver" (25:11). "Like a ring of gold or an ornament of gold is a wise man's rebuke to a listening ear" (25:12). "A man finds joy in giving an apt reply—and how good is a timely word!" (15:23). "A cheerful look brings joy to the heart, and good news gives health to the bones" (15:30). "An honest answer is like a kiss on the lips" (24:26). "The tongue of the righteous is choice silver" (10:20). "The words of a man's mouth are deep waters" (18:4). "Through patience a ruler can be persuaded, and a gentle tongue can break a bone" (25:15).

Inasmuch as a fitting word at the proper time meets up with so many variations in Proverbs, we realize how important this notion was to those speaking and listening. The value of speech is measured according to what it accomplishes in common, everyday life.[23] In this regard, there is another facet to be observed: that which is appropriate, that which is fitting, is at the same time beautiful speech. This is conveyed clearly in the comparisons of 25:11; 25:12; 10:20 (something precious); 24:26 (a kiss on the lips); and 16:24 (honeycomb). This sort of speech produces joy (12:25 and 15:23). That appropriate speech is simultaneously beautiful speech finds correspondence in the Greek *kalós k'agathós* as well as the Hebrew *tôb*, which can signify "good" as well as "beautiful." In these proverbs, what is proper correlates closely to what is beautiful. The realm of the aesthetic is not some other, special realm; one has pleasure in that which is appropriate and that which is beautiful. It is a thing of beauty when one succeeds in offering an appropriate response (12:15, 23); people delight in this as over a costly vessel (25:11).[24]

All of these sayings represent moments in the outworking of an event. We have no real difficulty imagining the situation in which they may have been spoken. In a number of these, the situation is even hinted at—for example, in 25:12, "a wise man's rebuke to a listening ear," where a word as a necessary warning prevents something bad. In 25:15, the audience will recall having experienced something similar.

It becomes apparent that this proverb was set together subsequently; vv. 15a and 15b are capable of having stood as independent sayings.

"Pleasant words are as honeycomb, sweet to the soul and health to the bones" (16:24). "A fountain of life is the mouth of the righteous" (10:11). "A patient tongue is a tree of life" (15:4). Each of these proverbs says something about good speech, related in part to godly wisdom (cf. esp. 18:4b).

In 16:24, "pleasant words are as honeycomb," we find the remarkable observation that appropriate speech is a healing force for the whole person—body and soul.

Most of the proverbs about appropriate speech have the form of a comparison, similar to the proverbs of human observation, with which they are closely related. With regard to form, both kinds of proverbs conform to the pattern of using analogies of thought.

Perverse, Destructive Speech

The proverbs of this group are also closely linked to those of human observation: "Reckless words pierce like a sword" (12:18a; 18b is a later supplement; cf. the African proverb: "Your mouth will turn into a knife"). "As the north wind brings rain, so a backbiting tongue brings angry looks" (25:23). "It is a snare for someone to make a vow rashly" (20:25). "Like a fluttering sparrow, like a darting swallow, an undeserved curse does not come to nest" (26:2).

We also encounter in this category witty proverbs that generate the same effect as those about words not spoken at the proper time: "As vinegar poured over a wound, so is the one who sings to a heavy heart" (25:20). "Death and life are in the power of the tongue" (18:21; cf. James 3:1–12). "There are those whose teeth are swords and whose jaws are knives" (30:14; cf. a similar saying found in the teaching of Merikare: "The tongue is like a sword, and speech is mightier than fighting").

The proverbs about perverse, damaging speech are closely related to human observations and also have the form of a comparison. (Further proverbs about speech—of both beneficial and damaging varieties—will be noted in the section dealing with characterization.) Malicious and devious speech belong to the proverbs of antithesis concerning the foolish and the wise. All of these sayings are aimed at the community, which is damaged by hurtful and disgraceful speech. In the background of 12:18 and 30:14 is the awareness of the extent to which people can be wounded through speech. This awareness has as its basis an esteem for human worth.

A shift in cultural perception becomes evident through the proverbs about wholesome and damaging speech. As seen in their polarity to each other, proverbs portray culture as the nurturing of speech in corporate life. They call attention to speech that is good, fitting, and beautiful, at the same time cautioning against what is destructive and harmful. According to modern sensibilities, all this would seem rather unimportant, since the cultivation of speech has been radically and completely objectified. This aspect of culture has shifted to the realms of literature, art, and educational institutions, where those doing the speaking are active and those listening are passive. The cultivation of speech, sadly, has evolved so that it is to be found not where people interact but rather where someone is explaining something to someone else. Society is fragmented into those who create culture and those who consume culture. This tendency is heightened in a powerful way by the mass media. Yet, in the process, we forget what actually constitutes the cultivation of speech. It is the *colere,* the nurturing of speech and interpersonal communication. Further, it respects what is beneficial and appropriate, and like the proverbs, it is repulsed by speech that is damaging and detrimental.

3. The Human Being and Its Social Standing, Work, and Possessions

The Work of the Farmer

The people among whom these proverbs originated lived by the work of their own hands. They were farmers, husbandmen, craftsmen, housewives, and servants.

On the other hand, priests and Levites, scribes, and civil servants are never mentioned in these sayings. It is a prosaic, stable, civil world into which these sayings lead us. Work, especially manual labor, is highly respected. We find no indication that any type of work is belittled or despised, nor that one vocational class looks down at another.[25] Work is never idealized. It is acknowledged to be both hard and difficult and, at the same time, an absolute necessity: "A worker's appetite works for him, for his mouth drives him on" (16:26).

An agrarian principle of life such as "first the work, then the feast" occurs here as well: "Finish your work outside and get your fields ready; then build your house" (24:27).

Where work is mentioned without any specific description, cultivating the field is almost always meant. It is work, per se. Texts such as 28:19; 10:5; 12:11 presuppose this as well. The raising of livestock is included in this; hence the short poem in 27:23–27. The basic attitude being conveyed is that "a righteous man cares for the needs of his animal" (12:10).

Other types of work are occasionally encountered (e.g., an artisan in 22:29).

However, never is there anything specific mentioned about a particular trade, as in the German expression, "Cobbler, remain at your work" (although such can be found in Sumerian proverbs).

What is striking is that where other types of work are mentioned elsewhere, they correspond only to the wicked and appear in the context of merely being recognized. The reason for this, at least in part, is the preeminence accorded to speech. "Like the cold of snow at harvesttime is a faithful messenger to those who send him" (25:13).

The faithful and the faithless messenger stand in bold contrast: "The villainous messenger plunges men into trouble, but a trustworthy envoy brings healing" (13:17).

Joy is produced as a result of the good news: "A cheerful look brings joy to the heart; good news refreshes the bones" (15:30). "Like cold water to a languishing soul, so is good news from a far country" (25:25).

Also, we find the wicked messenger being rebuked: "Like vinegar to the teeth and smoke to the eyes, so is the sluggard to those who send him" (10:26). "Like cutting off one's feet or drinking violence is the sending of a messenger by the hand of a fool" (26:6).

This repeated mention of the messenger found in Proverbs presupposes the great significance of the messenger in the ancient world (see C. Westermann [1964]).

The Idle and the Diligent

Of the seventeen texts given to the idle and the diligent, ten present them in the form of an antithesis. They are seen as polar opposites; they are understood and considered in this contrast, standing in juxtaposition to each other. "A slack hand causes poverty, but the hand of the diligent brings wealth" (10:4). "He who tills his land will have plenty of bread, but he who follows worthless pursuits has no sense" (12:11). "The idle man does not catch his prey, but the diligent man will accrue wealth" (12:27). "In all hard work there is profit, but mere talk leads only to want" (14:23). "The one gathering in summer is prudent, but the one sleeping during harvest brings shame" (10:5). "The way of the idle is overgrown with thorns, but the path of the diligent has been leveled" (15:19). "The idle man does not plow in the autumn, so at harvesttime he looks but finds nothing" (20:4). "The hand of the diligent will rule, while the slothful will be put to forced labor" (12:24). "The idle man craves yet gets nothing, while the desire of the diligent is fully satisfied" (13:4).

In this contrast, it should be noted that diligence is viewed as a means of upward social mobility in only one of these proverbs—12:24, "the hand of the diligent will rule." Even the statement "the hand of the diligent brings wealth"

(10:4) is foremost a statement not about surpassing riches but about having enough: "He will have enough bread" (12:11). We find in these sayings no antagonistic censure of the lazy; they are not subject to a stern condemnation. Rather, in the proverbs they are reminded in sober fashion of the consequences of their idleness. As it is, they are tolerated in the community; they are part of it. Idleness is something human, and there will always exist the opposites of the idle and the diligent. The patient toleration of the idle and of sloth is particularly communicated in the abundant caricatures that are aimed at them—for example, 26:15 ("The idle man buries his hand in the dish, yet he is too lazy to bring it back to his mouth") and 26:14. Proverbs 15:19 ("The way of the idle is overgrown with thorns") is precisely this kind of ridicule; the second half of the saying, "the path of the diligent has been leveled," is a subsequent addition for the sake of parallelism. We may also note 22:13: "The idle man says, 'There is a lion outside!'" The aforementioned proverbs of scorn—26:15; 26:14; 15:19a; and 22:13—are distinguished from other proverbs contrasting the idle and the diligent inasmuch as they say something only about the idle. They possess the form of a characterization. A number of other sayings belong to this category as well: "Laziness brings on deep sleep, and an idle person goes hungry" (19:15). "Drunkards and gluttons become poor, and drowsiness clothes them in rags" (23:21). "Whoever is slack in his work is a brother to him who destroys" (18:9). "Like vinegar to the teeth and smoke to the eyes, so is the sluggard to those who send him" (10:26).

Moreover, in 20:13 we encounter a general warning against idleness: "Do not love sleep, lest you grow poor; open your eyes and you will have plenty of food."

The proverbs about the idle and the diligent bear consistent testimony that steady, industrious work performed where one is planted is right, good, and brings the promise of success. When a person through subtlety, audacity, or violence quickly gains wealth, such is without exception held to be suspect and is not esteemed, since riches thus accumulated are incapable of bringing blessing.

The proverbs about the idle and the diligent are important for an understanding of the book of Proverbs as a whole, because they reflect so clearly the character of a people's folk wisdom. These sayings—particularly with their humor—are absolutely genuine in the sense that they are not thought out. Rather, they emerge from a specific situation to which they speak. They presuppose an audience that has experienced in its surrounding world the contrast of the idle and the diligent just as we find it described here—a description that causes its hearers to laugh. The echo of this laughter is preserved in these proverbs to such an extent that even today we still can appreciate it. Such clever formulations are a sure indication of an oral beginning for such sayings. Wit is most effective when it is spoken to someone. When it is in written or printed form, wit is effective when it is retold, as is often the case, for example, with political satire. Mention of the idle and the diligent has been a universal part of proverbial folk sayings for millennia. It has retained its form because of its suitability. To maintain the contrary, that there are no proverbial folk sayings in the Old Testament, only didactic literature or maxims that a group of sages had contrived, is scarcely tenable. No one familiar with proverbial folk sayings of other milieus, times, and places would concur. Over and above this, if the proverbs concerning the idle and the diligent had, in fact, arisen in the context of a school of sages where they had been in use, then one would have to assume that idleness and diligence were occurring in the school during the actual learning process. Such, however, was not the case.

On the contrary, we find mention of the idle and the diligent in a small circle of people living together in the same place where all are dependent on the work of their hands. Indeed, the same is still true today. One thinks of neighbors whose fields or gardens border on one another. This sort of discourse belongs to everyday life, and the contrast presented here is confined to the realm of ordinary language. This can be further seen by the fact that idleness is not the object of commands or laws.[26]

All of the proverbs concerning the idle and the diligent apply to the sphere of agriculture (even though the contrast is valid for many other types of work). Likely, this is because, at a time when agriculture and cattle breeding were predominant, farming was deemed the primary work, since it was indispensable for maintaining a normal living. It is probable that craftsmen carried on some farming on the side, and vice versa.

In 26:13–16, we find a small collection containing proverbs concerning the idle: "The idle man says, 'There is a lion in the road! A fierce lion is roaming the street!'" "As a door turns on its hinges, so a sluggard turns on his bed." "The idle man buries his hand in a dish, yet he is too lazy to bring it back to his mouth."

Humor and ridicule characterize the idle in vv. 13–15. This characterization consists of one or two main points. The remark in v. 13b, "a fierce lion is roaming the street," is added to accommodate the parallelism. One-sided proverbs are also found in 18:9; 19:15; and 20:4. There are a number of sayings comparing the idle and the diligent that give the impression that half of the verse was added on at a later time—for example, 28:19, "The one tilling his land will have plenty of food, but the one following worthless pursuits will have plenty of poverty." Here the structure of the comparison is artificial and yet is effective. There are quite a few examples of such artificially constructed proverbs of comparison, most of which, however, due to their mere verbal repetition, sound prosaic. In some instances, the two halves do not correspond at all to each other—for example, 21:5, "The plans of the diligent bring an abundance, but whoever is hasty suffers want." It is also possible to identify a secondary connection in 10:5; 12:17; 19:15; and 13:4.

The Poor and the Rich

The proverbs dealing with the poor and the rich make no attempt to articulate the difference in principle between the two or to negate their difference. There are poor and there are rich, and one must live with this fact. Hence, the diverse ways in which to react to this reality are left open, and the variety of points of view are not reduced to any common denominator. Such sayings would be inappropriate for use in a school, since the context in which they appear is not in the least didactic.[27]

The following proverbs suggest the reality of both rich and poor: "Where there are no oxen there is no manger, but an abundant harvest comes by the strength of an ox" (14:4). "Rich and poor have this in common: Yahweh is maker of them all" (22:2). "All the days of the oppressed are wretched, but a cheerful heart has a continual feast" (15:15). "A man's riches may ransom his life, but a poor man hears no threat" (13:8). "The poor plead for mercy, but the rich answer harshly" (18:23). "One pretends to be rich yet has nothing; another pretends to be poor yet has great wealth" (13:7). "A rich man is wise in his own eyes, but a poor man who has discernment sees through him" (28:11).

This group of proverbs belongs to the category of human observations; at the very least, they are closely related. Proverbs 22:2, which alludes to the Creator, affirms this reality. A proverb of great density, which causes its hearers to reflect on it, is susceptible to many conclusions. It would be a mistake for a modern interpreter to attempt to establish with precision exactly how the proverb should be understood or to attempt to extract dogma from it. This open-endedness of the reflection on the poor and rich serves the juxtaposition of both elements, for example, in 15:15 and 13:8, which express both the positive and the negative aspects of the comparison. According to 15:15, it would appear as if life for the rich consists of one unbroken chain of good days. Yet 13:8 shows that the rich are capable of being extorted, an exceedingly painful experience; meanwhile, the poor person "hears no threat."

Consider the social character of the following: "The poor man is shunned even by his neighbor, but the rich man has countless friends" (14:20). "Wealth attracts many friends, but a poor man is deserted by his friends" (19:4). "All the brothers of a poor man shun him; how much more do his friends avoid him!" (19:7). "The rich rules over the poor, and the borrower is servant to the lender" (22:7). "Many seek the favor of a noble, and everyone is a friend of a man who gives gifts" (19:6).

These statements about the rich and the poor as well have sprung out of observations. They would not have been coined had they not grown out of such experiences. The observation that the poor man has no friend, to the point that even his relatives disavow him, is saying nothing more than this: it really is so; this is the way we experience it. Yet, such statements, functioning as sober appraisals, challenge the hearer to muse, Must it really be this way? Is the difference separating the rich and the poor not, in fact, too great? With this in mind, it is important to take into consideration the words of Jesus as recorded in the Gospels.

The antithesis that is mentioned in 18:23 and 22:7 can result in a situation whereby the poor person is in a position of servitude before the rich.

Moreover, we find a particular group of sayings in which it is acknowledged that wealth can grant security of a sort, but not such that offers any guarantees: "A rich man's wealth is his fortified city; poverty is the ruin of the poor" (10:15). "A rich man's wealth is his fortified city; it is an unscalable wall in his imagination" (18:11).[27a]

When wealth has no solid foundation, however, a different picture emerges: "Wealth hastily gotten dwindles away, but whoever gathers little by little will increase it" (13:11). "An inheritance acquired hastily in the beginning will not be blessed in the end" (20:21). "A faithful man will be richly blessed, but whoever hastens to get rich will not go unpunished" (28:20). "A miser hastens after wealth and is unaware that poverty awaits him" (28:22). "A greedy man stirs up strife, but whoever trusts in Yahweh will prosper" (28:25). "Acquiring riches by falsehood is a fleeting vapor and a snare of death" (21:6).

Indeed, security through riches has other limitations:"Riches are worthless in the day of wrath, but righteousness delivers from death" (11:4). "When a wicked man dies, his hope perishes; any expectation of abundance comes to naught" (11:7). "A good name is more desirable than great riches; favor is better than silver and gold" (22:1).

The behavior of the rich toward the poor is the emphasis of the following sayings: "The one who is kind to the poor lends to Yahweh, and he will reward him for what he has done" (19:17).[28] "The one giving to the poor will not lack, but the one closing his eyes to them will receive many curses" (28:27). "The one increasing his wealth by much interest gathers it for him who is kind to the poor" (28:8). "What is desired in a man is his goodness, and a poor man is better than a liar" (19:22). "A generous man will prosper, and the one watering will himself be watered" (11:25).[28a] "People curse the one who withholds grain, but blessing crowns the head of the one selling it" (11:26). "From the fruit of his lips a man is satisfied with good, and the work of a man's hands comes back to him" (12:1). "One man gives freely, yet gains even more; another withholds unduly but suffers want" (11:24). "Whoever mocks the poor shows contempt for his maker; whoever is glad at calamity will not go unpunished" (17:5). "The one oppressing the poor to increase his own wealth and the one giving gifts to the rich will only come to poverty" (22:16).

Although the proverbs take a somewhat sober yet impartial view of the reality of rich and poor and what they signify, they are quite partial when it concerns the behavior of the rich toward the poor. They stand clearly on the side of the poor and declare that the needy will be helped. It is no accident that here we encounter a reminder of Yahweh's working: he will punish the one who mocks the poor and will reward the one who helps the poor. This identification with the poor is reminiscent of several statements in the Gospels. We might note here how there are occasions when small groups of proverbs complement one another. The statements of observation establish that the poor lose their joy and that their sense of worth is violated. It is precisely this correlation that is made by the proverbs that are indirect admonitions to turn one's heart toward the poor. This claim is not stated explicitly; personal insight should inspire such help.

Several paradoxical proverbs that summon the listener to reflection presuppose discernment on the part of the person being addressed—for example, 11:24, "One man gives freely, yet gains even more," as well as 11:25 and 22:16. These paradoxical sayings indicate that there is intrinsic value in helping the poor. One should not judge according to material standards. The increasing gap between rich and poor presents a danger to the whole community; thus lessening the distance between the rich and the poor must necessarily benefit the whole community. Such is expressed in the words of Jesus in the Gospels. Alleviating need does not injure anyone who will risk doing it: "The gain of the person is his goodness" (19:22).

In terms of form, we must distinguish between those sayings about the poor and the rich in which the contrast is critical for their interpretation and those in which this is not the case.

In the two-part proverbs of antithesis, contrast is essential to their understanding: "The poor plead for mercy, but the rich answer harshly" (18:23). "Rich and poor have this in common: Yahweh is the maker of them all" (22:2). "All the days of the oppressed are wretched, but a cheerful heart has a continual feast" (15:15). "A man's riches may ransom his life, but a poor man hears no threat" (13:8). "One pretends to be rich yet has nothing; another pretends to be poor yet has great wealth" (13:7).

These sayings are evidence that two-part proverbs about the poor and the rich in fact developed orally and were in oral usage.

And yet, a word pair such as poor–rich stimulates the formulation of antithetical proverbs, whereby a one-part saying involving the poor or the rich is expanded into a parallelism.[29] Even when it cannot be demonstrated with certainty, a number of proverbs of antithesis involving this pair would appear to have been one-part sayings—for example: "The rich man's wealth is his fortified city" (18:11a). "Riches are worthless in the day of wrath" (11:4a). "The one who is kind to the poor lends to Yahweh" (19:17a). "The one giving to the poor will not lack" (28:27a). "A poor man is better than a liar" (19:22b).

It is worth noticing that these single-verse sayings often produce a stronger effect in their contracted form than some proverbs having a double construction. This is another evidence for their origin and use in oral tradition.[30]

4. The Human Being in
Community and Family

H. Wolff and E. Gerstenberger have spoken of a "clan ethic" that is present in Proverbs. I would concur with this to the extent that both men place the proverbs in an early period of Israel's history—approximately from the time of the Judges (so C. R. Fontaine as well)—and to the extent that they assume an early stage of oral transmission of proverbial sayings. However, the designation "clan ethic" would seem to me to be questionable on two counts. The community expression "clan" (which extends beyond family, i.e., father–mother– child) does not occur in the book of Proverbs. Nowhere do we find reflection and conduct applied to a wider form of community, nor to more distant relatives. Thus, it is problematic to speak of a "clan ethic."

The other reason for concern is this: "clan" can only signify a family-structured form of community. Yet, the proverbs deal with the subjects of family, family proceedings, relationships between family members, or family problems in very few instances. Only in the sphere of instruction does the family play any significant role. Outside of this, the few proverbs that allude to family do not offer much occasion to speak of "family ethic." This stands in contrast, for example, to Leviticus 18, which has entirely to do with family relationships. The scenario portrayed in Proverbs, on the contrary, is clearly and unequivocally one of life in a small farming village.[31]

Four strata of family relationships are visible.

The Old and the Young

"The glory of the young is their strength; the honor of the old is their gray hair" (20:29). "Gray hair is a crown of splendor; it is attained through a righteous life" (16:31). "A crown of the old are children's children; the glory of children are their parents" (17:6).

These three sayings are of a general nature. They all say essentially the same thing: that is, they establish, by means of the juxtaposition of young and old, the commandment to honor one's parents, inasmuch as they value the significance of age. These statements possess a didactic character and assume an unmistakable place in the context of education. Thus, they show a familiarity with the proverbs of instruction in chapters 22–24. Compare the Egyptian Onchsheshonqy: "Do not despise an old man in your heart" (see Appendix).

Brothers

The proverbs seldom speak of brothers (and sisters) and their relationship to one another. In Psalm 133 we find an expanded proverb: "Behold, how good and pleasant it is when brothers dwell in unity." This is also a didactic saying, with an exhortatory ring. A comparative proverb, Prov. 27:10c, reads, "A friend who is nearby is better than a brother who is far away" (cf. 18:19, below). The virtual absence of brotherly relationships in the proverbs is even more conspicuous when compared to their place of prominence in the patriarchal narratives.

Man and Wife

"A wife of noble character is the crown of her husband, but a disgraceful wife is like rottenness in his bones" (12:4). "Like a gold ring in a pig's snout is a beautiful woman who shows no discretion" (11:22). "A continual dripping on a rainy day and a contentious woman are alike" (27:15). "Better to live in a desert than with a contentious and ill-tempered woman" (21:19). "A quarrelsome wife is like a constant dripping" (19:13b).

Proverbs 12:4a is explicit and unreserved praise of a woman and is expanded into a poem about a wife of noble character in 31:10–31. This praise, however, through 12:4 is made part of a proverb of comparison that contrasts the disgraceful wife with the noble one. The other proverbs of this category are words of ridicule intended for the quarrelsome, disgraceful, or indecent woman. (Notice that the forms of these sayings differ: 28:19 and 25:24 are proverbs of value judgment, whereas 10:22 and 27:15 are comparisons.) Such words of witty ridicule about contentious women are to be found among many peoples—for example, an African maxim, "Two women are two pots full of poison" (see Appendix). Here, as elsewhere, they have arisen and have been passed down in male circles. They would be extremely questionable if viewed as components of a clan ethic. It is scarcely thinkable that they arose within a larger family circle and passed on in such an environment, since women had considerable say in the matter of educating the children. Rather, these proverbs presuppose a situation in which the men had come together alone—for example, the *sōd* (a circle of close friends) (L. Köhler, 1953). It is further improbable that these sayings were the subject of wisdom teachers. If such teachers were, in fact, sages, they would have been careful to teach in such a way that their students might genuinely learn. However, these sayings are inappropriate to be considered exemplary of scribal wisdom. Rather, it is more plausible that the beautiful poem about the noble housewife in 31:10–31 represents a protest against such slanderous words. Note, for example, the Egyptian Onchshe-shonqy: "A good wife of excellent character is like bread that arrives at a time of famine" (see Appendix).

In light of this isolated group of sayings satirizing the contentious woman, we conclude that a genuine comparison of man and wife and their relationship one to another is absent. The reason for the negative characterization of the woman here is that a company of men is being heard. A counterbalance to this grouping is opposition of the foolish and the wise man, where the negative characterization presents a much more poignant and diversified critique of the man who is a liability to the community. The wrong behavior of men (i.e., the fools) constitutes a far greater threat to society.

It is striking that relationships between the sexes and the question of sexuality as such are almost totally absent from the proverbs. Where they do play a notable role is in the didactic poetry of later wisdom in Proverbs 1—9. There we encounter the warnings about loose women that presuppose a context of municipal community. The absence of sexuality as a threat to the community in early proverbial wisdom stands in contrast to the early Christian ethic as well as that of the medieval period, in which it had a determinative significance for the whole of ethics.

Parents and the Upbringing of Children

In an important group of texts there is conformity among all sayings, inasmuch as they speak to the relationship between children and their parents. However, they are interested in just one aspect of this relationship: upbringing. "A wise son brings joy to a father, but a foolish son brings sorrow to his mother" (10:1). "A wise son brings joy to a father, but a foolish man despises his mother" (15:20). "A foolish son brings grief to his father and bitterness to the one who bore him" (17:25). "A foolish son is his father's ruin, and a quarrelsome wife is like a constant dripping" (19:13). "To have a fool for a son brings grief; there is no joy for the father of a fool" (17:21). "The father of the righteous has great joy; he who has a wise son delights in him. Let your father and mother be glad; let her who bore you rejoice" (23:24–25). "A man who loves wisdom brings joy to his father, but a companion of harlots squanders his substance" (29:3). "He who keeps the law is an intelligent son, but a companion of gluttons shames his father" (28:7). (Two other proverbs belong to this group as well: 15:5 and 13:1.)

In each of these sayings, the concern is whether the children are wise or foolish, whether they are a source of joy to the parents or a source of worry. The sheer repetition alone communicates in a clear fashion. All of the sayings are implicit admonitions to school-age children that, as a result of their exposure to wisdom, they behave in such a way as to be a cause for joy and not worry to their parents. Teachers authorized by the parents are instructing young people through these sayings and thereby carry on the instruction of the parents.

In this light, punishment using the rod is justified several times: "Folly is bound up in the heart of a child, but the rod of discipline drives it far from him" (22:15). "Strike a scoffer, and the simple will learn prudence; correct a man of understanding, and he will gain knowledge" (19:25). "The one who spares the rod hates his son, but the one who loves him is diligent to discipline him" (13:24). "The rod and reproof give wisdom, but a child left to himself brings shame to his mother" (29:15). "Discipline your son, and he will give you rest; he will bring delight to your soul" (29:17).

The normal explanation of these many proverbs, namely, that parents are being exhorted to a strict upbringing of their children and consequent use of the rod, does not quite convince me. It is scarcely imaginable that parents are in need of being motivated to use the rod. They need no motivation to do this! Rather, I am assuming that these statements are to be understood in light of the preceding group of sayings. The teachers are justifying themselves over against the parents in their occasional use of corporal punishment. The "fathers" in this case are in fact the teachers.

The two categories dealing with upbringing being considered thus far are not those that originated orally; rather they have been copied in the atmosphere of a school, like that established by Jesus Sirach in the later postexilic era. Evidence of the late development of such sayings is the didactic, abstract language that prevents the context from being recognized. These are to be distinguished from the few proverbs about upbringing that differ notably from the aforementioned: "A rebuke goes deeper into a man of understanding than one hundred blows into a fool" (17:10). "Even a child is known by his actions, by whether his conduct is pure and right" (20:11). "Train a child in the way he should go, and when he is old he will not depart from it" (22:6). "An offended brother is more unyielding than a fortified city, and disputes are like the barred gates of a citadel" (18:19).

In 17:10, a certain critical opposition to the rod surfaces. To be sure, it is not excluded or condemned; rather, the implication is clear that correction with words is capable of achieving more than the rod. The rod is not to be used indiscriminately.

Proverbs 20:11 conveys a rather astonishing and clear-sighted observation for that time, which is of considerable significance for the task of educating children: the fact that a child's disposition is already recognizable and that such observations must be taken into consideration in raising a child.

Proverbs 22:6 belongs, along with the preceding two sayings, to the category of human observations. Although it is formulated as admonition or advice, the introductory imperative can also be understood in the sense of the protasis as a conditional clause. This observation reflects the experience of someone who has noticed the difference between an upbringing that was adequate to the demands of life and one that failed—that is, one that did not concern itself with such demands. Only the one was able to stick it out. This is an amazingly farsighted observation with which we can still concur today.

The same applies to 18:19. Disappointments that were experienced in one's youth ("an offended brother") consequently manifest themselves for a long period of time in one's behavior. It is important to be aware of this in order to compensate for it.

The contrast between both groups of sayings on raising children is striking. The aforementioned four exceptions are concrete and applicable to specific situations and have grown out of human observation. The majority of proverbs about upbringing, on the contrary, tend to be abstract, general, and dealing in principles, without any connection to concrete situations. Because these two groups deal with the same subject in such a distinct manner, they cannot have derived from the same source. They illustrate a necessary distinction between two strata of tradition. This distinction, however, can only be understood inductively.

5. The Human Being in Public Life

Business

Business seldom appears in the proverbs. Ancient Israel was a genuinely agricultural people. Only after the exile did the vocation of merchant acquire greater significance.

From the beginning, defrauding in business is strongly condemned, in full accordance with the prophets of judgment: "Differing weights and differing measures—Yahweh detests them both" (20:10). "A false balance is an abomination to Yahweh, but a just weight is his delight" (11:1). "A just balance and scales are Yahweh's; all the weights in the bag are his doing" (16:11).

In these three statements are found the designations ("differing weights," "false balance") for a deceitful business transaction. In all three it is Yahweh who watches; such practice is an abomination to him. Those who deal deceitfully are characterized as those who commit abominations. In terms of form, these sayings belong to the category that characterizes behavior.

These three proverbs amply demonstrate the freedom of formulation that one finds in proverbial composition. The same proverb can be found in three different formulations. All three existed side by side. More than likely the basis for each was the simple, single-verse formulation: "False weights and false measures are an abomination to Yahweh."

This notion is extended into a parallelism in 20:10 through the addition of "both." In 11:1, this characterization of deceptive behavior is transposed into a proverb of comparison: that which pleases Yahweh and that which is an abomination. In 16:11, the statement is further modulated into a formulation that gives added stress to Yahweh's working. The three sayings illustrate that in the proverbs the same statement can take on an entirely different form.

Also strongly condemned is speculating with grain: "The one withholding grain the people curse, but blessing crowns the one selling it" (11:26).

This, too, is a proverb characterizing behavior. In this context, it is bound up with the results of the person's behavior—curse or blessing. Such a saying reflects the governing function of these proverbs: namely, to serve the welfare of the community.

A very different sort of proverb is one that is expressed tongue in cheek: "'It's no good! It's no good!' says the buyer, then off he goes and brags about his purchase" (20:14).

As an observation about people, this proverb is simply a citation of a cagey buyer that allows the listener to laugh.

Legal Process

In the judicial proverbs, we notice strong corroboration with the prophets of judgment: "Acquitting the guilty and condemning the innocent—Yahweh detests them both" (17:15). "To punish an innocent man is not good; nor to flog men for their integrity" (17:26). "Partiality in judging is not good; whoever says to the wicked, 'You are innocent,' will be cursed by peoples and abhorred by nations. But it will go well with those who rebuke the guilty, and a good blessing will come upon them" (24:23–25). In the same vein, partiality regarding a person's appearance is condemned: "It is not good to be partial to the wicked or to deprive the righteous of justice" (18:5). "Like a club or sword or sharp arrow is a man who bears false witness against his neighbor" (25:18). In both of these sayings a judgment is formed; in 25:18, it is expressed through a comparison.

Several proverbs are exhortations to proper conduct in court: "Do not exploit the poor man because he is poor, and do not trample the afflicted at the gate" (22:22).[32] "Do not testify against your neighbor without cause, and do not deceive with your lips" (24:28). "What you have seen with your eyes do not bring hastily into court, for what will you do in the end, if your neighbor puts you to shame?" (25:7–8).

These three admonitions relating to legal procedure show that the judicial process was a concern of the community at large. Everyone shared responsibility in seeing that no corruption was to surface. The indictment voiced by the prophets could well be based on this popular notion of justice as found in certain proverbial sayings. On the other hand, these texts indicate that the proverbs apparently had a significant influence on the judicial process.

Consider the proverbs that denounce the false witness: "A corrupt witness makes a mockery of justice" (19:28). "A false witness utters deceit" (12:17). "A faithful witness does not deceive, but a false witness breathes out lies" (14:5). "A truthful witness saves lives, but one who utters lies is a deceiver" (14:25). "A false witness will not go unpunished, and the liar will not escape" (19:5; cf. 19:9, "will perish"). "A false witness will perish, but the man who has listened may speak" (21:28). " . . . a false witness who breathes out lies . . . " (6:19).

The many proverbs condemning the false witness are indicative of the important place of testimony in the whole judicial process, in addition to the great, sober consequences associated with it. This characterization also serves the proverbs' primary function: in becoming audible, the unanimous condemnation of the false witness by the entire community is voiced.

Bribery is also the subject of proverbial warning: "One who is greedy brings trouble to his household, but the one who hates gifts will live" (15:27). "A wicked man accepts a bribe in secret to pervert the ways of justice" (17:23).

In all of these sayings alluding to judicial process, it should not be overlooked that they have a critically important function in the life of the community. Here it is not necessary to inquire into their particular *Sitz im Leben,* since it is already clear. One cannot really classify these proverbs as "wisdom" or wisdom sayings. They are, rather, sayings that govern a particular facet of public life and serve the maintenance of a functioning judicial process. In this context, they have a purely social significance—one that has application for the life of the community.[33] Yet, they are not the expression of a wisdom that emerged over time in and of itself; rather, they simply deal with conduct that is harmful to the community. They resemble the proverbs of nonliterate peoples to the extent that proverbs extend to all facets of communal life.

Politics and War; the Cult

A topic such as politics does not surface in the proverbs, apart from allusion to the king and kingship. Not once is war or a battle mentioned—in and of itself a noteworthy phenomenon, since just the opposite is true of the prophetic books. At no time do we encounter the results of war, downfall, devastated cities, refugees, war casualties, or anything related. And yet something just as astonishing also strikes the reader: one never encounters in the proverbs a historical consciousness or belonging to a particular tribe or the juxtaposition of Judah and Israel. There is, moreover, no trace whatsoever of patriotism or national identity to be detected.

That tribal association or tribal designation never occurs in Proverbs (as contrasted with the Psalms!) is evidence that tribal affiliation was the subject of very little discussion in the everyday life of a village or small town. Notwithstanding the many investigations of the past several decades in which much energy was spent in determining whether particular traditions were to be located in the north or south or in a specific tribe, Proverbs at least illustrates that there existed domains in which people did not ask about tribal origin. Hence, it is not possible to ascertain precisely where a particular tradition may have originated.

The lone discernible reason for this is that the proverbs emerged and were passed on in localities such as villages and small towns and that they were confined solely to the "private" life of the people there. Proverbs constituted a form of oral tradition that was molded exclusively for this kind of life.

This very same reason can also account for the religious cult playing virtually no role whatsoever in the proverbs. Inasmuch as the people among whom proverbs originated and circulated all came in contact with the cult through various sacrificial offerings, festivals, and processions, this lack of mention of the cult is astonishing. Yet, in this regard it should be noted: the cult possessed its own language and linguistic patterns, as evidenced so strongly in the Psalms. Until the time of the exile, the linguistic patterns found in proverbs and in the cult did not come in contact at all. Only during the exile and afterward did there no longer exist fixed boundaries. Proverbial statements made their way into the compilations of the Psalter, and subsequently, there arose a devout form of wisdom—proverbs that came to express piety. This notwithstanding, it remains astounding that up to the time of the exile these fixed linguistic boundaries for proverbs existed. It is necessary to trace this phenomenon as it compares with proverbs of other people.

6. The King

The Action of the King

"It is the glory of Yahweh to conceal a matter; to search out a matter is the glory of kings" (25:2). "As the heavens are high and the earth deep, so the hearts of kings are unsearchable" (25:3). "Remove the dross from the silver, and out comes a vessel for the silversmith; remove the wicked from the king's presence, and through his throne righteousness is established" (25:4–5). "A wise king winnows the wicked; he drives the threshing wheel over them" (20:26). "The lips of a king speak as an oracle, and his mouth should not betray justice" (16:10). "Kings abhor wrongdoing, for a throne is established by righteousness" (16:12). "When a nation is rebellious, it has many rulers, but one having understanding and knowledge maintains order" (28:2). "When the righteous thrive, the people rejoice; when the wicked rule, the people groan" (29:2). "If a king judges the poor with fairness, his throne will always be secure" (29:14). "For lack of guidance a nation falls, but many advisers make success certain" (11:14). Regarding form, 25:3; 25:4ff.; and 20:26 take the form of a comparison; 25:2; 28:2; 29:2; and 11:14 are proverbs of antithesis; and 16:10; 20:26; and 29:14 are characterizations.

All these sayings acknowledge the king, whether directly or indirectly. It is granted that the king establishes a matter (an example being the wise verdict of Solomon). For this task, there is a special empowerment for this one man, the king (25:3). Thus, a royal proverb (e.g., 25:4ff.) can be compared to a work of art. Standing in connection with the judging aspect of the king's work is the removal of the wicked person (25:5; 20:26), by which the throne gains stability (25:5; 16:12; 28:2; 29:14). The office of the king is an enduring office. For this reason, the proverbs show a notable interest in the stability of kingship. It is exactly the same with African proverbs (see the later discussion). Stability is ensured through a just rule of the king. Among many proverbs, note " . . . and his throne will be established through uprightness" (25:5). "The king passes a just verdict" (16:10); "injustice is an abomination to him" (16:12). Wisdom is integral to the pronouncement of a just verdict (11:14; 25:3; 28:2).[34]

The King's Favor and the King's Anger

The king's majesty is established in the possibilities of his action. He is mighty in his grace and in his wrath: "A wise servant pleases the king, but his wrath is toward the one acting shamefully" (14:35). "Kings take pleasure in righteous lips, and the one who speaks uprightly he loves" (16:13). "The wrath of the king is a messenger of death, but a wise man will appease it" (16:14). "In the light of a king's face there is life, and his favor is like a rain cloud in the spring" (16:15). "Like the roar of a lion is the king's wrath, but his favor is like dew upon the grass" (19:12). "Like the roar of a lion is the king's wrath; the one provoking him forfeits his life" (20:2).

Regarding form, 16:13 is a characterization; the others are proverbs of antithesis. It might be asked, however, whether several proverbs of characterization were later augmented in order to produce a parallelism. Such could apply to 19:12 and 20:2, both of which agree in the first half of the verse. More than likely 19:12a (= 20:2a) was originally a single-verse characterization of the king, just as is 16:14a (16:14b is praise of the wise person). The same is possible for 16:15.

All these statements, whether individual descriptive statements or comparisons, characterize the king. They are neither praise nor reproof, neither acknowledgment nor criticism. They merely express the uniqueness of the king as perceived in his impact on the common people. This is most probably a group of proverbs that arose soon after the establishment of the monarchy, at a time when the phenomenon of kingship was still relatively new. These sayings attest to a certain amount of reflection; they also appear in the form of exhortations or warnings. Something new and striking is expressed in the sayings: into the hand of this one man, life and death have been placed; "the wrath of the king is a messenger of death" (16:14a; cf. also 19:12; 20:2).

What the King Promotes

"In a multitude of people is the glory of a king, but without people a prince is ruined" (14:28). "For a lack of guidance a people falls, but there is safety in an abundance of counselors" (11:14). Similar are 14:35 and 16:13.

These statements focus reflection not on the person of the king but rather on his rule. They ascribe to him the greatness of the people—a theme that is also encountered in African proverbs (see below)—as well as signify that his work is guided by good counsel and wise advisers (cf. Genesis 37–50). Reflection such as this on what kingly rule requires is in full harmony with what we find in the historical books concerning the early period of the monarchy. In this regard, see F. Crüsemann, *Der Widerstand gegen das Königtum* (1978). He also notes parallels found in African proverbs.

Criticism of the King

"Like a roaring lion or a charging bear is a wicked man ruling over a poor people" (28:15). "The more a ruler is lacking understanding, the crueler is his oppression" (28:16). "If a ruler listens to falsehood, all his officials will become wicked" (29:12). ". . . but the man who is greedy for bribes ruins it [the land]" (29:4b).

In form, each of these four proverbs constitutes a critical portrayal of the king—28:15 and 16 are characterizations, 29:12 expresses a consequence, and 29:4b is one side of an antithesis.

It is unlikely that the four proverbs were composed by sages in the royal court or for school instruction. They are open criticism, not of the monarch as such but rather of a king who fails in his office and thereby does harm to the people. They can only have arisen among the people, coined by persons to reflect specific experiences with particular kings—for example, a king who robs the poor among his people in a wanton manner; or a king who is lacking in wisdom and who oppresses his people with his limitations; or a king who is no discerner of spirits, who listens to lies and thereby corrupts the whole royal court; or a king who ruins his entire nation through high taxes.

In the criticism of these four proverbs is a good deal of courage and political wisdom emanating from those who wish to affirm the monarchy as such and avert damage. It is highly significant that we also find in African proverbs clear parallels to this.

Admonition to the King

Proverbs 31:1–9, the sayings of Lemuel, is a wisdom poem from a later period that assumes an awareness of Egyptian teachings. Nevertheless, many echoes of the royal proverbs from the earlier period remain. The queen of Massa exhorts her son in vv. 2–5 about his personal conduct (drinking and strange women, as in Proverbs 1—9) and in vv. 5–9 about his royal office— judging on behalf of the poor (vv. 5b, 9), the widow and orphan (vv. 8–9).[34a]

The King and Yahweh

"Like streams of water, the king's heart is in Yahweh's hand; he turns it wherever he pleases" (21:1). "It is the glory of God to conceal a matter, but the glory of kings is to search a matter out" (25:2).

Proverbs 21:1 is a characterization of the king that honors him, yet not without a slight, critical reservation. The writer points to the limits of royal power, just as Proverbs often finds the limits of human power in the activity of Yahweh. There are a number of passages in Proverbs that speak of God and the king together.

Proverbs 25:2 reflects an esteem for the king's working. It is the honor of a king "to search out a matter." In comparing the operation of the king to that of Yahweh, it can be said that while the two are not on equal footing, they are nevertheless comparable.

It seemed certain up until now that the royal proverbs arose in the royal court. Thus, H. J. Hermisson (1968): "With regard to the royal proverbs we can readily see that they can in no way be considered the work of the people" (p. 71). Holding a contrary view, F. W. Golka in "Die Königs- und Hofsprüche und der Ursprung der israelitischen Weisheit" (*VT* 36, 1 [1986]: 13–36) establishes that royal/chieftain proverbs exist among African folk sayings. At times, these sayings are quite similar to those in Proverbs. No one as of yet has claimed that the African royal proverbs (some of which are listed by R. Finnegan, 1970) are anything other than popular adages. The African sayings contain motifs such as the king's justice, his strength as seen through the number of his people, the special empowerment of the king, as well as potent criticism and references to the limits of his power. All of these themes are found as well in the book of Proverbs.

The few samples of African proverbs listed below, cited from F. W. Golka's article, are sufficient for illustration: "If the headmen are wise, the people are also wise" (p. 23). "When the chief's breast has plenty of milk, it is for all the world to drink" (i.e., the king as mediator of blessing; p. 23). "The chief has no relatives" (he is impartial; p. 24). "The king is the lake" (he is there for all; p. 24). "The centipede's legs are strengthened by a hundred rings"; "If Otsibo says he can do something, he does it with his followers" (the king's dependence on his subjects; p. 15). "God is generally on the side of the chief" (p. 23). "A canoe is not partial to a prince; whoever upsets it gets wet" (p. 15); "Better to be hated by the prince than hated by the people" (criticism of the king, limitations of royal powers; p. 16). "Authority (power) is the tail of the water-rat" (it is easily lost; p. 16). "Dew soon does dry up, so will chieftaincy" (p. 16). "When the chief limps all his subjects limp also" (p. 17).

If the motifs found in African proverbs are so similar to the royal sayings in the book of Proverbs, and if, conversely, parallels in form are not to be found in Near Eastern wisdom literature, then it is indisputable that these are a popular folk material. It will suffice, however, to note that the critical remarks in Proverbs aimed at the king would not have originated in the royal court or in the royal school.

There is another aspect to this as well. In the royal sayings in Proverbs, there is no mention of splendor and might, which would be unfurled in the royal court and which would be a sign of a portrait or evidence of merit. If we were to compare the language of these proverbs with that of the Forty-fifth Psalm, the contrast would become abundantly apparent. Psalm 45 can have originated only in the royal court or in its environs; the royal sayings from the book of Proverbs show no trace of the language of the court.[35] One further element surfaces in examining the royal proverbs of the Old Testament alongside their African counterparts. In both cases, a moderating influence is recognizable— a form of wisdom that guards against excessive royal power and glorification. Today this would be formulated in terms of an explicitly democratic orientation: unbridled royal power is always dangerous. An excessive veneration of the ruler is prohibited by these sayings. They serve as a source of critical attentiveness.[36]

7. The Messenger

"Like the coolness of the snow at harvesttime is a faithful messenger to those who send him" (25:13). "Like cold water to a weary soul is good news from a distant land" (25:25). "Like cutting off one's feet or drinking violence is the sending of a message by the hand of a fool" (26:6). In 25:13, a dependable messenger is praised by means of a comparison. Proverbs 26:6, an upbraiding of the messenger, is more a saying about the fool. The first two proverbs suggest a connection between the inhabitants of Judea and people of foreign nations. Whether it concerns family relations or commercial transactions is difficult to say. We can only assume that a link to people in far countries was present and important for those among whom these sayings originated. All three texts are genuine proverbs of comparison. Moreover, all three belong to the collection of chapters 25—31. The messenger sayings are a subgroup of the cluster dealing with salutary speech (hence, the news).[37]

8. Summary

In a particular group of proverbs, appearing in the form of comparisons or declarative statements, observations and discoveries are reproduced—for example, the enigmatic phenomenon of breathing, the uniqueness of the individual person, or the observation that no face of any particular person is exactly the same as that of another. This is a discovery by means of analogy, which progresses from the realm of the known to the unknown. Because these were individual observations and identifications that originally possessed a meaning of their own, they are preserved in the form of a proverb, by which they retain their special significance and are passed on. This speech form is easily remembered due to the nature of comparison. These sayings were not brought together to form a broader linguistic context; the specific form of each saying was able to preserve the wonder that was registered and that originally accompanied the discovery. The form expresses the ability of the creature, bestowed on him by the Creator, to understand himself and to find his way in the world. This is the very same consciousness of being created that we find in Psalm 139. Such requires no teaching on what it means to be human or about the world into which humans are born; rather, it is an awareness that aspires to and is capable of self-observation, discovery, reflection, and insight. It is precisely this that the proverbs seek to communicate and pass on. Such is the nature of being human![38]

This primary feature of observation and discovery is present throughout various other realms and subjects in the proverbs. In addition, there are other tendencies that result from this chief characteristic: for example, that perception at times must be critical, that it can be complex (as evidenced by proverbs of paradox), and that any perception must acknowledge its own limitations.

Antitheses such as joy and sorrow, hunger and satiation, wholesome and destructive speech, the human condition in relationships to work and possessions, the idle and the diligent, the poor and the rich reflect that a human being lives in a magnetic field, as it were, between two poles. He is incapable of being locked into one particular constant mode of existence—a reality that is established by his being a creation suspended between birth and death. To illustrate, the polarity between joy and sorrow corresponds to that of lament and praise found in the Psalms. They share the same understanding of what it means to be human. Part of this awareness is an understanding of the nature of speech (which is also a polarity of good and evil), by which a transaction occurs between the speaker and the listener. Given the nature of proverbs as an originally oral form of communication, we are dealing here with oral discourse that is rooted in a particular situation. The value of a saying is measured according to its effect in corporate life. As the comparisons illustrate, the proverbs display a love for beauty.

As to questions of social status, work, and personal belongings, the polar opposites in the work of the farmer and craftsman play an important role. Here we find the somewhat exaggerated character of popular sayings reflected in the use of humor, which can, at times, exhibit itself by satirizing the idle yet at the same time by a serious and even profound reflection on the contrast of the poor and the rich. At times, some of the proverbs directly mirror the situation out of which they arose. Where the concern is the simple reality of contrast between poor and rich, the proverbs often assume the form of a comparison. Any social commentary as to this contrast or the limitations of wealth or the behavior of the rich and the poor is absent.

In considering a person's relation to the community, we encounter the contrast of young and old, man and wife, parents and children. As it stands, there are relatively few of these sayings, the one notable exception being that of the contentious woman. Particularly striking about this category of proverbs is the contrast between the number of sayings dealing with instruction and wisdom found in chapters 22—24 and the relatively few sayings on instruction that belong to the category of human observation. Here a time lag is evident (e.g., 17:10; 20:11; 22:6). The same applies to the proverb about the brother who is betrayed (18:19) and the one about the wife of noble character (12:4), who is presented as a contrast to the immoral woman. It is striking that in the sayings directed to husband and wife, the entire realm of sexuality is all but absent.

Proverbs gives only a little advice to the person in public life. One area that is addressed is fraud in business; such practice is sharply rebuked. A number of diverse proverbs deal with the messenger, who at that time had a significant role.

The whole sphere of politics does not surface in the proverbs; neither does that of war or of the cult. There is, however, a special group of sayings devoted to the king.

II. PROVERBS ABOUT HUMAN CHARACTER

1. Form

An especially important subject of the proverbs is that of human character—encompassing seventy-eight texts—related to people living in community. This theme manifests itself in proverbial statements, in proverbs of antithesis, and in comparisons. The original form of characterization is a simple statement; this grammatical form accommodated a social function. As such, the characterization is not easily recognizable for the simple reason that in its origin it is single-verse. In the compilation of proverbs, however, it occurs only in the form of a parallelism. It can be extended to a parallelism by means of proverbial contrasts and comparisons but also through the addition of another characterization.

The original single-verse nature of characterization can be recognized, for example, in 16:27–30, which consists of proverbs of antithesis on the theme of the wicked and the righteous. These sayings are composed of four elements. In these verses, four texts dealing with the actions of the wicked are united in a sequence; one may conclude that the redactor viewed these as belonging together. Each of the four describes a specific action of the wicked. In each case the saying is molded into a parallelism by means of the addition of a second wicked deed: "A wicked man plots evil, and his speech is like a scorching fire" (16:27). "A perverse man spreads strife, and a talebearer separates close friends" (16:28). "A violent man entices his neighbor and leads him in a way that is not good" (16:29). "The one winking his eyes plots perverse things; the one pursing his lips is bent on accomplishing evil" (16:30).

It is clearly recognizable here that the characterization was originally single-verse and that a second component produced the parallelism.

The same is true in the proverbs of antithesis dealing with the theme of the foolish and the wise. In these sayings, we find a proverb that typifies the foolish and then subsequently is expanded. The amplification here is of a different kind: the action of the fool is set over against the praise of the wise. "Whoever trusts in himself is a fool; but he who walks in wisdom is kept safe" (28:26). "A fool finds pleasure in doing wrong, but a man of understanding delights in wisdom" (10:23).

What is apparent in these proverbs occurs rather frequently: both halves of the stanza are often later adapted to each other. As such, each statement can often stand independently, with no natural connection to the other. Both halves may even fail to match altogether. In cases where this is ascertainable, we may be virtually certain that the halves of each verse in many cases have been adapted to each other at a later point in time.

Observation and experience lie at the root of characterization as well. A separate examination would be necessary to inquire into precisely how the definitive verdict that we find in assorted characterizations came about or to analyze what factors were involved in this process and what was the related purpose for the selection of such characterizations.

Stock Phrasings in the Characterizations

In these characterizations, we meet certain characteristic forms that, before they were incorporated in the literary device of the parallelism, were independent. Stock phrasing is typically employed: "Whoever plots evil will be known as a mischiefmaker" (24:8). "Whoever mocks the poor shows contempt for his maker" (17:5). "Whoever winks the eye causes trouble" (10:10). "Whoever winks the eye plots perversity" (16:30). "Whoever goes around as a talebearer reveals secrets" (11:13). "Insight is a fountain of life to the one possessing it" (16:22). "Whoever withholds grain will be cursed by the people" (11:26).

The characterization is normally stated in the context of a particular case illustration: "Whoever assaults his father and drives away his mother is a son who causes shame and disgrace" (19:26). "Whoever robs his father or mother . . . is a partner to him who destroys" (28:24). "Whoever loudly blesses his neighbor, rising early in the morning, will be counted as a curse" (27:14). "A man lacking judgment by taking a pledge becomes security for his neighbor" (18:1).

The characterization in its form is similar to the definition: "'Scoffer' is the name of the proud; haughty is the man who behaves with arrogant pride" (21:24). This would include the proverbs that begin with the phrase "Do you see the one . . . ?"—"Do you see a man skillful in his work? He will stand before kings; he will not stand before obscure men" (22:29); "Do you see a man wise in his own eyes? There is more hope for a fool than for him" (26:12); "Do you see a man hasty with his words? There is more hope for a fool than for him" (29:20)—as well as the description of the deeds of the wicked man: "The wicked man listens to evil lips; a liar gives heed to a malicious tongue" (17:4). "A worthless witness mocks at justice; the mouth of the wicked devours iniquity" (19:28). "The violence of the wicked will drag them away, because they refuse to do what is right" (21:7). "The soul of the wicked craves evil; his neighbor finds no mercy in his eyes" (21:10). "With his lips the malicious man disguises himself; in his heart he harbors deceit" (26:24). "Wicked men do not understand justice; but those seeking Yahweh understand it fully" (28:5). "An angry man stirs up strife, and a hot-tempered man commits many sins" (29:22). The characterization can also be an admonition or warning: "Do not be envious of the wicked . . . for in their heart they plot violence and their lips talk of mischief" (24:1–2). "My son, give me your heart, and let your eyes observe my ways" (23:26). "With his lips the malicious man disguises himself; in his heart he harbors deceit . . . do not believe him!" (26:24–25). "A man tormented by the blood of another is a fugitive until death; let no one support him" (28:17). It would appear that the redactors of Proverbs also viewed characterization as a single and originally independent form, as evidenced by the short poem found in 30:11–14, which strings several characterizations together in a sequence: "There is a generation that curses its fathers and does not bless its mothers; a generation that is pure in its own eyes but is not cleansed of its filth; a generation whose eyes are so haughty and whose eyelids are lifted up; a generation whose teeth are swords and whose jaws are knives, devouring the poor from the earth, the needy from among mankind."

It is possible that 21:4—"Haughty eyes and a proud heart, the lamp of the wicked, are sin"—is a fragment taken from a similar poem.

In this case as well, the compiler placed together what seemed to belong together. Each of the verses in 30:11–14 is a typical example of what was originally a single-verse characterization.

An important criterion for recognizing the function of characterizations is the fact that negative depictions far outweigh positive ones. For both speaker and listener, the use of the negative characterization was more important than the use of the positive. The social function of the negative depiction can thus be more precisely defined: it is regulative in its function. A negative portrayal of conduct, speech, or action on the part of an individual typifies that which threatens the welfare of the community. The purpose of the characterization is to take sayings that had developed orally and were suited for oral transmission and publicly censure an individual by means of a negative judgment made strictly on a popular level.

EXCURSUS 1
The Relationship of the Proverbs
to Old Testament Laws

The advantage of proverbs over against laws lies in their popular appeal and public character. They live in the people, they are spoken and heard again and again, and they are employed where they can bring about a certain effect. The laws do not possess this inherent capacity, with the notable exception of the commandments.[39] They are re-corded and familiar only to relatively small circles, as indicated by the technical nature of their language. In contrast, the regulatory function of proverbs of characterization allows them to have a far greater effect. They touch everyone, and they do so continually. For the people, it was the familiar proverbs informing their behavior that had force; it was from these that behavioral guidelines were derived.[40]

2. Types of Character That Endanger the Community

One can discern small collections of sayings in 26:1–28 that were placed together by the compiler according to catchwords: the fool (vv. 1–12), the slug-gard (vv. 13–16), the quarrelsome (vv. 17–22), and the malicious (vv. 23–28). The compiler has taken mostly unarranged individual sayings and begun to arrange them according to content. In the transition from oral to written tradi-tion, this kind of grouping would have facilitated reading. The way in which the malicious, the quarrelsome, the fool, and so forth should be characterized is summarized. To this end, different forms are utilized: in 26:17–22, all the proverbs are comparisons; in vv. 23–28, proverbial statements are introduced through a comparison; vv. 1–12 are mostly comparisons (with the exception of vv. 4–5, which are hortatory); and in vv. 13–16 we find one comparison, with the rest being statements.

The Malicious

See 26:23, 24–25, 26–27, 28; 22:5; 17:4; 16:27. A complex comparison is found in 26:23. Here a contrast from another realm is placed alongside a con-trast that is displayed in a malicious person: "Like the glaze coating over earth-enware are passionate lips with an evil heart" (26:23).

The apparent genuineness proves not to be so; the malicious person is not a sound person. Tacitly, by means of comparison, attention is brought to the potential danger posed by the malicious person: "With his lips the malicious man disguises himself, but in his heart he harbors deceit; for though his speech is charming, do not believe him! For seven abominations are in his heart" (26:24–25). "His malice may be covered with deception, but his wickedness will be exposed in the assembly. The one digging a pit falls into it, and the one rolling a stone, on him it will turn" (26:26–27). "A lying tongue hates its vic-tims, and a flattering mouth works ruin" (26:28).[41] "Thorns and snares lie on the path of the perverted; the one guarding his soul will keep far from them" (22:5). "The one doing evil listens to wicked lips; a liar gives heed to a malicious tongue" (17:4). "A wicked man plots evil, and his speech is like a scorching fire" (16:27).

Proverbs 26:24–25 says the same thing as 26:23, though without a comparison. The warning is stated at the end of the proverb. Proverbs 26:26–27 says the same as well, except that here the mention of the consequences of guile takes the place of a warning: it will be revealed before the court. Verse 27 can also stand independently, inasmuch as it consists of two comparisons that are conjoined and that announce to the deceiver the penalty for his actions. Proverbs 22:5 serves to warn him further. Proverbs 17:4, not unlike an observation about people, adds an additional aspect: the malicious man is bent on collaborating with his own type. This proverb also contains a warning element.

The cluster of sayings that function as characterizations work differently from those of human observation, which mirror an inquisitive attentiveness. And yet the characterizations in no way attempt to say something clever or ingenious. Rather, they all have the clearly recognizable aim of warning the malicious man of his speech and conduct. Such brings attention to the menace he represents to the common good. The concern being expressed here is markedly social in nature. An awareness of accountability for the welfare of the community is being expressed. At the very same time, something is being communicated about the speaker. To describe him as a sage is appropriate to the extent that his wisdom is practical. His wisdom grows out of an awareness of responsibility for the community that he endeavors to serve and make a difference in.[42]

Contention

"Like one seizing a dog by the ears is the one passing by who meddles in a quarrel not his own" (26:17). "Like one going mad and shooting arrows is the one deceiving his neighbor and saying, 'I am only joking'" (26:18). "For lack of wood a fire goes out, and where there is no talebearer, gossiping ceases" (26:20). "As charcoal to embers and as wood to fire, so is a quarrelsome man for kindling strife" (26:21). "The words of a talebearer are like choice morsels; they go down to the innermost parts of the body" (26:22). "A perverse man spreads strife, and a talebearer separates friends" (16:28). "The one who loves transgression loves strife" (17:19).

In 26:17–22, we find a cluster of proverbs set together that are also all comparisons. Strife, which disturbs the peace, is viewed by the compiler as an important theme of the proverbs. The short compilation of 26:17–22 deals with one specific aspect: strife that is frivolously kindled by a "disturber of the peace." Each of the sayings concerns the quarrelsome person. In this vein, it is naturally assumed that, in any community, conflict can appear and, under certain conditions, is necessary. There is no warning against conflict per se, rather only against those who carelessly "ignite" or fan a conflict (thus, vv. 20 and 21). The first of the proverbs in this group, v. 17, employs a comparison. The emphasis here is that the one who meddles creates needless conflict. Both comparisons of vv. 20 and 21 are also predicated on the idea that a damaging conflict need not arise if there exists no one to stir it up. When people still speak today of fanning or kindling strife, the genesis of this metaphor can be traced to the proverbs. This particular metaphor is especially fitting because conflict can fly out of control and consequently gather irresistible momentum. In 26:22, humor is injected. The saying is intended to call attention to the ease with which slander occurs and yet the enormity of damage that can be served up. A similar proverb is 18:6, which involves the foolish.[43]

The Concealer

"The accomplice to a thief hates his own life; he hears the curse but discloses nothing" (29: 24).

Pride, Arrogance

See 16:18; 18:12; 11:2; 13:10; 21:4; 17:19.

"Pride goes before destruction, and a haughty spirit before a fall" (16:18).[44] (Cf. the African proverb: "Do not walk erect, so that you are not bent.") "Haughty eyes and a proud heart, the lamp of the wicked, are sin" (21: 4). "Before destruction a man's heart is proud, but humility comes before honor" (18:12). "Whoever makes his gate high invites destruction" (17:19).

In the proverbs about the arrogant man, either his fall is indicated or he is contrasted with humility. This accords with the nature of arrogance, the effect of which on the life of the community is not so rapid or obvious. Yet the frequency with which the proverbs speak of the peril of arrogance is based on the connection between haughtiness and a tenuous relationship to God. Arrogance can scarcely bear honor being given to Yahweh. For this reason, the very same judgment concerning pride is pronounced in the words of Jesus: "Whoever makes his gate high invites destruction" (17:19).

Deception

See 26:27; 28:10; 16:30.

"The digger of a pit falls into it, and the one rolling a stone, on him it will turn" (26:27). "Whoever leads astray the upright on an evil path will fall into his own trap" (28:10). "The one winking his eyes plots perversity; the one pursing his lips is bent on accomplishing evil" (16:30).

Deception is very similar to malice. Here, too, we find the frequent comparison with the pit into which falls its digger. This statement is in no way meant to express the necessary consequence; rather, it is the unforeseen, that which takes the deceiver by surprise, that he did not even suspect.

Violence

"The violence of the wicked will sweep them away, because they refuse to do what is right" (21:7). "A violent man entices his neighbor and leads him on a path that is not good" (16:29).

Callousness toward the Lowly

"The greed of the wicked strives for evil and his neighbors find no mercy" (21:10). "If you close your ear to the cry of the poor, you will cry out and not be heard" (21:13).

It is typical of the book of Proverbs to come back again and again from many different angles to one's conduct toward the lowly. In every place where Proverbs speaks to this issue, it indicates that if one refuses to help, the human consequences are significant. It is not merely an issue of omission that is being criticized; rather, the person's whole orientation to life is being characterized. Here again, the book of Proverbs concurs with the words of Jesus.

The type of person being characterized in this way exhibits many other traits as well: he does evil, punishes the innocent, mistreats his parents, initiates malicious talk, and slanders others. Such persons mock and wound with words, lead others astray, bring trouble, bear false witness, bribe, and lead a dissolute life.

It should be noted here that capital crimes—murder, theft, robbery, breaking in, to name a few—do not receive mention; the community as a whole and the courts are responsible for these. In this characterization, rather, the concern is wrongs that do not go before court or that are unknown, which nevertheless are very significant for community life. To illustrate, while robbery as such is not mentioned, the case of depriving one's parents in a way that goes unatoned for and unreported is addressed.

It is the function of each of these proverbs to regulate, warn, and protect. Yet they are operative in situations only to the extent that they are cited and called to remembrance.

3. Characterization of Behavior

In one category of proverbs, not persons but actual behaviors are exemplified, usually in a comparison. "Like clouds and wind and yet no rain, so is a man who boasts of a gift he does not give" (25:14). "Like a bad tooth or a lame foot is trust in the unfaithful in the day of trouble" (25:19). "The north wind brings rain; so a backbiting tongue brings angry looks" (25:23). "The one who flatters his neighbor is spreading a net for his feet" (29:5). "Like a muddied spring or a polluted well is a righteous man who falters before the wicked" (25:26).[45] "A strong man who oppresses the poor is like a driving rain that leaves no crops" (28:3). "Like a club or a sword or a sharp arrow is a man who bears false witness against his neighbor" (25:18). "The mouth of an adulteress is like a deep pit; the one angry with Yahweh falls into it" (22:14).

These comparative sayings, all of which fall in chapters 22—29, personify by comparison behavior that does not serve or that constitutes a threat to the community. All these sayings mirror a critical intent. Such a characterization says something that is designed to make a person think, so that he can appraise himself as to whether his conduct is serving corporate life. The use of comparison gives the concerned party freedom to decide for himself. Implicit in these sayings is an admonition or warning for those individuals who through such behavior could be exposed to danger. While all these comparisons are well thought out, one can, on occasion, notice that a number of them have been adapted to the characterization—for example, "clouds and wind yet no rain" (25:4); "like a driving rain that leaves no crops" (28:3); "a muddied spring" (25:26). One can also observe how the comparisons are graduated according to the sharpness and weight of the criticism—an example being the way 25:14 differs from 25:18.

The boaster, who brags of his gift (25:14), is scolded because he disappoints his fellow citizens and thereby arouses distrust. The obtrusive neighbor (25:17–18) is reminded of what his obtrusiveness can create. The "unfaithful in the day of trouble" (25:19) is urged to consider the consequences of his unfaithfulness. The gossiper (25:23), as sure as the north wind bringing rain, is certain to cause ill will. The flatterer overdoes it (26:28) and, as a result, produces the opposite effect; as a matter of fact, he can even cause severe damage (29:5). The righteous one who falters before the godless (25:26) disappoints his friends, because they have expected the opposite from him. All these actions have consequences! The false witness (25:18) threatens the life of his fellow neighbors; he is reminded of this risk by means of a pointed contrast.

With all these comparisons, an actual incident in the life of the community is being addressed to which the behavior is related and from which it arose.

These incidents were regularly repeated in the community's life. One could, with a little imagination and effort, form a narrative out of them. In the juxtaposition of incidents taken from human experience, they comprise a sort of common sense that makes it easier for the person being exhorted to accept the intended message. The proverbs of comparison provide the opportunity of exerting influence on others in a helpful and instructive manner, without the person in view having to feel patronized. There is a point of identification with the object of the comparison, and humor added here and there facilitates this.

4. Characterization of the Fool by Comparison

A group of proverbs in 26:1–12 deals with the fool (translation by H. Ringgren): "Like snow in summer and rain at harvesttime, so honor is not fitting for a fool" (26:1). "A whip for the horse, a halter for the donkey, and a rod for the backs of fools" (26:3). "Like cutting off one's foot or drinking violence is the sending of a message by the hand of a fool" (26:6). "Like a lame man's legs that hang limp is a proverb in the mouth of fools" (26:7).[46] (The text of v. 8 is uncertain.) "Like a thornbush in the hand of a drunkard is a proverb in the mouth of fools" (26:9). (The text of v. 10 is uncertain.) "Like a dog returning to its vomit is a fool repeating his folly" (26:11).[47] "Do you see a man who is wise in his own eyes? There is more hope for a fool than for him" (26:12).

The above are sufficiently witty, ingenious sayings that one can feel them; they express the true confrontation of real people in their common life. They reflect the extent to which people in this particular circle have had experience with fools. They also illustrate the extent to which wittiness has a place in this exchange and the degree to which it can serve normal discourse (e.g., 26:7, 9, 11).

Esteem and wisdom simply are not suited to a fool. The speech and conduct of the fool are inferior to that expected of the average citizen; he does and says "what is not fitting." And because it is essential to corporate life that individuals hold to that which is fitting, this sort of demarcation of the fool is necessary. At issue is the quality of the community's life. Proverbs 26:9 is particularly instructive. One must be careful with a thornbush; it would be especially hazardous "in the hand of a drunkard." Just as dangerous is "a proverb in the mouth of fools," that is, someone who only pretends to be wise. What poses a threat is the fact that someone can allow himself to be deceived. This proverb is similar to those that speak of appropriate speech at the proper time. (Incidentally, 26:7 and 9 demonstrate that proverbs have their origin in oral usage.)

Foolishness does not allow itself to be expelled: "Though you grind a fool in a matter as grain with a pestle, his folly will not depart from him" (27:22;

cf. also 26:3 and the Egyptian Onchsheshonqy: "Don't be provoked by a fool"). "Stone is heavy and sand is a burden, but a fool's provocations are heavier than both" (27:3; see also 26:6 and, perhaps, 26:10).

Certain occurrences are remembered by those coining the proverbs. Perhaps someone had sent a fool as a messenger and consequently was taken in. The fool is dangerous due to his loutishness; again and again he is troublesome. Proverbs 27:3 is formulated in the pattern of the comparison. It takes the abstract notion of "burden" and concretizes it by comparing it to a heavy weight; in this way, the metaphor "burdensome" comes alive.

5. Characterization of the One Who Promotes the Community

Characterizations depicting someone who furthers the community are encountered far less often in the proverbs. It is only natural that those who coined proverbial sayings concerned themselves more with those individuals posing a threat to community life. The positive form of characterization applies to (1) conduct affecting others and (2) one's own personal conduct.

Doing Good and Demonstrating Compassion

"A generous person will be enriched; the one who waters will himself be watered" (11:25). "Whoever lends to the poor lends to Yahweh, and he will repay him for his deed" (19:17). "What is desired of a man is his goodness, and better is a poor man than a liar" (19:22). "A man with a generous eye will be blessed, for he shares his food with the poor" (22:9). "The one who covers an offense promotes love, but one who repeats a matter separates friends" (17:9). "If your enemy is hungry, give him food to eat, and if he is thirsty, give him water to drink" (25:21).

Also added to the list of good works are forbearance with the angry (19:11) and reproof where it is necessary (28:23). When someone is managing his belongings properly, this will include voluntary and generous giving. The alleviation of shortage and need is a part of life in the sight of God. It is always a personal and direct expression of giving that meets a need encountered. This group of proverbs is especially important for the spirit of the community, from which these sayings emanate. Israel experienced its God again and again as the one who looked on its needs and had compassion for his own. It is a response to this work of God that is reflected in those who, by looking to him, minister compassion to others whom they encounter along their way. The Gospel narratives speak of this as well. Matthew 5:7, for example, corresponds to Prov. 14:21: "Blessed is he who is kind to the needy."

Personal Behavior

"Whoever watches his mouth guards his life" (13:3). "A heart at peace gives life to the body" (14:30). "The one who holds his tongue is wise" (10:19). "Whoever restrains his words is a man of understanding" (17:27). "It is an honor for a man to avoid strife" (20:3). "Whoever guards his mouth and tongue keeps himself from calamity" (21:23). "The highway of the upright avoids evil; the one who guards his way guards his life" (16:17). Qualities such as forbearance under the weight of suffering (18:14), skill in one's vocation (22:29), and faithful service (27:18) are also mentioned. We encounter as well positive characterizations in the proverbs of antithesis involving the foolish and the wise.

These are the "beatitudes" among the characterizations, even when only one proverb is formulated as such ("Blessed is he who is kind to the needy," 14:21). Jesus' saying "What you have done to one of the least of these my brethren you have done to me" corresponds to 19:17. In proverbs such as 13:3; 10:18, 19; 17:27; 20:3; 21:23; and 16:17, the virtue of restraint is underscored. Accordingly, esteem is not bestowed on someone who distinguishes himself in the presence of others through conspicuous actions, rather on a person who is disciplined enough to hold his tongue and hinder strife. The Greco-Roman notion of "virtue" is not in the background here, since such a conceptualization of virtue always has the individual as its focus. Rather, positive characterization in Proverbs is aimed at that which promotes peaceable communal life.

6. Conclusion

The proverbs of characterization deal with perception and action relative to one's conduct. Both stand in reciprocal relationship to each other. The nature of the characterizations in Proverbs is predominantly negative, since they are aimed foremost at that which detracts from the community. These can be exhibited by types of persons—both in terms of orientation and in mode of conduct—or by individual situations; this is as far as they go. It is not their intent to explore thoroughly "human nature," nor do they seek to present themselves in wider connections or provide explanations. The characterizations stick to what is real and tend to avoid generalizations such as "humans are wicked" or "humans are always and everywhere sinners." They are based on the premise that people have been thus created, that they can fail, and that they do fail, yet only in the spectrum of situations presented by the examples themselves. The proverbs always say only something that accords with real life—for example, that the quarrelsome person is quarrelsome. Never do they seek thereby to condemn the person entirely; and neither do they intend to show that a person at all times is quarrelsome. Rather, the malicious person in the proverbs is portrayed in the context of his malice, and others are consequently warned. Both positive and negative aspects are referred to for the sake of communal tranquility. The characterization is for the well-being of the community, and this not in a manner that directly reproaches or threatens the offender or condemns him morally. Neither does it provide protection for society from the wicked person. Rather, it states a situation (e.g., 26:24) and calls both parties involved to vigilance and reflection.

The characterization concerns that which we would call human understanding. It is human inclination to want to be aware of those who will cross our path, the result of which is that we are then able to form an opinion about them and adapt accordingly. The characterizations are similar to the proverbs of observation. They can be more precisely identified when they appear in a series of comparisons that are more effective in profiling a type than mere lists of attributes or abstract categories. Nevertheless, the forming of an opinion is accomplished in different ways by different groups of sayings, as the comparisons well illustrate.

But characterization in these proverbs also has to do with personal behavior, which stems from the aforementioned perception. The proverbs are conditioned entirely by a social impulse. Thus the characterizations do not merely address individuals. For example, 26:24, "With his lips the malicious man disguises himself, but in his heart he harbors deceit," is spoken to two parties. The malicious person is uncovered and presented in his falsehood, and the potential victims are at the same time warned.

It is certainly no accident that the proverbs of characterization are rarely investigated in the more recent literature on the book of Proverbs or that, despite their great number, their significance is scarcely if at all probed. Only when one assumes that sayings were oral in their development and usage is it possible to recognize their meaning.

That the proverbs of characterization do, in fact, effect change and that they indeed were heard and heeded is evidenced by their very nature. They bring to expression a "common sense" that has been conditioned by the transmission of the wisdom of the fathers, with whom the majority of people would concur, even when some had varying opinions and interests.

III. PROVERBS OF ANTITHESIS:
THE FOOLISH—THE WISE

1. Originally Double-Verse Proverbs
and Those Editorially Constructed

Virtually all of the proverbs of antithesis dealing with the foolish and the wise are found in the collection of 10:1–22 and chapter 15. In chapters 22—24 and 25—27, they are totally absent. Among these are found some that were originally distinct from others that were later brought together as proverbs of antithesis.[48]

Following are numerous sayings that were double-verse in their original form: "A prudent man sees danger coming and takes refuge, but the simple-minded one keeps going and suffers for it" (22:3). "Mockers stir up a city, but wise men turn away anger" (29:8).[49] "A fool gives vent to his anger, but a wise man restrains himself" (29:11). "Precious treasure is found in the dwelling of the wise, but a foolish man devours it" (21:20).[50] "A rebuke goes deeper into a man of understanding than a hundred blows to a fool" (17:10). "One of understanding keeps wisdom in view, but the eyes of a fool wander to the ends of the earth" (17:24). "Lady wisdom builds her house, but with her own hands folly tears it down" (14:1). "The talk of a fool brings a rod to his back, but the lips of the wise protect them" (14:3). "The wisdom of the prudent man is to discern his way, but the folly of fools is deceiving" (14:8). "The simple-minded believe everything, but the prudent man considers his steps" (14:15).[51] "In everything the prudent man acts with knowledge, but a fool exposes his folly" (13:16). "The one despising his neighbor lacks judgment, but a man of understanding restrains his tongue" (11:12).[52]

Several of these sayings are from the very start aimed at presenting opposition—for example, 22:3, "The wise person sees danger coming and takes refuge, but the simple-minded one keeps going and suffers for it." Proverbs 29:8; 14:1; 17:10; and 14:15 are similar. Above and beyond this, however, all these proverbs share in common a particular situation in which the contrast between wise and foolish behavior is best understood. This situation links both components of the proverb together.

Secondarily Constructed Proverbs

The literary device of parallelism found in these sayings serves the purpose of a straightforward complement to the characterization of the one type or the other. Examples of this are statements such as 10:1, "A wise son brings joy to his father," which originated as single-verse. Someone then added a simple complement: "but a foolish son is sorrow to his mother." This sort of augmentation has been done to many of the sayings.

With other proverbs the later addition is conspicuous, where it only partially succeeds or where it does not match particularly well—for example, 10:21 ("The lips of the righteous nourish many, but fools die for lack of judgment") or 19:13 ("A foolish son is a father's ruin, and a quarrelsome wife is like a continual dripping"). The same can be said of 14:7; 10:8, 14; 13:10, 16; 15:21; and 17:7. We can be virtually assured of a later addition in those cases where the supplementary statement is an extolling of wisdom or the wise person—for example, 10:23, "As sport to a fool is the doing of evil, but wisdom is the delight of a man of understanding" (the actual antithesis is contained in v. 23a).

Proverbs of Instruction

Here we encounter a category of antithetical proverbs about the foolish and the wise that finds its context rooted in instruction and the teaching of wisdom: "The one who loves discipline loves knowledge, but the one who hates correction is stupid" (12:1). "On the lips of the discerning is wisdom found, but a rod is for the back of the one lacking judgment" (10:13). "The wise in heart heed commandments, but a babbling fool will come to ruin" (10:8). "The fear of Yahweh prolongs life, but the years of the wicked are cut off" (10:27). "Strike a mocker and the simple will learn prudence; reprove a man of understanding and he will gain knowledge" (19:25). "Punishments are established for mockers and floggings for the backs of fools" (19:29). "When a mocker is punished, the simple man becomes wise; when a wise man is instructed, he acquires knowledge" (21:11). "Folly is bound up in the heart of a child, but the rod of discipline drives it far from him" (22:15). "The one who heeds wholesome admonition will abide among the wise" (15:31). "The one who ignores discipline despises himself, but the one who heeds admonition acquires understanding" (15:32).

Particularly striking is a subgroup of proverbs in which parallelism has become an empty form—an observation also made by G. von Rad. Here it is possible to speak of "idling" or "echo" (*Leerlauf-*) parallelism, inasmuch as both halves of the verse say the same thing without any notable correlation. What we have here is not synonymous parallelism, in which case both halves of the proverb say something independently; rather, these sayings deal with the antithesis of wisdom and foolishness as such: "The crown of the wise is their wealth, but the folly of fools yields folly" (14:24). "The tongue of the wise commends knowledge, but mouths of fools spew out folly" (15:2). "The heart of the discerning seeks knowledge, but the mouths of fools feed on folly"

(15:14). "Understanding is a fountain of life to those who have it, but folly is the punishment of fools" (16:22). "The heart of the discerning acquires knowledge, and the ear of the wise seeks it out" (18:15).

2. Proverbs Dealing Exclusively with the Foolish and the Wise

Characterization

Because it is not always possible to ascertain with certainty which proverbs were originally double-verse and which ones were originally single-verse, the one-sided caricatures of the foolish and the wise are included here.

The Foolish

The speech, actions, and thinking of the foolish are so clearly portrayed in the proverbs that one would think those being depicted were being directly observed. The rendering "fools" could be misleading to the extent that some might understand these to be dumb people. A lack of intelligence, however, is only a marginal stigma. There is no word that corresponds precisely to the Hebrew *kesil*. The fool is an unreflective speaker and actor who, since he does not stop to consider the consequences of his words and deeds and thereby endangers the community, will eventually be destroyed. He is "antisocial," "asocial" in the literal sense of the word.

The Fool

"The one troubling his own household will inherit the wind, and the fool will be servant to the wise" (11:29). "The mocker does not like being corrected; he will not go to the wise" (15:12). "Of what use is money in the hand of a fool, since he has no intention of obtaining wisdom?" (17:16). "A fool takes no pleasure in understanding, rather only in expressing his opinion" (18:2). "A fool's lips bring strife, and his mouth invites a beating" (18:6). "A fool's mouth is his ruin, and his lips are a snare to his soul" (18:7). "The one answering before hearing—to him is folly and shame" (18:13).[53] "A man's own folly prevents his way, and then his heart is vexed against Yahweh!" (19:3). "A man wandering from the path of understanding comes to rest in the company of the dead" (21:16). "'Scoffer' is the name of the proud and arrogant man; he acts with insolent pride" (21:24). "Do you see a man who is hasty with words? There is more hope for a fool than for him" (29:20; cf. the African proverb "Hurry! Hurry! has no blessing" [see Appendix]).

The Speech, Actions,
and Thought of the Foolish

The thought expressed in 12:23, "The heart of a fool blurts out foolishness," is especially prominent in the fool's behavior. This trait stands in contrast to the restraint of the wise. The fool is always compelled to speak his mind immediately: "A fool shows his annoyance at once" (12:16). Whereas the wise man would rather hold his tongue, "the heart of fools blurts out folly" (12:23), "the fool exposes his folly" (13:16), "the mouth of the fool spews out folly" (15:2), and "every fool bursts loose" (14:16). What is typical of him is that he interrupts others: "The one who gives an answer before hearing—to him is folly and shame" (18:13); "Do you see a man who is hasty with words? There is more hope for a fool than for him" (29:20). It does not occur to the fool to think about what he should say: "A fool takes no pleasure in understanding, rather only in expressing his opinion" (18:2). He is not concerned about what risks he might thereby run: "A fool gives full vent to his anger" (29:11). Because "the mouth of a fool feeds on folly" (15:14), his mouth leads to ruin (18:7). Furthermore, the fool inflicts damage with his speech on corporate life: the mouth of the fool is virtual ruin (10:14); he encounters his neighbor with derision (11:12) and spreads slander (10:18). He produces strife through his presumption (13:10; 18:6), and if someone reproaches him, he is only defiant (14:9). Should anyone attempt to speak with him, he "rages and scoffs, and there is no peace" (29:9).[53a]

The Actions of the Foolish

The proverbs say only a little about the actions of the foolish. Fools apparently have no power to do extensive damage, but they are aggressive. They destroy their own household and bear the fruit thereof (11:29). What wisdom has erected, foolishness tears down (14:1). The foolish person squanders the abundance that has been entrusted to him (21:20). "Mockers stir up a city" (29:8), yet they achieve thereby no success.

The Thought of the Foolish

It is characteristic of the foolish that they are thoroughly content in their folly: "As sport to a fool is the doing of evil" (10:23); "Folly is a delight to one having no sense" (15:21). They are impudent in their presumption (21:24), they are undisciplined, and they give full rein to their anger: "A quick-tempered man acts foolishly" (14:17); "The one with a quick temper exalts folly" (14:29). "It is for fools repugnant to turn from evil" (13:19). They are without knowledge: "Fools mock guilt" (14:9). Wisdom is not to be found among them (14:33): "The heart of the foolish is inverted" (15:7); "The mocker searches for wisdom and does not find it" (14:6). Even if he would desire to purchase wisdom, it is of no use, since "he has no understanding" (17:16). He is foolish and simple-minded: "The simple-minded one believes every word" (14:15). He engages thoughtlessly in what is wicked (14:16) and, as a result, will not listen to anyone: "The mocker does not like being corrected" (12:1; 15:12). Not even blows with the rod have any effect on him (17:10). He is, anyway, always right: "The way of a fool seems right" (12:15). Nevertheless, "whoever relies on his own understanding is a fool" (28:26); "the eyes of the foolish wander to the ends of the earth" (17:24).

Isolation of the Foolish

One consequence expressed in the proverbs involving the foolish is an initial setting apart of both sides—both the foolish and the wise: "a companion of fools suffers harm" (13:20). Moreover, "fine speech is not becoming of a fool" (17:7), and "it is not fitting for a fool to live in luxury" (19:10). Conversely, "the mocker . . . will not go to the wise" (15:12). These sayings mirror a recognizable trend toward isolation.

Punishment of the Fool

"The punishment of fools is folly" (16:22), for "a fool's mouth is his undoing, and his lips are a snare to his soul" (18:7). That his misfortune is to be attributed to himself is emphasized repeatedly—for example, "A man's own folly ruins his life, yet his heart rages against Yahweh" (19:3); "The simple-minded keep going and suffer for it" (22:3; 27:12); and, in a rather graphic saying, "The talk of a fool brings a rod to his back" (14:3). Attention is drawn in a similar fashion to their death: "A man who wanders from the way of understanding comes to rest in the company of the dead" (21:16); "Fools die for lack of understanding" (10:21); and "Fools bear shame" (3:35).

Characterization of the Wise

The Wise Promotes the Community

The Work of the Wise Man, His Speech, and His Thought

"The speech of the righteous covers hatred" (10:18). "The lips of the righteous nourish many" (10:21). "The one who overlooks an insult is prudent"

(12:16). "Among the upright is found good will" (14:9). "The wisdom of the prudent man is to consider his way" (14:8). "Choice aplenty is found in the house of the wise" (21:20). "Wise men turn away anger" (29:8). "If a wise man pleads with a foolish man . . ." (29:9). "A wise man is able to hold himself back" (29:11).

In these sayings, the wise person has a function in the community: he contributes to the maintenance of peace, he quiets anger where it surfaces, he appeases the strife of fools, and he attempts to communicate with them. His lips "cover hatred," even when in the process he himself must absorb abuse. He guards the abundance that has been entrusted to him. He contributes toward goodwill. His words are capable of refreshing many. To this group of sayings can be added 11:9; 12:18; 16:14; 20:22; 24:3–5; and 28:2.

The Wise Man Restrains Himself

This group of proverbs belongs with the aforementioned group to the extent that it expresses in a variety of ways how the wise person exercises a positive influence on the community. "Wise men store up knowledge" (10:14). "A man of understanding holds his tongue" (11:12). "The lips of the wise preserve them" (14:3). "The one who restrains his words has knowledge" (17:27). "In everything a prudent man acts with knowledge" (13:16). "The prudent man considers his steps" (14:15). "A man of discretion is patient" (14:17). "A man of understanding walks uprightly" (15:21). "One who is even-tempered is a man of understanding" (17:27). "The prudent person sees danger coming and takes refuge" (22:3). "With those who take advice is wisdom" (13:10).[54] "With the slow to anger is great understanding" (14:29). "A rebuke goes deeper into a man of understanding" (17:10). "It is an honor for a man to avoid strife" (20:3).

Three discernible features tend to characterize the behavior of the wise. The wise man restrains himself in his diagnosis and in his speech. Where speech is unnecessary, he is silent; he sets a guard over his lips.

Furthermore, his actions are in harmony with his speech. He does everything with forethought. He gives attention to his steps. In critical situations, the prudent man remains calm. He holds to a straight path, and as a judicious person, he remains composed. If he sees calamity approaching, he takes refuge at the proper time.

Wisdom also is manifest in a person's inner constitution; it is found among the humble. The person who bears an insult is prudent. The one who is forebearing is the wiser; he takes seriously any criticism. Keeping his distance from strife is, for him, not cowardice, rather an honor.

Here we find manifest a view of the wise person that is motivated by an awareness of accountability to the community of which he is a part. These proverbs are molded not by a differentiation that is either political or religious in nature, rather solely by a particular notion of collective life that has its specific limits, precisely as it is found in many places. The responsibility of the "wise," who are communicating through these sayings, stems from a commitment to preserve the very essence and health (the *shalom*) of the community.[55]

When the sense and purpose of this proverb group are correctly perceived, a harmony results: that is, they correspond to the social function of the proverbs as a whole, which is to maintain peace.

In sum, it can be said that the proverbs of antithesis involving the foolish and the wise, with their one-sided characterizations, provide amazingly rich and precise insight into the social relations and occurrences of the period of the monarchy. They mirror tensions and subsequent reflection on such tensions that would have been typical of life in a village or small town. If ancient Israel's social history is to receive its due consideration, the proverbs of antithesis, namely, those dealing with the foolish and the wise, need to be given greater attention than has been heretofore accorded them. Such an investigation, made possible only through an inductive method of examination, proceeds from saying to saying and group to group in its analysis of inherent contrasts. It probes into the spheres in which these contrasts occur, into the dispositions represented on both sides of the contrast, and into prevailing human interests. It is astonishing what emerges in terms of recognizing social conditions and sociological insight as a result of a more precise classification of proverbs (a classification that in the present study is intended to serve only as a broad overview). We may further clarify the result of this analysis: proverbs of antithesis concerning the righteous and the wicked form a later stratum and yield virtually nothing in the way of insights as to social conditions, for they concern themselves only with an antithesis of worldview.

3. The Wisdom of the Wise in Transition

A character sketch of the wise reveals the contours of yet another group of sayings. Although wisdom is understood primarily as functional in the previously mentioned proverbs, a wisdom that promotes the community in various ways can also manifest itself as an abstract entity, existing unto itself: "The one listening to a life-giving exhortation will dwell among the wise" (15:31). "The wise in heart is called discerning, and pleasant speech promotes instruction" (16:21). "The heart of the wise makes his speech prosper, and his lips promote instruction" (16:23). "The one who restrains his words has knowledge, and the one who is even-tempered is a man of understanding" (17:27). "The heart of the discerning acquires knowledge, and the ear of the wise seeks knowledge" (18:15). "The one who acquires wisdom loves his own soul; the one who seeks insight will prosper" (19:8).

To this category belong numerous other sayings that all contribute to the praise of wisdom, whether directly or indirectly. In all these sayings, wisdom still exists for its own sake; these proverbs say nothing about any function in the community.

The Wisdom of the Wise;
Praise of the Wise (or Wisdom)

These proverbs say only that the wise man is a wise person, each using different terms and significations. They exist solely as a direct or indirect means of extolling wisdom: "The crown of the wise is their wisdom" (14:24). "Wisdom abides in the heart of the discerning" (14:33). "The tongue of the wise dispenses knowledge" (15:2). "The lips of the wise spread knowledge" (15:7). "The wise in heart is called discerning" (16:21). "The heart of the wise makes his speech prosper" (16:23). "One of understanding sets his face toward wisdom" (17:24). "Wisdom is a delight to a man of understanding" (10:23). "The wise person listens to counsel" (15:14). "The heart of the discerning seeks knowledge" (12:15). "The heart of the discerning acquires knowledge, and the ear of the wise seeks knowledge" (18:15). "Walk with the wise and be wise" (13:20).

Wisdom as Gain for the Wise

"The prudent are surrounded with knowledge" (14:18). "Insight is a fountain of life to the one having it" (16:22). "The one acquiring wisdom loves his own soul; the one seeking understanding will prosper" (19:8). "The one walking in wisdom is delivered" (28:26). "The wise inherit honor" (3:35). (Cf. also 10:13; 12:1; 13:14; 14:16–18; 15:32; 18:4b; 21:11b.)

In surveying this group, one is initially struck by how much these sayings resemble one another. All extol wisdom; all seek to show how valuable wisdom is. Through this lauding of wisdom, these sayings also extol the wise; it is an honor to identify with wisdom. In these proverbs, wisdom has become a merit in and of itself. Removed from its everyday function, it is an abstract understanding of wisdom, the same understanding that is dominant in Proverbs 1—9.

Included in this group as well are the proverbs of antithesis that join in the praise of wisdom and contribute in the proverbs of instruction.

We appear to have before us a category of texts in which the transition from early to late wisdom has been accomplished or, at the very least, has been prepared.[56] Evidence for this is the emergence of one particular group of proverbial statements belonging to the general heading of characterization: the contradistinction between the wise and the foolish. This group in its form belongs to early proverbial wisdom, yet in its content is clearly to be differenti-ated, due to its movement from an instrumental wisdom to one more focused on the reality of wisdom itself. From the contrast of the foolish and the wise (also classified as characterization) there emerges an offshoot of sayings in which the wise are portrayed somewhat differently than in earlier comparisons. This leads to the suggestion that the transition from earlier to later wisdom in fact was a gradual process.

IV. COMPARISONS

One can presume that the high number of comparisons in Proverbs is indic-ative of their significance.[57] This weight, however, cannot be universalized; each saying must be considered on its own merit. From the outset it can be said that the comparisons are not embellishment in the sense that Aristotle under-stood it (see C. Westermann, *Vergleiche und Gleichnisse im Alten Testament und Neuen Testament,* 1984); they have more than a mere aesthetic value (cf. Bult-mann's *"ornamentale Elemente"*). Further, they are not "images" that exist to il-lustrate a "matter" (*Sache*). Seen positively, two things can be said. First, the subject matter of comparative proverbs needs to be considered. This can hap-pen only when the comparison itself is allowed to speak. Second, every genuine comparison contains something provisional; one cannot press it too far. It can-not be forced; rather, it should be permitted the freedom of being able to ex-press what it will. This is all the more valid, inasmuch as the majority of comparisons here reflect occurrences that are merely being hinted at yet whose contours are not being specifically delineated.

The most important factor in the distribution of the comparisons is their inclusion in the category of proverbial statements. In the words of exhortation they have no real function. The one being addressed in the exhortations and warnings becomes the one who reacts, normally being challenged to a particu-lar action. The proverbial statements, on the other hand, are aimed at a thoughtful (i.e., comprehending and reflective) response. The comparison serves the person whose inclination is toward pondering things.

In chapters 25—26 (and part of 27) we find a collection of comparative proverbs. Otherwise, they are scattered through Proverbs as a whole. The con-centration found in Proverbs 25—26 demonstrates that comparison for the compiler had a singular importance. Hence he has placed them together (cf. also 1 Kings 5:12–13).

In a group of proverbial statements that either belonged already to later wisdom or is found in the transition to it, comparisons drop fully out of sight—

for example, notably among the proverbs that extol wisdom. Here we can see that in this phase, wisdom becomes an abstract notion. The concrete nature of the comparison is here not well suited to the depiction of wisdom and is no longer needed. In what follows, it is possible only to cite certain examples; some discussion has already appeared in preceding sections. The examples being cited can be categorized according to the headings already given: observations and experiences with related contrasts and characterizations of wise persons and wise behavior. The proverbs of antithesis are closely linked to the characterizations. This is especially true of the foolish–wise sayings, in addition to other smaller groups.

1. The Content of the Comparisons

Through the comparisons the world in which ancient Israel lived comes to expression in all its diversity and fullness and has a share in what the proverbs want to express. Because the world was understood as created, it is capable of communicating. The actions, speech, and thought realm of humanity are indeed those of a creature, who, along with everything else in the created order, has his origin in the work of the Creator. It is this work of the Creator that makes possible the comparisons. The comparisons make mention of the following domains:

heaven and earth: clouds, wind and rain, winter and summer, snow, rain and steady dripping on a rainy day, the abyss, the realm of the dead, darkness and the deep waters, fire and smoke, gold, silver, and iron;

terrain: street, path and road, desert, thorn hedge, stones and gravel, pits, bubbling brook and murky springs, corrupt fountain, pile of stones, dew on the grass, early green foliage and withering leaves, pasture for cattle;

plants and animals: trees (tree of life), grass, thorn branch, foliage, roots in the soil, birds in flight, doves, swallows and starlings in their nest, bear, growling lion, roaming dog, pig, snake, viper;

human being: heart, body and soul with its division and its senses, body parts and bones, face, mouth and lips, tongue and breath, heart and spirit;

clothing and sustenance: ornament and decoration, wreath and crown, bread, honey and honeycomb, apple, delicacies, wine, vinegar, perfume and ointment, "a golden apple in a setting of silver," a golden ring, precious jewels, a purse with precious stones, "earthenware with silver glaze";

work, dwelling, trade: field, goods and property, winnowing and threshing of grain, grain and fruit, goldsmith;

buildings: house, cabin, roof and door, door hinge, castle and fortress, wall
and sliding bolt, city and gate, wall and dam, collapse of a house, tin of
the roof;

implements and tools: furnace and melting pot, light and lamp, rod, hammer,
wood and coal, axe;

illness: wound, medicine, healing, consumption, hopping of the crippled,
intoxication, sore tooth, staggering foot;

weather: snow in the summer, rain at harvest, rain that runs off;

weapons: sword, arrow, flaming arrow, spear;

hunt: pit, trap.

It is the world of the farmer, the tiller of the soil, and the tradesman that
opens before our eyes in these comparisons. It is this realm of the simple person and his everyday life out of which the proverbs have grown. The wisdom
of the proverbs is the wisdom of this uncomplicated world and unpretentious
people. The thought and action of such people are determined by the elements
that surface in the comparisons. The wisdom of the proverbs serves the purpose of assisting right thinking and right action on behalf of those living in an
uncomplicated world.

In accordance with the brevity of the proverbs, the object of comparison is
always treated in abbreviated fashion; normally, it is expressed by either one or
two terms. In listening to the proverbs, one must visualize the setting that is
being hinted at in each individual case: the bubbling brook, the flying bird,
the bread, the ornament, the city with walls and a gate, the winnowing of
grain, the harvest, the furnace, and so forth. Only then does the fullness with
which the comparative sayings have been formulated open up to us. There
exists a connection between the abundance and the fullness of the comparisons
and their concreteness in their briefer forms, which is explainable only by inductive analysis.

When we consider the totality of subject matter being utilized, we come to
the following conclusion: everything belongs to the experiential realm of normal people living in a village or small town. Any reference to a wider context,
realm, or dimension is missing. Absent is anything having to do with a big city,
other nations or peoples, the military, commanders and war, voyages, commerce and trade, the Temple and Palestine, works of art, or civilization. This
renders it highly improbable that the proverbs arose in a royal or cultic school
of wisdom or that their authors were part of a more highly educated stratum.
The reason that this element has not been given sufficient attention in research
done up to the present is that comparisons have been accorded no significance.[58]

When we compare the compilation of topics in Proverbs with descriptions of proverbs attributed to Solomon (1 Kings 5:12–13), the thought occurs that a collection of proverbs of comparison is on display.

That the proverbs are closely linked to poetry (or that they are an early form of poetry) can be explained by their "poetic" form and the numerous poetic devices, on the one hand, and the relative significance of the comparisons for the proverbs, on the other. It is not at all possible to deprive the comparisons of their poetic artifice and charm; they can be smirking, serious, nonthreatening or shocking, familiar or summoned from the unknown, brilliant or melancholy—all of which play a part in proverbs, arousing the reader to contemplation, reflection, and imaginative deliberation. Sometimes they are only suggestive, other times paradoxical, but always, they are striking.

The proverbs as linguistic vehicles of wisdom in ancient Israel do not merely reflect the relationship between an individual and his world. They also link wisdom to the very diverse world in which the audience lives. The sayings connote a wealth of imagination, broad in scope and quite varied, that is able to adduce correlatives linking the "saying" with the world in which it is spoken. The resultant effect is that the world makes itself known in the proverb. What is farthest removed from these proverbs and their wisdom is an abstractness in its conceptualization. Rather, it is precisely their proximity to real life that is being mirrored in the comparisons. The wisdom on display is very much at home with humor and wit, and it is far more concerned with events that occur than with the realm of the thought world. The characteristic analogy being employed here is foremost one of occurrences and secondarily one of *analogia entis*.

2. The Form of the Comparisons

Although the basic structure of the comparisons is always the same, namely, a = b, the abundance of forms of individual sayings is quite extraordinary. Only a sample of these is provided. Normally, the saying is a strophe consisting of two verses. Infrequently, there are two strophes; rarely do more occur. The reason for the linguistic uniqueness is that both verses of the proverb, which often are unrelated though placed side by side, seldom are joined by a "like" (*ke*) or even an "as . . . so . . . " Hence the Hebrew proverbs of comparison sound different from their translations, which require the particle "as–so." The linguistic efficacy of the Hebrew comparisons can be attributed to their extreme brevity, which permits the listener himself to think through and complete the relationship of the verses to one another. (The translations below follow H. Ringgren.) Comparisons come in a variety of forms:

1. The linking of two unrelated nominal clauses, placing subject and predicate in close connection: "Like a gold ring in a pig's snout is a beautiful woman who rejects discretion" (11:22). "A word aptly spoken is like apples of gold in settings of silver" (25:11a; cf. 18:4). "Like a gold ring or an ornament of gold is a rebuke from the wise to a listening ear" (25:12). "Like clouds and wind without rain is a man boasting of a gift he does not give" (25:14).

2. A single-verse predicate clause that conforms to the category of human observation: "There is reckless speech that is like the piercing of a sword" (12:18a; v. 18b was probably added on later to this saying composed in 3–2 meter; 18a is a complete comparison). "A wise king scatters the wicked and drives the wheel over them" (20:26). "In the light of a king's face there is life, and his favor is like a rain cloud in spring" (16:15). "A worthless man plots evil, and his speech is like a scorching fire" (16:27). "Acquitting the guilty and condemning the righteous— both are an abomination to Yahweh" (17:15).

3. The linking of two originally independent sayings in 17:19 and 17:22: "A cheerful heart is like good medicine, but a crushed spirit dries up the bones" (as a result of the addition of v. 22b, a proverb of antithesis is formed out of the comparison found in 22a).

4. Simple, single-verse nominal clauses extended into predicate clauses: "The words of a talebearer are as delicious morsels; they go down to a person's innermost being" (18:8). "The name of Yahweh is like a strong tower; the righteous person runs into it and is safe" (18:10). "The spirit of Yahweh is like the lamp of a man; it searches out his innermost being" (20:27; cf. also 20:5, 17; 21:1).

5. A nominal clause with an attached parallel: "The wealth of the rich man is his strong city, like a high wall protecting him" (18:11; v. 11a is itself a complete comparison). "An offended brother is more unyielding than a fortified city, and quarrels are as the bars of a castle" (18:19). "As the roar of a lion is the king's rage, but his favor is like dew on the grass" (19:12).

6. A predicate clause extended into another predicate clause: "A wise man attacks the city of the mighty and tears down the stronghold of their trust" (21:22).

7. The juxtaposition of two nominal clauses: "As the heavens are high and the earth deep, so the heart of kings is unsearchable" (25:3).

8. The juxtaposition of two predicate clauses, both of which begin with an imperative in a conditional sense: "Remove the dross from the silver, and the smith has material for a vessel; remove the wicked from the

king's presence, and his throne will be established in righteousness"
(25:4–5).

9. Two predicate clauses juxtaposed to each other, both of which can
   function as independent proverbs: "Through forbearance a ruler can be
   persuaded, and a gentle tongue can break a bone" (25:15).

10. Three nouns on the one side and a nominal clause on the other: "Like
    a club or sword or hammer is the man bearing false witness against his
    neighbor" (25:18).

Particularly effective are comparisons involving polar opposites, which are
found in the proverbs of many peoples—for example, 11:22 ("a gold ring in
the snout of a pig") and 26:8 ("a jewel in a sling"). (A more thorough discussion
of the forms of comparison is found in J. Schmidt [1936] and in H. J. Hermisson [1968], pp. 137ff.)

3. The Uniqueness of the Comparisons Exemplified

In genuine proverbs of comparison, the proverb and the comparison are
identical; that is, the proverb in its entirety is a comparison. On the whole,
comparisons are statements that are seldom linked to an admonition and seldom posed as a rhetorical question. The comparison normally serves as a form
for human observations and characterizations.

Several examples that are distinct deserve some comment:

"A cheerful look brings joy to the heart; a good word refreshes the bones"
(15:30). This proverb is not an explicit comparison, since it does not have the
a = b structure. Nevertheless, it belongs to this category. Its particular subtlety
lies in the dual parallelism—heart–body, look–word. A seemingly mere physi-
cal occurrence is discovered to be something in which the entire person is
involved (heart–body). By grasping this, the reader is indeed caused to reflect
and might consequently discover what this proverb is capable of communicating.

"Like a bird that strays from its nest is a man who strays from his home"
(27:8). Just as the prophet Jeremiah observed concerning the work of the pot-
ter, in the same way the author of Prov. 27:8, 17 has watched with his eyes the
flight of a bird and a blacksmith at work. Iron is sharpened by iron, and, in
the same way, one man sharpens another. The author has thought through his
observations and recalls them as he considers a similar phenomenon; he
reaches a conclusion from analogy. When we understand these statements not
merely as illustrating pictures, rather as comparisons, which they, in fact, are

meant to be, it becomes clear that the thinking process among the people of ancient Israel was considerably more empirical than had been presumed by those of us who are biased as a result of our abstract, Western reasoning. These people lived in a world in which they actively took part—observing it, making comparisons, being struck by similarities, and drawing ever-increasing conclusions from the realm of the known to the unknown. In this way, they discovered with great eagerness (cf. Prov. 27:20) something new. Moreover, a verse-by-verse analysis bears out that they perceived themselves as creatures among other creatures to a far greater extent than we have thought up to now. Their wisdom, likewise, was not some abstract, esoteric notion of wisdom, rather, a wisdom that made it possible for God's creation (even when it at times is conferred on animals!) to be at home in the rich and variegated fullness of creation. When the observations about people converge with and complement those involving the rest of creation, then what is said about creation in the rest of the Old Testament amounts simply to this: human beings understand themselves as humans, insofar as they perceive themselves as part of the whole of creation.

Comparisons are normally not required in the proverbs of antithesis, for the point lies in the contrast itself. In 15:13a, "A glad heart makes a cheerful countenance," the comparison serves to reinforce the wholesome power of joy. In two contrasts between the poor and the rich—"The wealth of the rich is his strong city" (10:15) and "A man's riches may ransom his life, but a poor man bears threat" (13:8)—one particular feature is emphasized that stimulates reflection about the ambivalence over riches. And yet, in this subgroup of poor and rich, comparisons relating to the behavior of both are absent. The reason for this is that these sayings contain an implicit admonition, and admonitions (concentrated in chaps. 22—24) do not intersect with comparisons.

"An honest answer is like a kiss on the lips" (24:26); "It is joy to a man to give an apt reply" (15:23). When the comparison in these and other sayings points to the appropriate moment for helpful words, such stands in continuity with speech as it is found throughout the Old Testament as a whole. All significant speech in the Old Testament is linked to a temporal context, from the primary context of creation to the very end of the scriptures. Every word retains its meaning foremost in a sequence of events. This encompasses, for example, the most weighty of words in the Old Testament, those of the prophets, whose speech was for a particular hour. The prophets were members of a people among whom speech was held in high regard, as is understood precisely in this group of sayings.

One particular experience is formulated in a comparison in a way that is not only witty and capable of being easily passed on but striking as well: "a soft tongue breaks a bone" (25:15b; with parallels in Sumerian sayings).

This typical folk proverb illustrates what can be achieved through conversational speech. Here the character of the wise person comes into play. He does not allow himself to be provoked to anger or to verbally attack the other person; rather, he remains cool and composed, thereby achieving more than the "heated one." "There is reckless speech that is like the piercing of a sword" (12:18). "A generation whose teeth are swords and whose jaws are knives . . ." (30:14).

It is noteworthy that the proverbs about harmful speech stand out from the proverbs about salutary speech. This impression is actually reinforced through the comparisons, since these, too, are sayings that have grown out of observation and experience. Those who coined them have observed and experienced how much speech can hurt a person. In the German language we describe the comparison by means of the figure of speech *ein verletzendes Wort;* yet the isolated participle *verletzend* ("hurting," "offending," hence "offensive") does not possess the linguistic force in a sentence that an event before one's eyes generates. Through such an example we can recognize the original oral function of the proverbs. Like sayings were formulated, heard, and preserved in order to protect the defenseless person hearing the tradition from injurious speech.

That the situation as well as the person speaking is an integral part of salutary speech is expressed in the pointed and profound saying "Like a thornbush in a drunkard's hand is a proverb in the mouth of a fool" (26:9).

Hence, even a "wise saying" can do damage and open wounds when it is spoken by an incompetent person at the wrong time. Such intricate background occurrences can be formulated in a saying that in another situation is able to increase understanding or even influence a decision.

Whoever endeavors to understand proverbs of this kind must first free himself from the erroneous misunderstanding that proverbs communicate general truths. Rather, it is particularity that is uniquely communicated (i.e., what is not inherent to all proverbs in a general sense), leading to their formulation and transmission. "The one digging a pit will fall into it, and the one rolling a stone will have the stone turn back on him" (26:27).

This saying occurs frequently and has numerous variants. It has also been preserved up to the very present. Indeed, a devious person has dug a grave for someone else to fall into. Yet, it is he, not the others, who falls in. The unexpected, which catches the devious person by surprise, has indeed happened. This occurrence has been observed and formulated in speech so that it can be newly applied in similar circumstances. However, the proverb will not say, "It always happens like this." Such an overarching understanding is a misunderstanding of the proverb. The proverb says, "It happened this way and it can happen this way again," not "it will always happen this way." The proverb warns the community of a danger it faces.

A companion picture, however, is another proverb that cannot possibly be misunderstood: "Like earthenware covered with glaze are burning lips with an evil heart" (26:23). This is one of many comparisons describing duplicity at work. Fraud and allurement coincide in the saying.

By no means is it incidental that comparisons, in referring to the quarrelsome, compare contention to violent forces: "Starting a quarrel is like one who breaches a dam" (17:14). "Without wood a fire goes out; where there is no talebearer, quarrel ceases" (26:20). "As charcoal to embers and wood to fire, so is a quarrelsome man for kindling strife" (26:21).

The potency of proverbs using comparisons such as the above is often underestimated. The devastating force of a quarrel is being perceived, along with its immeasurable consequences, at the same time that the destructive nature of this development at its inception is being recognized: "one who breaches a dam." In other words, the one who precipitates this is no longer in control of the forces he unleashes.

Such destructiveness can be ignited by clumsy thoughtlessness: "Like one seizing a dog by the ears is the one passing by who meddles in a quarrel not his own" (26:17).

What sets these proverbs apart is their concern for preserving the welfare of the community in the narrow zone that exists between tranquility and disturbance. Neither a governmental power nor the worshiping community is ultimately responsible for this; rather, the community of people as a whole—that is, its adult members—are. Proverbs are the linguistic (and, therefore, the nonviolent) vehicle by which commissions and omissions relative to the welfare of the community are regulated. They are aimed at those who acknowledge the collective character of their content. The efficacy of these sayings, especially the comparisons, is due to the fact that people carefully set out to preserve and protect public welfare, and they see this as a task that is transmitted from generation to generation.

Thus, it is confirmed that in much of what they say, the proverbs are in agreement with prophetic indictment. The prophet Isaiah pronounces the fall of everything that is exalted, while a proverb says that "the one building a gate too high invites destruction" (17:19; cf. also 26:27).

The effect of the proverb is produced by taking an inner attitude and translating it into a linguistic precedent—a precedent that is valid.

"Like a club or sword or sharp arrow is the man who bears false witness against his neighbor" (25:18). The passion of prophetic indictment is being communicated through this saying: the person who falsely charges his neighbor is wielding deadly weapons!

As is the case in prophetic accusations, here also we encounter the oppression of the lowly: "A ruler who oppresses the poor is like a driving rain that leaves no crops" (28:3). "Like a muddied spring or a polluted fountain is a righteous man who gives in to the wicked" (25:26).

The prophets did not shrink from criticizing an esteemed and respected man if, in fact, such a one stooped to the level of a transgressor.

On the other hand, mercy knows no limits with those who are suffering, and one particular saying is assimilated into the proclamation of Jesus (Rom. 12:20): "If your enemy is hungry, feed him . . . thus you will gather burning coals on his head" (25:21–22).[59]

Among the proverbs of antithesis involving the foolish and the wise we encounter comparisons in the proverbs that characterize only the fool, and particularly imaginative ones at that (26:1, 6, 7, 9, 11). These communicate something of the tension that takes place in a small community between those who are concerned for the community's improvement, harmony, environment, and general conduct and those who do not care about these things. It is the former who must constantly direct their efforts in resisting the latter, whose interests are blatantly selfish in nature: "Like snow in summer and rain in harvest, so honor is not becoming of a fool" (26:1). "Like cutting off one's foot or drinking violence is sending a message by the hand of a fool" (26:6). "Like a lame man's legs that hang limp is a proverb in the mouth of fools" (26:7). "Like a dog returning to its vomit is a fool repeating his folly" (26:11). "A stone is heavy and sand is a burden, but a fool's provocation is heavier than both" (27:3).

Each of the above is a word of derision aimed at the foolish; all are colloquial expressions. It should be noted, however, that they all are guided by a basic predisposition of forbearance. Even when the fool is a genuine burden, he must be endured nevertheless, for without this forbearance there is no peace whatsoever. These particular sayings involving the foolish and wise stand in notable contrast to those involving the righteous and wicked, where tolerance would appear no longer to exist. Note again the distinguishing mark here: forbearance goes hand in hand with humor; where it ceases to be, humor ceases as well.

Let us summarize our discussion of comparisons. Because the function of the comparison in the proverbs traditionally has not been recognized or sufficiently valued, the contribution of this unique method of utilizing analogy has not been brought to light. Yet, it is not possible to understand rightly ancient Israel's views about people and the world apart from observing this component part. It is noteworthy in this vein that, both in Israel and outside, comparisons are profusely developed in the earliest strata and that in later strata they recede markedly in favor of abstract, didactic discourse. The latter, which no longer is conversant with the comparison, has lost its connection to real life; it is merely "morality."

V. PROVERBS OF VALUE JUDGMENT
(COMPARATIVE PROVERBS)

Value Judgment in Chapters 10—22

"Better to be lacking in honor and have a servant than to pretend to be important and lack food" (12:9). "Better is a little with the fear of Yahweh than great wealth and trouble with it" (15:16; cf. Amenemope: "Better is poverty from the hand of God than treasures in stockpile" [see Appendix]). "Better is a meal of vegetables where there is love than a fattened ox and hatred" (15:17). "Better is a little with righteousness than great revenue with injustice" (16:8). "Better is a dry morsel with peace and quiet than a house full of sacrifices with strife" (17:1). "Better is a poor man walking in integrity than a man whose speech is perverse and who is a fool" (19:1). "What is desired of a man is his loyalty; and better is being poor than being a liar" (19:22). "Better is living in the desert than with a contentious and ill-tempered wife" (21:19). "A good name is more desirable than great riches; favor is better than silver and gold" (22:1). "Better is living on a corner of the roof than sharing a house with a contentious wife" (21:9). "Better is a patient person than a warrior, and controlling one's temper than capturing a city" (16:32).[59a] "Better is being lowly in spirit and numbered among the poor than sharing spoil with the proud" (16:19).

Proverbs of Value Judgment

"To obtain wisdom is better than gold, and to choose understanding rather than silver" (16:16). "There is gold and an abundance of precious stones, but lips of knowledge are a rare jewel" (20:15).

Proverbs of Value Judgment
in Chapters 25—31

" . . . for it is better to be told 'Come up here' than . . . " (25:7). "Do you see a man wise in his own eyes? There is more hope for a fool than for him" (26:12). "Wrath is cruel and fury is overwhelming, but who can endure jealousy?" (27:4). "Better is open rebuke than hidden love" (27:5). "Trustworthy are the wounds of a friend, but many are the kisses of an enemy" (27:6). "Better is a neighbor who is near than a brother who is far" (27:10). "Better is a poor man walking in integrity than a rich man perverse in his ways" (28:6). "To show partiality is not good, yet for a piece of bread a man will do wrong" (28:21). (See also the proverbs of value judgment in Qohelet.)

The proverbs of value judgment have as their goal contemplation based on a standard of value. These sayings have a simple and logical structure: better A than B (with no accompanying substantiation). This structure allows us to deduce with a fair amount of certainty that these sayings developed and were passed on orally. They presuppose a situation in the life of the community in which it is possible or even necessary to decide between two alternatives. The proverb has the function of offering advice to someone who stands before a decision. It also purposes to be a succor to someone else who must effect a decision. In the "better . . . than . . . " sayings, nothing is prescribed and nothing is exacted. The saying can even serve as a consolation to someone who is dissatisfied with what he has (e.g., 15:17).

The majority of proverbs from this group deal with having little and having much. Inasmuch as everyone wishes to have much (the "have-not" is not despised in these sayings), a juxtaposition is created between striving (greed and covetousness) and having little, which is depicted in some cases as the superior state—or at least, potentially so. The lowly person is capable of being the better, and making up one's mind in favor of the lowly can be, in fact, the wise decision. Normally, the subject matter here is the poor and the rich—for example, "Better is a little with righteousness than great revenue with injustice" (16:8). Or take several similar proverbs—for example, 12:9; 15:16–17; 17:1; 19:1 (= 28:6); 19:22; 22:1a–1b. All these are concentrated in chapters 10—22; the only occurrence in chapters 25—31, 28:6, is a replication of 19:1. This also is a sure indication that the collections of 10—22 and 25—31 evolved separately. It can be assumed that in the evolution of chapters 10—22 (or parts thereof), the relationship of the poor to the rich was particularly problematic.

The notion that it is better in certain cases to have little than to have much is more precisely defined by a consonance found in the proverbs—"Better is a little with righteousness" (16:8)—even when it can be stated in many variations. A somewhat critical disposition toward wealth tends to be reflected in all of these sayings. This criticism is not a general condemnation of wealth; the possibility that a rich man can be an upright man is left entirely open. The generally skeptical inclination, nevertheless, is based on experience, which indicates that it is possible for a rich man to accumulate his wealth through less-than-upright means or not to use it in the right way. This notion is prominent as well in the proverbs of antithesis involving the rich and the poor.

"Better is a patient person than a warrior, and controlling one's temper than capturing a city" (16:32). "Better is being lowly in spirit and numbered among the poor than sharing spoil with the proud" (16:19). In contrast to the glorification of a warrior or military success, the "better" here is patience and self-control.

"Better is open rebuke than hidden love" (27:5). "Trustworthy are the wounds of a friend, but many are the kisses of an enemy" (27:6). In these two proverbs, the significance of carefully weighing values is especially emphasized. In the relationship to one's neighbor, showing an overt friendliness can constitute a lesser value, for everything is dependent on sincerity (as is precisely the case with speech!)—a quality that does not shrink from correction. Both of these proverbs demonstrate quite admirably an element that is universal. Indeed, there exists no single human community that would not concur with this!

Ridicule of the contentious woman, which we met in the proverbs of comparison, can also take on the form of a proverb of value judgment, such as 21:19 and 21:9. Both proverbial forms establish a point of comparison. Several other proverbs could be added to this category as well: 27:10 ("Better is a neighbor who is near"), in addition to 25:6b–7; 27:4; 28:21; and 19:22. In each of these texts, the precise wording varies, as is the case with some nineteen proverbs of value judgment found in Qohelet.

Proverbs 16:16 and 20:15 are proverbs of value judgment that have been imitated. These two sayings are sufficiently distinct from all others that they can be clearly identified as later imitations. In the other proverbs of value judgment, the assessment "better . . . than . . . " relates to a concrete situation. But here the form of the evaluation is borrowed for the purpose of extolling wisdom's virtue: wisdom is superior to gold, silver, and coral. We can hereby detect the transformation of the sense of "wisdom": in the proverbs of value judgment, the wise decision is depicted as a decision in favor of something specific (e.g., a pot of vegetables with surrounding peace), whereas wisdom in the imitated proverbs is abstract, becoming an impartial value in and of itself.

Inasmuch as the oral development of the majority of the proverbs of value judgment is incontestable, they must have possessed early on considerable importance for everyday living, even before the corpus of the law was formed. They would have been widely distributed, since they were passed on orally, and they would have provided important guidelines for assistance in decision making. An integral part of corporate life was the constant assessment of and reflection on values that affected life in the community—a continual weighing of what was desirable and what was less desirable. Such a comparative probing is fundamentally different from a static teaching on values, in which the distinction between good and bad is decreed once for all, whether in the political, social, religious, or personal realm.[60] This notable distinction is reflected in these few sayings where an entity is often represented as being better than something else, based on public perception. Thoughtful consideration takes into account the situation. A situation can arise in which a reprimand or severity will be helpful, and not an affirmation (27:5–6). The same can be said of the poor and the rich: in certain instances, it is better to be numbered among the poor.

Regarding form, the proverb of value judgment is one of the simplest forms found in the book of Proverbs. In addition to the drawn-out form (e.g., 15:16: "Better is a little with the fear of Yahweh than great wealth and trouble with it"), we also encounter a short form (e.g., 19:22: "A poor man is better than a liar").

Comparative probing into what is better—a scrutiny that is thoughtful yet does not postulate absolute opposites (e.g., poverty is good—wealth is bad)—holds further meaning for the tension between poor and rich. When this tension, which is relative in nature, is viewed dogmatically and in absolute terms, it can lead to such regrettable contrasts as were manifest, for example, in the medieval church, where poverty achieved an absolute status through monasticism and where the institutional church simultaneously amassed an inordinate amount of wealth through buildings and the like. Such interpretation inevitably leads to unfortunate consequences.

Alongside those proverbs with the "better . . . than . . . " structure are also those with a "worse . . . than . . . " formulation. Only a few examples, however, have been preserved—for example, 27:4, "Wrath is cruel and fury is overwhelming, but who can endure jealousy?" and 17:12, "Let a man encounter a bear robbed of her cubs rather than a fool in his folly" (cf. also the discussion found in the characterization of the fool).[61]

The proverbs of value judgment stand in contrast to a notion of the law by which the law clearly establishes how someone is always to conduct himself when faced with an ambivalent situation—he is obligated to do what the law prescribes. In such a context, the proverbs of value judgment would lose the sense in which they are intended; they would be superfluous. In contradistinction to this approach to the law, the proverbs of value judgment presume not only the freedom of a person to decide but also the freedom to consider independently what is prudent in a given situation. During the preexilic period, final codices of the law did not yet exist or they were known only in certain circles.

One of the most important features of comparative proverbs is that they offer no substantiation. Not a single one of these sayings gives any supporting reason. The absence of such indicates that the comparative tōb-min possesses the character of a summons. It is a call to contemplate a decision; it calls the person specifically to decide in favor of what is more advantageous. In other words, it constitutes in some situations an appeal to embrace the "lesser": Do not consider the "better" to be what everyone else considers to be the better; rather, decide after you have reflected on whether it is truly the better! Such is meant to serve as counsel for the person being addressed. The underlying assumption is that a person is free to make a decision on his own.

The appropriation of this linguistic form in Jesus' preaching would indicate that for him, the freedom to decide—even when it was contrary to the norm—was foundational to human behavior in any given situation.

The function of the "better . . . than . . . " proverbs for the community is made even clearer when we consider the extent to which contrary public opinion can sway people. Inasmuch as most spheres of public life tend to be decided by quantitative and qualitative standards (the constant need for what is more, bigger, higher, faster, or louder), there is consequently no more place for reflection or moderation, both of which have great potential for benefit. Rather, moderation must be silenced! From the vantage point of those who spoke and pondered such proverbs, however, the absolute tyranny of the law of increase on all levels could only be considered unfathomable folly.

That the "better . . . than . . . " sayings are popular proverbs needs no proof. One is vividly struck by their universal distribution, on the one hand, and their sheer abundance and variety, on the other. The compilation of G. Vanoni[62] shown below can serve to illustrate. Cited are only a few examples: "Better be hated by the prince than hated by the people" (Malagasi, Africa). "Mieux vaut être l'esclave du rîche que l'époux du pauvre" (Hindi). "Un sage ennemi vaut mieux qu'un ignorant ami" (Sanskrit). "El huero es más prudente que la galina" (Anam). "An old grandmother in the house is better than an empty house"; "The antelope says, 'It is better to break a leg than land in the soup'" (Krobo, Africa). "Un seul fils d'éléphant vaut mieux qu'une multitude de francolines"; "Un véritable ami vaut mieux qu'un parent méchant"; "La case où tombent les gouttes est meilleur qu'un beau tombeau"; "Le travail communautaire est bien meilleur que le travail individuel"; "Le don de Dieu vaut mieux que le don de l'homme" (Korangasso, Africa).

In addition to these, we find samples of "better . . . than . . . " proverbs in Egypt, Mesopotamia, Africa, and Sumatra that appear in the Appendix. It would indeed be very strange if this form of speech, which is found throughout the entire world in the form of a popular proverb, should be included in the book of Proverbs as sayings emanating from a school of wisdom.

VI. NUMERICAL PROVERBS:[63]
COMMENDATIONS AND RIDDLES

"The serial numerical proverb brings into focus comparable phenomena."[64] Outside of Israel we encounter it in Ugarit and in the Ahiqar narrative. The most frequent sequence of numbers is two–three. The Ugaritic counterpart presents a threefold negative caricature in the context of a banquet; the Ahiqar narrative presents three modes of conduct that provide Shamash pleasure. These sayings point in the direction of instructional wisdom. In the Old Testament, apart from Proverbs, we encounter a similar form of saying—for example, Ps. 62:11–12, "One thing has the Lord spoken, two things have I heard, that you, God, are mighty, and that you are loving" (cf. Sir. 25:9–16; also Sir. 26:5–6; and besides the five numerical proverbs in 30:15–33, see also 6:16–19).

The numerical proverbs utilize the medium of enumeration in order to extend the form of the short saying. The result of this is a poem. Enumeration does not merely serve as a technical medium; rather, as H. W. Wolff (1964) notes, the numerical proverbs bring into focus comparable phenomena. However, it is important to be able to explain their intended purpose. The content of various numerical proverbs found throughout the Old Testament is so diverse that it is difficult to identify the purpose of enumeration—a category to which amplification also belongs.

When we inquire as to which classification the numerical proverbs resemble, the likely answer is human observations. In Prov. 30:15–33, the numerical proverbs would seem to be categorized according to the heading of observation. Yet these are not merely observations about people; they also encompass one's surroundings. Verses 24–28 are the fruit of attentively observing the animal kingdom, which also surfaces in numerous other proverbs. In vv. 18–19, it is the wonder of motion that unites the four observations. A particular phenomenon of creation that is found in very different forms is perceived here as being held in common. The proverb expresses the amazement of the person who is pondering this commonality: "Three things are for me extraordinary, indeed, four that I do not understand . . . " An initial step in human understanding consummates here in awesome wonder: "motion" in all its astonishing heterogeneity is discovered to be that which links diversity. (There is no Hebrew equivalent of the abstract noun "motion.")

In 30:29–31, a certain dignity is reflected in the motion of a stride. It presents unusually vivid contrasts such as the stalking of a lion, the strutting of the rooster among hens, the stride of the he-goat, and a king passing before his people. This enumeration communicates how creatures, typified in four examples, are united by means of the phenomenon of motion. Dignity is a mode of creaturely nobility in which even animals take part. The majesty of motion is able to link human beings and the animal kingdom.[65]

In 30:15–16 and 30:21–23 are two negative or frightening phenomena that also have entirely differing outward forms but nevertheless, in the eyes of the beholder, share something in common: insatiability (vv. 15–16) and insufferability (vv. 21–23). This is another example of how a particular notion stem-

ming from many different observations can develop and encompass so rich
a diversity.

Finally, four animals are listed in 30:24–28 that are numbered among the
smallest yet that accomplish amazing feats. The purpose of this proverb is to
show the translation of wisdom into the realm of nonhuman creation, even
among the smallest of creatures. Here wisdom is understood as the capacity to
do the extraordinary.

Proverbs 6:16–19 is a very different type of numerical proverb: "There are
six things that Yahweh hates . . . " Following are six wicked phenomena, all of
which are mentioned elsewhere in other proverbs as deeds of the wicked or
of the foolish. In this case, the numerical proverb is only a technical means of
enumeration. What we have here is actually an imitation of the numerical
proverb.

Earlier we mentioned that numerical proverbs are similar to human observations. This assertion can be extended: In form, the observations about people
are in fact proverbs of comparison. The occurrence of a comparison is at the
root of the numerical proverb. It is precisely when we view the numerical proverbs together with the many proverbs of comparison (i.e., an analogy) that the
significance of the comparison for Israel's wisdom becomes apparent. In the
comparison or juxtaposition of creatures resides an essential ingredient in understanding both the world and people, in addition to people and nonhuman
creatures. Because a human being and the surrounding world are one from the
standpoint of their createdness, comparison can serve as a useful tool in human
understanding. Both aspects of creation derive their existence from the Creator—from the smallest to the greatest.

Regarding form, it has already been noted that numerical proverbs are an
outgrowth of observation and comparison. And yet, they are designed to be an
enumeration, as accentuated by the numbers themselves. In contrast to other
instances of listing,[66] the particularity and uniqueness of the numerical proverbs found in 30:15–33 lie in their contemplative character, which is suited to
the proverbs that are observations about people. In sum, the enumeration issues out of the awareness that the things being listed are related on the basis
of recognizing a particular unifying criterion or mutual trait that binds them together.

The Commendation "Blessed Is the Man . . . "

Statements that begin with *'ašrē* ("happy/blessed is the one") are not wisdom
sayings, rather well-wishing or commendations—a special form of salutation.
They occur forty-five times in the Old Testament. Among these are twenty-six
occurrences in the Psalms, eight in Proverbs (scattered among several sections),

and once in 1 Kings 10:8 (= 2 Chron. 9:7) in the primary sense of commendation (on the occasion of a meeting between the queen of Sheba and Solomon, spoken by the former: "How blessed are your wives, how blessed are your servants!"). Here the commendation has the connotation foremost of a confirmation. Similar to this is a commendation of Israel in Deut. 33:29, "Blessed are you, O Israel, who is like you . . . !"; Ps. 33:12, "Blessed is the people whose God is Yahweh"; also Pss. 89:16 and 144:15. An individual can be commended in the same way, as in Ps. 127:5 or Ps. 40:4, "Blessed is the man who makes Yahweh his trust," among numerous examples in the Psalms. In another group of sayings, a person is commended in a way that manifests a point of contact with wisdom—for example, Ps. 1:1, "Blessed is the man who does not . . . , rather . . . ," or Ps. 128:1, "Blessed is everyone who fears Yahweh." Those who fear Yahweh are to be commended. In the place of the fear of God, wisdom also can be substituted—for example, Prov. 3:13, "Blessed is the man who acquires wisdom." The commendation can be viewed either as something that resembles the explicit lauding of wisdom (cf. 8:34) or as an indirect extolling of wisdom. To the extent that commendations of wisdom are classified according to the "praise of wisdom" motif, they can be ascribed to wisdom in a wider sense; as such, commendations constitute a special form of salutation.[67] (Several of the Psalms are extended poetic commendations, examples being 127:3–5 and 128:1–4.)

The Riddle

Riddles are normally treated together with proverbs. Yet, they represent an independent genre. For further discussion, see H. P. Müller, "Der Begriff Rätsel im Alten Testament," *VT* 20 (1970): 465ff.

VII. PROVERBS OF ANTITHESIS: THE RIGHTEOUS—THE WICKED[68]

1. Basic Fourfold Thematic Structure

"The one walking in integrity walks securely, but the one on crooked paths will be exposed" (10:5). "The righteousness of the blameless man keeps his way straight, but through his own wickedness the wicked man falls" (11:5). "The integrity of the upright guides them, but those acting unfaithfully are destroyed by their own duplicity" (11:3). "The righteousness of the upright delivers them, but by evil desires the unfaithful are taken captive" (11:6). "The one who seeks good seeks after favor, but evil seeks out the one who searches for it" (11:27). "The one who trusts in riches will certainly fall, but the righteous will flourish as a green leaf" (11:28). "The fruit of the righteous is a tree of life, but the souls of transgressors are taken" (11:30). "The one who despises instruction becomes a pledge for it, but the one who honors a command will be rewarded" (13:13). "Good sense brings favor, but the way of the unfaithful is ruin" (13:15). "Do not those devising evil err? But loving-kindness and faithfulness are for those who plan good" (14:22). "Through his evildoing the wicked man is brought down, but the righteous man finds refuge in his integrity" (14:32). "The one greedy for unjust gain troubles his family, but the one who hates bribes will live" (15:27). "A man who is kind does his soul well, but a cruel man troubles himself" (11:17). (Cf. also 21:12; 12:13; 13:6; 28:18, 20; 29:6.)

In these nineteen texts, all four of the elements belonging to the proverb of antithesis are summarized in one saying. Other categories of proverbs contain only some of these. By way of containing all four elements, a totality, to which each element belongs, is shaped by the sayings of this group. In each of the sayings the same subject is expressed: the antithesis of the righteous and the wicked in action and in fate. This type of fixed schematic in which all the proverbs actually say the same thing while at the same time varying in some unique way is found only in this complex set of proverbs. The possibility of this schematic having arisen from oral proverbs is out of the question, since a calculated thesis is developed within each statement. At the root of this model is a perceived observation, a conceptualization that has been thought out. Accordingly, the individual statements on the action and fate of the righteous and wicked are consistently of a general nature—for example, 11:5, "The righteousness of the blameless keeps his way straight, but through his own wickedness the wicked falls." Here, anything concrete is altogether missing. There is no indication of a situation to which the saying could relate; the statements are purely general and theoretical, corresponding to the schematic of the whole with its fourfold division.

Thus, we can be certain that these proverbs are artificially constructed. Their function is to propound a teaching or theory about the wicked and the righteous. One can only admire the inventiveness with which these sayings express the same thing in different words or combinations of words. Their style is somewhat reminiscent of Psalm 119.

The Deeds of the Righteous—
The Deeds of the Wicked

"The heart of the righteous ponders how to answer, but the mouth of the wicked spews out evil" (15:28). "The thoughts of the righteous are just, but the counsels of the wicked are deceitful" (12:5). "The mouth of the righteous is a fountain of life, but the mouth of the wicked covers violence" (10:11). "The tongue of the righteous is as choice silver, but the heart of the wicked is of little value" (10:20). "The lips of the righteous know what is fitting, but the mouth of the wicked knows only what is perverse" (10:32). "The righteous man has regard for the life of his animal, but the mercy of the wicked is cruel" (12:10). "The righteous person hates falsehood, but the wicked person acts shamefully and disgracefully" (13:5). "The one despising his neighbor sins, but blessed is the one displaying kindness to the poor" (14:21). "A wicked man exhibits a bold face, but an upright man gives thought to his ways" (21:29). (Cf. also 11:13, 17; 13:10; 28:1, 4, 5; 29:7, 10, 27.)

All of these proverbs say essentially the same thing: they juxtapose the thinking, speech, and action of the wicked with that of the righteous. On the one hand, the cause for this on the part of the wicked person is enumerated: his heart is cruel, lacking in virtue; his meditation is on deception; he is arrogant and quarrelsome; he manifests a defiant countenance; his craving is wrong; his mouth spews forth wickedness or perversity; he conceals violence; he is a slanderer and false witness; he behaves disgracefully and shamefully; he despises his neighbor, oppresses the lowly, and is alarmed where righteousness is pronounced. Precisely the opposite is said of the righteous in these sayings and thus needs no reiteration. When we allow all of this recounting of all that is good about the one and bad about the other to take effect, it becomes clear that we are dealing with a purely theoretical construct, the purpose of which is only to articulate a contrast. Here it is important to note that in this group and in the next, emphasis in the sayings is given entirely to the coexistence and/or antithesis of the righteous and the wicked, and not to the consequence of their deeds and punishment. Every single one of these proverbs has the structure of antithesis; the design of portraying opposition governs them all.

The Fate of the Righteous—
The Fate of the Wicked

"The wage of the righteous is life, but the reward of the wicked is sin" (10:16). "In the way of righteousness there is life, but the way of error brings death" (12:28). "The light of the righteous shines brightly, but the lamp of the wicked is extinguished" (13:9). "The memory of the righteous will be blessing, but the name of the wicked will rot" (10:7). "When the storm passes by the wicked person is gone, but the righteous person stands firm forever" (10:25). "The fear of Yahweh prolongs life, but the years of the wicked are cut short" (10:27). "The prospect of the righteous is joy, but the hopes of the wicked perish" (10:28). "The righteous person is delivered from trouble, and it visits the wicked instead" (11:8). "The wicked are overthrown and are no more, but the house of the righteous stands firm" (12:7). "No harm befalls the righteous, but the wicked have their fill of trouble" (12:21). "The righteous man discerns his place of rest, but the way of the wicked leads them astray" (12:26). (Cf. also 10:30, 31; 11:2, 18, 19, 21, 23, 31; 12:8, 20; 13:2, 6, 21, 22, 25; 14:11, 19, 32; 15:6.)

Out of all the groups of texts, one finds in this largest group (thirty in number) the clearest expression of what the proverbs of antithesis seek to convey. This rather lengthy series from beginning to end has the sole function of presenting the fate of the righteous and the wicked by accentuating in each saying something different about the inherent contrast. There are two controlling features of this group. First, in every verse the wicked person is contrasted with the righteous and vice versa. In this way, it is not only intimated but rather driven home that there is no other possibility. One either is included among the righteous or he is numbered with the wicked, *tertium non datur.* The second feature is just as obvious and prominent: there is prosperity only for the righteous; evil alone awaits the wicked. Just as both groups are contrasted, their fate is compared as well. Prosperity or trouble applies absolutely for either the one or the other: "The light of the righteous shines brightly, but the lamp of the wicked is extinguished."[69]

This has been formerly described as the doctrine of retribution or the phenomenon of cause and effect; it has also been referred to as "schicksalwirkender Tatsphäre" (K. Koch).[70] However, in both of these significations, the succession of guilt and fate is emphasized. The texts of Proverbs, on the contrary, leave a very different impression. Linguistically, this is highlighted through their incessantly repetitive structure of juxtaposing verse halves and coexistence, as well as contrast. This applies to both the actions and the fate of the righteous and the wicked. This general pattern, created by the stringing together of polar opposites, is a characteristic feature.

There are several texts that deviate from this usual pattern. In 10:31, the action of the righteous and the fate of the wicked are contrasted; in 13:2, the action of the wicked is contrasted with the fate of the righteous. In each of these three texts, the secondary link between the righteous and the wicked is apparent.

The mistaken interpretation of this category of sayings as a cause-and-effect correlation is partly a result of viewing them solely on the basis of their content without sufficiently paying attention to their form. Such a reading would require a form in which the verse was arranged so that the action appeared in the first half of the verse and the fate appeared in the second. However, the controlling pattern of this proverb group is the juxtaposition of both types in the same verse. It is with this antithesis that the composer is primarily concerned.

The Deeds and Fate of the Wicked (Unilateral)

"If a man returns evil for good, evil will not depart his house" (17:13). "Severe chastisement awaits the one forsaking the way; the one hating correction will die" (15:10). "An evil man seeks only rebellion, and a merciless official will be sent against him" (17:11).

2. Proverbs of Antithesis:
The Righteous—The Wicked in Chapters 25—29

The twenty proverbs of antithesis that occur in chapters 25—29 are not found in a fixed block; rather, they are scattered over five chapters. This makes the virtual conformity of the clusters in which these sayings are arranged all the more remarkable.

The action of the righteous person is depicted as follows: his behavior is blameless (28:18); he is a man of trustworthiness and faith (28:20); the righteous seek Yahweh and as a result understand all things (28:5); the righteous man is bold as a lion (28:1); he retains instruction (28:4); he is concerned about justice for the lowly (29:7) and sympathizes with them. Doing wrong is, for him, an abomination (29:27).

It is said of the wicked man that his ways are perverse (28:18); he is eager to get rich quickly (28:20); he is snared by his own sins (29:6); he does not comprehend what is just (28:5); he abstains from instruction and praises the wicked (28:4); he is not concerned about the lowly (29:7) and is a companion of thieves. An entire poem (30:11–14) describes a generation whose teeth are like swords for the purpose of devouring the poor. This person digs a pit so that others will fall in and seduces the upright on evil paths (28:10).

Regarding the fate of the wicked man, he falls into the pit that he had dug for others (28:18; 26:27; 28:10); he is suddenly destroyed (29:1); he does not go unpunished (28:20); he is snared by his own sin (29:6).

As to the fate of the righteous man, he receives help and is richly blessed (28:20); he can sing and be glad (29:6); the innocent man achieves prosperity (29:18b). All of these sayings are so general, with no particular situation, that we learn virtually nothing about the groups of people in contrast here or about what is happening between them. The things mentioned are the things customarily said about the righteous and the wicked.

3. What Happens between the
Righteous and the Wicked

Either one group or the other rises to power. Only in a few proverbs is there any mention of what actually transpires between the righteous and the wicked: "When the righteous triumph, there is great elation; but when the wicked rise to power, men go into hiding" (28:12). "When the wicked rise to power, people go into hiding; but when the wicked perish, the righteous thrive" (28:28). "When the wicked thrive, sin increases, but the righteous will see their downfall" (29:16).

This group of sayings is unique and striking for different reasons than other groups. Events are presupposed here that would have reflected a small city, among whose citizens there were groups competing for leadership. At one time, the one group had authority; at another time, the other group. Unfortunately, the proverbs do not tell us anything in the way of specifics. They do, however, give evidence that the authors were concerned about the coexistence of those designated as wicked and righteous.

There is one similarity between these proverbs and several from the compilation of chapters 10—22: "When it goes well with the righteous, the city rejoices; and when the wicked perish, there are shouts of gladness" (11:10). "Through the blessing of the upright a city is exalted, but by the mouth of the wicked it is destroyed" (11:11). "Righteousness exalts a nation, but sin is a disgrace to any people" (14:34).

In the above sayings there is also something that is transpiring between the righteous and the wicked: there is competition between them. In 11:10–11, they form factions, whose controlling influence in the city is in flux.

Another group of sayings could be included here. The wicked man persecutes the righteous, and the righteous man escapes from him: "With his mouth the godless man destroys his neighbor, but through insight the righteous escape" (11:9). "The words of the wicked lie in wait for blood, but the speech of the upright rescues them" (12:6). "An evil man is ensnared by the sin of his lips, but the righteous man escapes from trouble" (12:13). "Thorns and snares are in the path of the wicked, but the one guarding his soul remains far from them" (22:5).

According to 11:9, the righteous are threatened by the wicked; in 12:6, their speech "lies in wait for blood"; and in 12:13 and 22:5, the righteous person is beset by trouble. However, the wicked man is not successful in achieving his evil goal: "through insight the righteous escape" (11:9; 12:6). Nevertheless, it should be noted that none of the sayings indicates a conflict going on, and in no case are the wicked threatened by the righteous, who apparently are the weaker of the two. This parallels the situation in the psalms of lament between the righteous and their enemies (cf. Ps. 22:13–18).

The contrast between the righteous and the wicked plays itself out in a public setting to which both belong. Further, these sayings indicate that the welfare and misfortune of the community are dependent on whichever of the two is dominant. The absolute character of this contrast in such a context should not be missed.

EXCURSUS 2
The Righteous and the Wicked
in the Psalms and Job

In order to appreciate the proverbs of antithesis concerning the righteous and the wicked, it is necessary to draw on two complexes in the Old Testament that present this antithesis in a similar fashion. The method of evaluation being utilized here is a statistical analysis of words that speaks for itself. The most frequently employed term associated with the wicked in the proverbs of antithesis is *rāšaʿ*. It occurs in only three complexes: out of 203 occurrences in the Old Testament, 78 are found in Proverbs (synonyms of the three groups inclusive), 82 in the Psalms, and 26 in Job. Outside of these three major groups, the term *rāšaʿ* occurs seventy-nine times in the rest of the Old Testament, though appearing nowhere else in such density (*THAT* 2.813ff.). Indeed, the lexical component alone would suggest a relationship of these three complexes to one another.

The Righteous and the Wicked in the
Psalms of Lament of the Individual

In my essay "Struktur und Geschichte der Klage im Alten Testament" (*ZAW* 66 [1954]: 44–80), I examined the third category of the lament—the accusation of one's enemies. This category of lament is dominant in the psalms of lament, and it is the most profusely developed. The abundant statements about the enemy have a twofold classification: according to the enemy's behavior and according to the existence of the enemy. Most of the statements relate to the attacks made by the enemies on the one lamenting. Their speech leads to action: they mock the person in lament and delight in his misfortune. In numerous psalms of lament, the existence of enemies emerges; hence, a characterization. The genre of lament thereby has undergone a change, inasmuch as the speech depicting the enemies is no longer a call to God. Rather, the enemies are being depicted as corrupt, wicked, and godless. All of the terms employed here appear as well in the characterization of the wicked found in Proverbs. The characterization is magnified through the theme of the enemies' fate: destruction and downfall are declared to them, an example of which is Ps. 52:3–9. A description of the enemies and their fate can dominate a whole psalm, as in Psalms 52; 53; and 58. We find in these psalms the very same sequences of motifs as in Proverbs, and these are significant in terms of their emphasis. One also finds the occurrence of verbatim agreement, such as the parallel between Prov. 11:28 and Ps. 52:10.

The Righteous and the Wicked
in the Speeches of Job's Friends

The second parallel of note—the speech of Job's friends—functions quite differently. Here we find an argument being presented in the speeches of Job's companions directed at Job. All of the speeches develop the theme of the fate of the wicked, yet the difference in form is apparent. The speeches are components of a rhetorical composition (*Der Aufbau des Buches Hiob,* 1956, 1977 [2d ed.], pp. 92–98). In the first round of conversation, the fate of the wicked is one argument among several; in the second, it is the primary one and is amplified: not merely the end, rather the whole life of the wicked is under scrutiny, and justification for the fate of the wicked is given. We find many parallels here, particularly in the way in which the theme is developed but also in the very pronouncement that the wicked will perish. The speeches by Job's friends openly presuppose this motif; they offer a variation of it, and they amplify it.

The theme of the fate of the righteous also occurs, but in another connection. In the first round of speeches, the three friends promote the theme of "the prosperity of the righteous"; in the second, it is wholly absent; and in the third, it resurfaces in the speech of Eliphaz, where it is substantially changed.

What should be gleaned from this state of affairs? When such a thematic inference can be found in three Old Testament passages, and when it is strengthened by the occurrence of the same statements as well as word clusters, we may assume that a link exists between them. They must have arisen at about the same period. Inasmuch as the postexilic origin of the book of Job is virtually certain, and additional evidence from other texts would indicate such, one can assume a postexilic origin for those three text groups. Furthermore, the parallels confirm that a coexistence, not a succession, is being implied by the "righteous–wicked" antithesis.

EXCURSUS 3
Comparisons in the Proverbs of Antithesis:
The Righteous—The Wicked

Comparisons are contained in ten of the proverbs of antithesis. Juxtaposition is the intent of these sayings, and comparison has the effect of strengthening this aim. Some comparisons mention both the action and the fate of the righteous and the wicked: "The one trusting in riches will certainly fall, but the righteous will flourish as a green leaf" (11:28). "The fruit of the righteous is a tree of life, but the souls of transgressors are taken" (11:30). Others compare their fate: "The light of the righteous shines brightly, but the lamp of the wicked is extinguished" (13:9). "The righteous man discerns his place of rest, but the way of the wicked leads them astray" (12:26). (See also 12:3, 7; 13:2; 14:11.) Yet others compare the action of the righteous and the wicked: "The tongue of the righteous is as choice silver, but the heart of the wicked is of little value" (10:20).

In all of these sayings, the comparison functions to intensify the contrast. It is not original in form, just as all of the comparisons in Proverbs are not original. These particular proverbs have a literary origin and have been constructed for the most part from diverse elements. The comparisons have, in part, been abbreviated into metaphors, and frequently, the same metaphor is repeated. At times, both halves of the verse do not fit that well together.

This group is important because it provides evidence that there are sayings in Proverbs that were placed together at a later time, coming from originally independent elements. It is also significant in that it shows later sayings to be a part of what is generally regarded as an early compilation: chapters 10—22. Here we find illustrated divergent usage of sayings in comparison to other proverb groups.

Yahweh Deals with the Righteous and the Wicked

Out of 117 proverbs, only 11 contain the name Yahweh. It is, in fact, only a small group of sayings in which Yahweh's working is associated with the righteous–wicked contrast. In five of these, it is expressed by means of a set idiomatic expression that the wicked in their behavior are an abomination to Yahweh—for example, 11:20, "An abomination to Yahweh are those of a perverse heart, but those of a blameless way are his delight" (note also the same or similar in 12:22; 15:8, 9; and 15:26).

Four proverbs that are all different from one another indicate Yahweh's response to the contrast between the wicked and the righteous: "Yahweh does not let the soul of the righteous go hungry, but he thwarts the craving of the wicked" (10:3). "Yahweh is far from the wicked, but he hears the prayer of the righteous" (15:29). "Blessings are on the head of the righteous, but premature grief stops the mouth of the wicked" (10:6). "A refuge of integrity is the way of Yahweh, but ruin to those doing evil" (10:29).

In two sayings, the contrast occurs in association with the fear of God: "The one who walks uprightly fears Yahweh, but the one who is devious in his ways despises him" (14:2). "The fear of Yahweh prolongs life, but the years of the wicked are cut short" (10:27).

Thus, we find only very few proverbs in which Yahweh is mentioned in connection with the contrast of the wicked and the righteous. Their purpose is not to inform us about Yahweh and his action, rather only to underscore the contrast of both groups. The allusion to Yahweh in these sayings does not have any special significance in and of itself.

4. Summary

The proverbs of antithesis dealing with the righteous and the wicked form the largest grouping in Proverbs—117 sayings. In chapters 10—22, they constitute, with some interruptions, a major block; in chapters 25—29, they are scattered. These sayings represent a particular stratum of tradition in Proverbs. They cohere not only because they contrast the righteous with the wicked but also because they are constructed according to four elements, all of which are distributed differently. The proverbs of antithesis concerning the righteous and the wicked are distinct from those dealing with the foolish and the wise, inasmuch as allusion to the former is only general and theoretical. We encounter no concrete situations whatsoever. A number of sayings deviate from the pattern to the extent that something transpires between the righteous and the wicked: the latter persecute the former, and the former escape. A shift of influence is occurring between the two groups, and it is the righteous who promote the welfare of the city. These sayings demonstrate the dynamic existing between the righteous and the wicked as that of two interest groups in a particular locale. Such would confirm that the nature of the proverbs of antithesis is one of coexistence and not succession (that is, cause and effect).

The parallels found in the psalms of lament and speeches of Job's friends are indicative of a postexilic period. The contrast encountered is also one depicting coexistence, in which the wicked are the enemies of the one who prays.

The four elements of the proverb group form a whole in which the subject is always the same. A well-conceived notion that constitutes an instruction or systematic teaching underlies this particular saying. This formal arrangement corresponds to the consistently abstract description of the righteous and the wicked. One effect of this type of methodological depiction in proverbial form is that an absolute antithesis is presented, embracing all things. There are only the righteous and the wicked.[71]

2. HORTATORY PROVERBS (IMPERATIVE SAYINGS)

I. TWO TYPES OF HORTATORY PROVERBS

Of the eighty-two verses in Prov. 22:17–24:34, most are individual words of exhortation (admonitions and warnings) that may have a brief or a more lengthy substantiation; or they may have none at all. Two groups of exhortations can be identified according to this proverb type. The first begins at 22:22. This group, from 22:22 through 23:11, contains exhortations (with 22:29 being the only interruption). They are then continued in 24:1, after the poem of 23:29–35, which concludes the complex 23:12–28, and stretch with several interruptions to the end of the collection at 24:29, where we encounter another concluding poem in 24:30–34.

The second group is a collection of exhortations and instruction. It is introduced at 22:17–21 with the summons to listen, a summons that is repeated several times—for example, 23:12, 15; 19:22, 26. Proverbs 22:17–21 is not an introduction for the general exhortations found in 22:22ff.; rather, it introduces 23:12–28, which picks up the summons to hear. The block 23:12–28 can be designated as instructional wisdom by virtue of the fact that the summons to listen is unmistakably the words of a teacher, and the exhortations refer exclusively to the process of upbringing. That the instruction as presented in the teacher's tutelage is carried on by the parents is stated expressly in 23:13–14 and throughout chapters 22—25.

The simple exhortations in the block 22:22–23:11; 24:1–29, however, all relate to corporate life of adults in a bounded environment. Most of these are aimed at conduct toward one's neighbor that benefits the community.

Apart from the proverbs of exhortation in the aforementioned two groups, chapters 22—24 contain individual imperatives and/or texts that are attached or that break them off. The first of these are two poems, both of which are clearly recognizable concluding units in terms of their composition. Proverbs 23:29–35, a warning about drinking, is placed at the conclusion of the instructional wisdom; 24:30–34, which concerns the field of the idle person, concludes the section of general exhortations. Both poems confirm that the tradition found in the two blocks was known by those doing the transmission.

A further component is the extolling of wisdom found in 24:3–7, 13–14. What remain, then, are several individual sayings that actually interrupt the literary context: two proverbs of characterization (22:29 and 24:8–9), a proverb of antithesis about the righteous and the wicked (24:24–25), and a proverbial statement (24:26) that is a human observation and, seemingly, out of place here. The warning in 29:1 belongs to the context of wisdom of instruction.

II. THE INTRODUCTION IN 22:17–21:
THE SUMMONS TO LISTEN

"Incline your ear and hear the words . . . " (v. 17). "If you keep them in your heart, they will be established on your lips" (v. 18). "So that your trust may be in Yahweh, I have instructed you this day concerning your way . . . " (v. 19) "that to the one who asks you, you can answer rightly" (v. 21).

These are unmistakably the words of a teacher of wisdom, directed at his students (similar to the teaching of Amenemope; cf. Appendix). The summons to listen is broadened in such a way as to expound the mind and purpose of the teacher. His agenda is contained in this introduction. Here it is made clear that the exhortation is the most important and, in fact, truest focus of didactic instruction on wisdom. At the same time, however, the material that follows makes it clear that the exhortation in the first place is that of the father or the mother; this parental instruction is simply being extended by the teacher of wisdom.

In the twofold aim of teaching found in vv. 19–21, a connection exists between wisdom and the fear of God. The student learns on the one hand that he places his trust in God (hence, the fear of God), but he also learns to accrue knowledge and understanding, which qualify him to answer questions.

Both this link between wisdom and the fear of God and the combination of the student being addressed and the summons to listen are typical of Proverbs 1—9. The later wisdom also agrees with the modified notion of wisdom that is being emphasized and developed here: "Have I not written for you . . . , teaching you knowledge" (22:20). It is wisdom, objectifiable, teachable, and learnable, that is in view here, and not the earlier, functional view of wisdom.

III. EXHORTATIONS CONCERNING INSTRUCTION

Proverbs 23:12–28 is interlaced with summons to listen—vv. 12, 15, 19, 22, and 26—and the role of the father and mother is especially conspicuous in vv. 15, 19, 22, and 26. These sayings exhort others to the acquisition of wisdom: "Buy wisdom, discipline, and insight" (v. 23); " . . . so that you keep your heart on the right path" (v. 19); " . . . let your heart be zealous for the fear of Yahweh" (v. 17). The exhortation is predicated on the notion that the son will acquire a future and a hope (v. 18). A governing motif is also that he thereby accords his parents joy (v. 25): "May your father and mother be glad." In addition to the general admonition to gain wisdom is the concrete warning against harlotry and drunkenness in vv. 20 and 27: "Do not join those who are winebibbers . . . for a harlot is a deep pit" (note the parallels here to chaps. 1—9). Added on in vv. 13–14 is the admonition toward a firm upbringing by the parents. The poem describing drunkenness in vv. 29–35 concludes the section in vv. 12–28 with a vivid allusion to the exhortation in vv. 19–21.

IV. GENERAL EXHORTATIONS

The general exhortations that do not relate to a child's upbringing form the main part of 22:17–24:34. In and of themselves, they constitute a block that in the present text is interrupted by the instructional wisdom of 23:12–28. In the second major block there are also several interruptions.

Most of the texts exhort the reader to a particular behavior in relation to his neighbor. Proverbs 22:22 warns against depriving the lowly (cf. Amenemope: "Guard yourself from depriving the poor!" [see Appendix]). Proverbs 22:28 and 23:10 are admonitions not to remove landmarks or the borders of the lowly. Proverbs 24:28–29 exhorts against accusing one's neighbor without a cause and warns against retaliatory measures against him or deceiving him. A warning is also issued against rejoicing over the fall of one's enemy (24:17–18), against fretting over the godless (24:19–20), and against lying in wait against a righteous man's house (24:15–16). Very striking is the exhortation to rescue those being led away to death (24:11–12).[72] There is an admonition to get one's fields ready before building one's house (24:27), as well as not to be concerned about riches, which are so often fleeting (23:4–5). Also found here is the admonition to fear God and the king (24:21).

One is advised to avoid certain types of people: the hot-tempered (22:24–25), those who put up security for debts (22:26–27), fools (23:9), the wicked (24:1–2). All these exhortations and warnings have to do with a more narrow circle of life of those being addressed; they focus especially on conduct toward one's neighbor. The language in these admonitions is quite different from that of instructional wisdom.

In some cases, the exhortation is based on the activity of God: Yahweh takes up the cause of the poor and needy (22:22–23; also 23:10–11; 22:28, although the latter gives no reason). Yahweh tests the hearts, and excuses do not hold up before him (24:11–12). Yahweh looks into the heart when someone gloats over the fall of an enemy (24:17–18).

At the same time, attention is drawn to consequences, whereby the exhortation is predicated on the welfare of the one being admonished. The hot-tempered can become ensnared (22:24–25); if one puts up security for debts, one's very bed can be snatched away (22:26–27); riches can quickly evaporate (23:4–5). (Here we might compare Amenemope [see Appendix]: "Possessions are as sparrows in flight . . . " and "Do not hang your heart on treasures" [cf. Matt. 6:15–21].)

Proverbs 23:1–8 (excluding vv. 4–5) contains rules for behavior at meals with those who are more highly placed in society. These words have been inserted here. They contain a series of admonitions on the same subject. These rules for behavior are, with few changes, taken over from Egyptian wisdom.

Beyond this, there remain only a few texts in chapters 22—24 to mention that are not exhortations. There are two characterizations: 22:29, "Do you see a man skilled in his work? He will serve before kings," and 24:8ff. There is also a proverb of antithesis about the wicked and the righteous in 24:24–25 and a human observation in 24:26: "An honest answer is like a kiss on the lips." Additionally, we encounter several isolated statements extolling wisdom in 24:3–7, 13–14. While vv. 13–14 clearly are a part of the context of instruction, vv. 3–7 are an extolling of wisdom that resembles earlier wisdom: "By wisdom a house is built."

EXCURSUS 4
The Structure of 22:17–24:24 and
Its Correspondence to the Teaching of Amenemope

It is possible to encounter in the book of Proverbs sayings that occur word for word or near verbatim in other collections of proverbs. Here an interdependence does not necessarily exist, since the saying may have arisen elsewhere under the same circumstances. Such, however, is not the case with the instances of correspondence between Prov. 22:17–23:11 and certain Egyptian texts. These parallels can have arisen only by way of accessibility to the wisdom teaching of Amenemope on the part of the compiler of Proverbs 22—24. One indication of this is that the dining etiquette of 23:1–3, 6–8 constitutes a wider degree of correlation. Here we find an entire cluster agreeing with an entire cluster. From this it can be inferred that the (partial) appropriation of the teaching of Amenemope in chapters 22—23 may have proceeded initially in a literary stage of transmission.[73] In principle, this is the same as the characteristic borrowing of non-Israelite headings of wisdom texts, such as in 30:1—14—"Sayings of Agur." This practice occurred initially in the postexilic period, when "sages" collected sayings that had been handed down, including among these even non-Israelite literary traditions.

Inasmuch as Prov. 22:17—24:34 amounts to only about one-third of the range of the teaching of Amenemope (so B. Gemser [1960]), one can characterize the text in Proverbs as a select, adapted "Blütenlese" (Gemser) taken from Egyptian instruction. The sequence of proverbs in chapters 22—24 differs vastly from that of Amenemope. A further significant difference is that the units in Amenemope are consistently much longer than those in Proverbs. The most conspicuous correspondence between the two sources is the break-off in 23:11 of material that parallels Amenemope; the division between vv. 11 and 12 in Proverbs is confirmed through this parallel. In light of the fact that the units in Proverbs 22—24 are shorter than those of its Egyptian counterpart, this is all the more conspicuous. If the units in chapters 22—24, consisting of four verse parts, are longer than those of chapters 10—22 and 25—29 and those in Amenemope are longer than the units of chapters 22—24, an evolving of saying to didactic poem is on display, as we find exhibited in chapters 1—9.

If a segment of a wisdom writing of another people can be appropriated into an Israelite collection of wisdom sayings, the assumption follows that these sayings, originating and passed down among other nations, can be recognized as such. This capacity has been conferred on human beings by their Creator. Such corresponds to the fact that what is said about God in the wisdom sayings relates to the work of God as Creator and in fact applies to all people; this is the implication of the early human history as presented in Genesis 1—11. Allusion to Yahweh's working as it touches his people Israel appears first in the later wisdom of the postexilic era.[74] (For a more thorough discussion of Amenemope, see the Appendix.)

V. HORTATORY WORDS IN CHAPTERS 22—24: SUMMARY

When we compare the tradition of proverbial statements with exhortations as they occur throughout the whole book of Proverbs, it becomes evident that the former exhibit a much more comprehensive and adaptable tradition than the words of exhortation. Proverbial statements dominate in chapters 10—22, 25—29, and 31. Words of exhortation are restricted to chapters 22—24 and the latter part of chapters 1—9; there are also several individual admonitions scattered in 10—22 and 25—29. Chapters 1—9, however, consist for the most part of didactic poems about instructional wisdom into which words of exhortation have been assimilated. Moreover, apart from 22—24, exhortations generally do not retain a pure imperative form; rather, they have been modified and expanded.

When the collection of 22:17–24:34 is isolated from 10:1–22:16 and 25—29, redactive evidence would suggest that the words of exhortation constitute a distinct line of tradition. They represent a fundamentally different type of proverb that reflects a different *Sitz im Leben*.[75]

An analysis of chapters 22—24, furthermore, makes a necessary differentiation. Within 22—24 there are plain exhortations that are to be distinguished from those relating to the realm of instruction. Instructional wisdom, with its attendant admonitions, is introduced in the prologue of 22:17–21 and is then developed in 23:12–28. Characteristic of these exhortations is the vocative "My son . . . ," the summons to listen, in addition to a given reason for wisdom's praise. The *Sitz im Leben* of this instruction is the school, as is clearly seen from the prologue 22:17–21. All these instructional elements find their parallel in the didactic section of chapters 1—9. Wisdom as instruction presupposes the superiority of the one teaching over the one learning. For this reason, exhortation also prevails in the Egyptian royal wisdom.

At the same time, there are to be found general exhortations in 22:22–23:11 and 24:1–34 (with several interruptions). The plain admonitions never concern themselves with abstract wisdom; rather they admonish toward cooperation with one's neighbor and are directed toward conduct in a narrow, restricted sphere of living. Although all are passed on in the form of parallelism, the possibility that these were originally single-verse exhortations is repeatedly exhibited. One special form in conjunction with this is that of counsel, which is given for a particular situation.[76]

The substantiations given in these sayings are virtually all pragmatic. The one exhorting draws attention to the consequences of a wrong action or wrong decision. The one being exhorted is thus taken seriously in terms of his own decision-making capability. In no case are motivations offered to the listener that could not, in fact, represent his own. Occasionally, an exhortation is predicated on an action of God. Other times, benefits are pointed out that observance of the admonition will bring: "Then you will have plenty." One could label such reasoning as utilitarian. The motivation is here appropriate but never devaluing, for the one exhorting wishes to serve the one being exhorted. He indeed desires to assist him in proceeding on life's journey. This type of motivation surfaces also in the New Testament—for example, Luke 14:7–11 and Matt. 5:44ff.

With regard to subject matter, the exhortations in 23:12–28 (which are introduced in 22:17–21) belong to the context of instruction; all find their parallel in chapters 1—9.

The largest section of 22—24 consists of exhortations of a more general character, corresponding to Egyptian parallels and reaching as far as 23:11. These twenty-four verses contain twenty-two admonitions, in addition to seven scattered individual sayings of various types. Normally, the exhortations have attached to them a substantiation or some indication of specific consequences. The topics contained in these general exhortations are arranged according to two primary concerns: conduct toward one's neighbor or personal behavior and self-discipline.

VI. SCATTERED PROVERBS IN CHAPTERS 22—24

Scattered proverbs in chapters 22—24 that are not exhortations occur only among the general exhortations and not among the eight instructional proverbs. The probable reason for this is that the instructional proverbs had a literary origin and arose as a unit.

VII. HORTATORY PROVERBS
OUTSIDE OF 22:17–24:24

Words of exhortation are still to be found—whether individual or in small groups—in the collections of chapters 10—22; 25—31; and 1—9 passim. Their appearance in each case as individual sayings or in small groups calls attention to particularities that need to be considered.

In chapters 10—22, there are eight exhortations. Three of these either resemble conditional clauses or take their place: "Walk with the wise and you will grow wise; for the one who is a companion of fools it does not bode well" (13:20). "Drive out the mocker and out goes strife; quarrels and insults cease" (22:10). "Commit your works to Yahweh, and your plans will succeed" (16:3).

The first two of these sayings, as seen through their function, belong to the proverbs of antithesis concerning the foolish and the wise. The imperative 16:3 is a rhetorical modification; it corresponds to Ps. 37:5, a conditional promise. A pattern can be seen in some instances in which an imperative is employed where it would not be necessary, the result being that a parenetic exhortation takes shape. Even more distinctive is this practice in cases where an exhortation is appended to a proverbial statement: "One who starts a quarrel is like one who breaches a dam; so before a dispute erupts, drop the matter" (17:14). "The one who goes around gossiping reveals secrets; so do not associate with a man who talks too much" (20:19).

The first part of both of these sayings is an independent proverbial statement. The admonition accompanying each was appended in time. We may observe here a phase in which proverbial statements were transformed for didactic purposes. This is also the case in 20:13: "Do not love sleep or you will become poor; open your eyes, and you will have food to spare."

In terms of content, this saying belongs to the proverbs of antithesis dealing with the idle and the diligent. It has been transformed into a word of exhortation.

"Do not say, 'I'll pay this evil back!' Wait on Yahweh and he will deliver you" (20:22). This saying also appears in 24:29, but without the second sentence. It is, in and of itself, an independent proverb, a summons to hope, similar to 16:3 (= Ps. 37:5). By means of the imperative at the beginning, it becomes an exhortation to piety.

The last of the eight texts in this group is a statement about instructional wisdom: "Cease to heed discipline, my son, and you will stray from the words of wisdom" (19:27).

The result is surprising: of the eight words of exhortation occurring in chapters 10—22, one is about instructional wisdom and seven are statements that have been shaped into admonitions.

In chapters 25—31, fourteen words of exhortation occur, with another four appearing in the poem of 31:1–9. The majority belong to the category of generic exhortations that deal with conduct toward one's neighbor in a restricted, communal setting. Here, however, one peculiarity is worth noting: a number of these exhortations are single-verse sentences; respectively, they admit to the possibility that they were at some later time appended. "Do not forsake your friend or that of your father, and do not enter your brother's house when disaster strikes" (27:10). "Do not slander a servant in the presence of his master; otherwise, he will curse you, and you will pay for it" (30:10). (See also 27:1–2; 25:16, 17, 27; 26:5; 25:6.)

Although it is true that not every instance can be proven beyond doubt, it is apparent that in chapter 25 (the chapter of similes), for example, both the sayings in v. 16 and v. 27 are parallelisms that have been amplified through comparison.

Several other proverbs possess a peculiar form. They are sayings that begin with the description of a particular situation for which advice has been extended: "If your eyes have seen something, do not bring it hastily to court; for what will you do . . . ?" (25:7–8). "If your enemy is hungry, give him food to eat" (25:21). "With his lips a malicious man disguises himself . . . though his speech is charming, do not believe him" (26:24–25; cf. 28:17).

All of these statments describing a situation that requires advice are reminiscent of legal language. Here wisdom exhortations and casuistic law come in contact with one another. Even the primary features of law are universal.

Finally, in this section two texts are found in the context of instructional wisdom, 27:11 and 29:17, in addition to one royal proverb, 25:6.

EXCURSUS 5
The Farewell Exhortation
in Tobit 4:3–19

Following the exhortations in Proverbs, there is reference to a small collection of admonitions found in the book of Tobit. These are admonitions given by Tobit to his son at his departure from home (4:3–19).

From the text it becomes apparent that here we have exhortations of diverse types and origins being passed on that have been placed together—small compilations of sayings from which the farewell speech has been woven. This is reflected in the repetition of vv. 7–11 and 16–17. In addition to the type of exhortations found in the book of Proverbs, there are other types as well. The hortatory speech contains two parts that are clearly recognizable: one segment related to the specific situation, the request for an honorable burial for the father and mother as well as care for the mother following the father's death (3–4); the other, the exhortation to take a woman from the kin of the father (12–13). But there is also a series of quite diverse admonitions that do not relate to the situation at hand and which could be assigned to an entirely different period: admonitions to piety (5–6), alms (7–16, 17–18), prompt payment of employees, a cultured mode of life, the golden rule ("what you yourself do not desire . . . ," 16a), moderation in drinking (18b), and accepting wise counsel.

This remarkable sequence can be readily explained. Only two exhortations—an honorable burial and selection of a wife from the father's family—belong to the narrative. Both of these elements belonging to patriarchal history are passed on in the same context: the last testament in which the father commissions the son (Genesis 47 and 24). Such concurs with a custom practiced through the centuries by many people since the earliest of time. The last will is well known everywhere as a *Sitz im Leben* for exhortation.

In Tobit 4, however, an approaching death is not the immediate occasion of the father's speech to the son; rather, the father is here sending the son on a trip. Accompanying the departure of a son or daughter leaving home is an admonition that in this context has a notable character (even though it is probably universal in practice). With the departure from home of the child, things such as daily care, guidance, warnings to keep oneself from harm, and awareness of potential danger all are rehearsed. The caring love attending the one leaving home comes to expression in the parental exhortation, yet it does so only to the extent that the words can be preserved. This type of admonition, associated with the blessing that accompanies departure, still surfaces in the novels of the nineteenth century—for example, in Charles Dickens.

Precisely here, in the words of farewell to a child, is displayed an important historical setting for the word of exhortation. As a result, there always remains a residue—if only a scant trace—of the original setting and of the caring parental love that should guard the child and pave his way.

It is only natural, then, that in the course of a long history of tradition, the individual exhortation or warning was separated from its original setting and would end up in compilations such as Tobit 4, where the individual admonitions have been strung together without any contextual link. Yet, the memory of such is never fully gone, as evidenced by the farewell speech of Tobit to his son.

It is possible to observe in the history of imperative sayings, when contrasted to indicative sayings, a movement having taken place. Although proverbial statements predominate in the collections of proverbs among preliterary peoples, in early Egypt,[77] and in Israel (as represented by Proverbs 10—22 and 25—29), proverbial statements recede in the later period and imperatives become more prominent (Proverbs 1—9 and the later Egyptian wisdom being exemplary). This very development is observable even down to detail, where, to illustrate, proverbial statements in Proverbs are modified or amplified in the exhortations.

The farewell exhortations in the book of Tobit suggest that exhortations stemming from exceedingly diverse situations had a particular milieu, from which only the farewell exhortations have been handed down.[78]

3. POETRY IN THE
BOOK OF PROVERBS

Some sixteen poems, which are absent from the older compilations 10:1–22:16 and 25—29 (exclusive of 27:23–27), occur in 22:17–24:34, in the Appendix of chapters 30—31, and in several supplements to the didactic material of chapters 1—9. They are well suited for this collection because most of them are extended exhortations. From this inventory we may make certain conclusions. The earliest stage is reflected by 10:1–22:16 and 25—29, material that with one exception contains no poems. These sayings were handed down without the use of poetry. Only with the transition to literary tradition were short poems added on in certain places. This tended to occur at the conclusion of shorter compilations (e.g., 23:29–35; 24:30–34; perhaps 27:23–27). In addition, poems were also placed at the end of Proverbs—chapters 30 and 31. The poems have a particular relationship to words of exhortation; the former arose as an amplification of the latter.[79]

The poem in 23:29–35 follows the exhortation that preceded in 23:20–21; it represents in poetic form the expansion of a word of exhortation: "Do not gaze at wine when it is red, when it sparkles and goes down smoothly, but later it bites like a snake . . . " (v. 31).

An introduction precedes this statement in the form of a riddle with a solution: "Who has woe and sorrow?" (v. 29). "Those who linger over wine" (v. 30).

Verses 33–35, then, develop the consequences of excessive drinking. The portrayal is humorous; even the connection to the riddle in vv. 29ff. gives evidence that the poem serves the purpose of amusement. Proverbs 31:4–5 is also a warning about drinking.

The poem 24:30–34 ("I went by the field of the idle . . . ") deals with diligence and idleness. Here the underlying exhortation is not assimilated verbatim into the poem, and yet the poem expands the warning about laziness and its characterization, expressed also in 20:13: "Do not love sleep, otherwise . . . " Even this poem emits a trace of humor, and its beginning has the character of a folk song. The person passing by observes the neglect of a field and takes to heart a warning that he has heeded through the words of another. Both poems conform to a similar pattern. There doubtless existed many others similar in nature.

"Be sure to know the condition of your flocks! . . . " (27:23–27). In addition to the warning about laziness there is a warning concerning diligence, specifically as it applies to livestock, composed in the form of a paraphrastic admonition. Proverbs 27:24 provides a twofold reason: a warning that riches vanish and another accenting the reward for diligence—"then you will have enough" (cf. also 20:13). This is developed in vv. 25–27.

In 6:6–11, we encounter a warning to the lazy person by means of a countercontrast linked with a reference to the diligent ant. This is, of course, also a humorous depiction.

Diligence is also the theme of 31:10–31, an extolling of the diligent housewife. This portrait is distinguished from the aforementioned through its fullness of detail. Yet, this poem takes as its basis the proverbs found in vv. 10 and 30.

The warning about security in 6:1–5, which we encounter in numerous proverbs, takes the shape of a short poem, creating a scenario in which someone is counseled on how to be free from security that he has put up.

In all of these poems, the issue is specific and focused: the preservation and upkeep of possessions and sustenance for the family. To provide for the family requires a diligence and willingness on the part of its members to take part in the family's care. For this reason, diligence and sloth are worthy of such a prominent place; idleness and drunkenness are capable of bringing the family to ruin in relatively short time. Hence, this is stated for the benefit of those for whom diligence and sloth concerning work are a question of existence: they are to give serious thought to this "appropriate word," an exhortation framed in a fitting poem that can be easily remembered and passed on. Most probably, these brief poems developed in circles where people's interests corresponded— for example, families living in a village as opposed to circles of wise men in a school atmosphere, where fundamental interests were quite different, as reflected in didactic poetry.

Three poems offer a characterization of the wicked. Actually, 6:12–15, "A worthless man, a villain . . . ," is not a poem, rather an extended proverb about the wicked man. In vv. 12–14 he is characterized according to all of his wickedness: " . . . who goes about with a perverse mouth." His ruin is announced in v. 15.

"There are six things that Yahweh hates . . . " (6:16–19). This, too, is a characterization of the wicked, clothed in the form of a numerical proverb.

"There is a generation that curses its father . . . " (30:11–14). This caricature of the wicked, though similar to the two preceding texts, resembles 9:1–8.

In these texts, which are actually enumerations rather than poems, one senses an animosity toward the wicked, which is given expression without necessarily employing a fixed form.

Thus, we have identified the short poems that are the products of expanding individual proverbs. There are still several texts, however, that do not precisely fit a particular category—for example, 31:1–9, words spoken by Lemuel's mother to him. These are admonitions directed toward him as a person (vv. 1–9 on drinking and loose women) and toward his future office as king, most notably an exhortation about defending the rights of the poor. This text, which has been drawn from foreign wisdom, resembles Egyptian instruction (on 31:8, see note 34a).

The so-called numerical proverbs are, in effect, poems. As such, they belong to the period of transition from oral to written tradition. Individual sayings are extended by means of lists of phenomena belonging together, thus resulting in a poem. In terms of content, the sayings belong to human observations. Included in this category, however, are observations about the surrounding world. Accordingly, the numerical proverbs of 30:15–31 are compiled on the basis of the criterion of observation, and they attest to the importance of this proverb group. Adapted to a particular group within the created order, these sayings express the wonder of commonality. Out of this amazement issues a particular observation.

Proverbs 30:15–31 is comprised of five principal parts: that which is insatiable (vv. 15–16); the mystery of motion (vv. 18–19); that which is unbearable (vv. 21–23); wisdom of the extremely small (vv. 24–28); and the stateliness of striding (vv. 29–31).

When we consider that these poems represent a larger stratum in the history of the tradition, we can investigate the preliminary form from which this poem has been constructed. To be sure, we can be certain that there existed short sayings that were intended to be used in this manner—an abundance of such, in fact. Thus, the proverbs attributed to Solomon in 1 Kings 4:29–34, "He spoke of trees . . . , of animals . . . , of birds, of reptiles and of fish," receive confirmation. In ancient Israel there existed proverbs about plants and animals that are presupposed in the numerical proverbs of 30:15–31.

Several additional texts have no relationship to the proverbs: for example, 30:1–4, written in the style of Qohelet, and 30:7–9, a prayer that is reminiscent of the proverbs.[79a]

A transition in proverbial evolution from oral tradition to literature can be observed in the poems of chapters 10—31 as a whole. The poem is meant to be read, even when it is passed on orally. It is no longer limited to the situation in which it was originally spoken, as evidenced, notably, by 24:30–34, the field of the idle. By means of this portrait, the exhortation is amplified into a small scene, a graphic narrative, in much the same way as 23:29–35: "Do not gaze upon wine when it sparkles in the cup . . . " These scenes relate to daily work and sustenance and in each instance vary according to the situation behind the saying. Often humor emanates through these poems. In this, they are at one with the proverbs.

In all this, the poems distinguish themselves unmistakably from didactic poems, from which chapters 1—9 derive (also 22:17–21 and 23:12–28) and which are characterized by the series of summons to listen with accompanying address as well as a substantiation in the form of wisdom's praise. The link to proverbial wisdom is hereby broken. The wisdom that is extolled in these poems is both abstract and yet functional; it can even be personified. The contrast between this idea of wisdom and another that surfaces in the text of Proverbs is confirmed by the poems themselves. Even in cases where the subject matter of the poems is similar, the didactic poems tend to be rigid and repetitive in their exhortations and warnings, whereas the proverbial poems are multiform, lively, and humorous.

The observation that a group of short poems are extensions of proverbs would suggest that one of the sources out of which the poems grew might be the proverbs themselves. This is likely, since all over the world we find proverbs as well as songs, which are actually poems that are sung. If this suggestion is valid, then we are simply observing everyday life being mirrored in proverbial amplifications.

The tendency to extend the formulations of proverbial sayings into poetry is subsequently taken up and carried on by Qohelet.

Numbered also among these poems are those in the Psalter, especially the songs of ascent found in Pss. 127:1–2, 3–5; 128:1–3, 4–6; and 133:1–3.

4. PROVERBS IN
THE OLD TESTAMENT
OUTSIDE OF PROVERBS 10—31

I. PROVERBS IN PROVERBS 1—9

In 3:27–32, we find five words of exhortation that are strung together in succession. Verses 27–30 include no substantiation, while vv. 31–32 are substantiated by Yahweh's working. In vv. 22–24, we find single-verse words of exhortation that were passed down alongside the existing collection. Proverbs 9:7–9 contains a word of exhortation that has been extended into a poem, and 3:33–35 is a proverb of antithesis about the righteous and the wicked. On several occasions we encounter individual proverbs that have been assimilated into a didactic poem. These scattered, individual sayings mirror a type of transitional phase from the earlier to the later wisdom. Another aspect of transition is reflected in 3:1–12 by the inclusion of four words of exhortation in a didactic poem that begins with a summons to listen and an extolling of wisdom. Here the words of exhortation are all applied to one's relationship to God.

Material containing individual proverbs that have been extended into brief poems includes 6:1–5, a warning against putting up security; 6:6–11, an admonition to diligence; and 6:12–15, 16–19, a characterization of the wicked. These short poems parallel those of chapters 22—24.

This transition is also intimated by the longer didactic poems of chapters 1—9 to the extent that they facilitate an amplification of individual sayings. These are reflective, nevertheless, of the later wisdom.

II. INDIVIDUAL PROVERBS IN QOHELET

Although only a portion of the texts are clearly identifiable as individual proverbs, Qohelet nonetheless contains numerous individual proverbs—in fact, more than had been assumed up until the present. "The Book of Qohelet, in both its form and way of raising questions, was rooted in the rich soil of common Israelite wisdom" (W. Zimmerli [1980], p. 124). In Zimmerli's translation, the short proverbs appear in bold type. His study concentrates solely on sayings from Proverbs 10—29. Parallel texts from chapters 1—9 do not appear. While it is true that only a few verbatim parallels are to be found, those that do surface belong to the same categories. In the first place, we should note the distinction between indicative and imperative sayings. In most of these cases we are able to distinguish between those that are attributable to the Preacher and others that the Preacher has borrowed. In the epilogue, 12:10, it is expressly stated that the Preacher was also a collector of proverbs. That the proverbs originated and were initially transmitted orally is confirmed by the Preacher, even when several compilations of sayings were accessible to him (so also R. Gordis, 1976).

Groups of Proverbs in Qohelet
That Were Borrowed

It is significant that, as a group, the comparative proverbs occur most frequently in this book: "Two are better than one . . . " (extended into a poem; 4:9–12). "It is better that you not vow than that you vow and not pay" (5:4). "Better a good name than a precious ointment" (7:1). " . . . for a living dog is better than a dead lion" (9:4). "Wisdom is better than strength" (9:16). (Cf. also 2:24; 4:6, 13–16, 17; 6:3, 5, 9; 7:2, 3; 7:5, 8, 26; 6:5; 9:7, 18.)

A portion of these proverbs evidently stems from the Preacher himself, for he is communicating his own reflections—for example, 6:3; 7:1b, 2, 3, 4, 8a; 2:24.

Another portion is derived from earlier proverbial wisdom: 4: 6, 9–12, 13–16, 17; 5:4; 6:9; 7:1, 5; 9:4; 16:17. Each one of these proverbs could just as well appear in Proverbs 10—29; none of them expresses wisdom that is specific to the Preacher.

A third section consists of proverbs that are a combination of borrowed sayings and statements made by the Preacher himself—for example, 7:1 and 7:8.

Proverbial Statements: Human Observations

Frequently, the Preacher states in introducing a section, "I saw that . . . " (2:13; 3:10, 16, 22; 4:1; etc.). That which the Preacher saw was an observation about people.[80] His observations are consciously individual. He also borrows observations from earlier wisdom that concur with his. He, too, understands people empirically, as evidenced by his own perceptions: "The eye is not satisfied with seeing, nor the ear with hearing" (1:8; cf. Prov. 27:20). "Whoever loves money never has money enough" (5:9). "Deference makes amends for great offenses" (10:4). "Money is the answer for everything" (10:19b). "Light is sweet, and it is pleasant for the eyes to see the sun" (11:7). (Cf. also 10:5, 9, 10, 19a; 3:1–8; 4:9–12 [both of which are amplifications]; 5:11; 7:8, 29; 12:1–6.)

The arenas of life to which these observations and experiences belong, the scenes against which they are played out, are the same as those in Proverbs. Many of these proverbs are elaborated by Qohelet—for example, 3:1–8, which is based on a brief characterization.

Proverbial Statements: Human Limitations

This category is evidently important to Qohelet, for it constitutes a major focus of his wisdom. He does this, however, in his discussions; only a few proverbs possibly belong to earlier wisdom—for example, 6:12, "For who knows what is good for man in his life?"; 7:13, "Who can straighten what he has made crooked?"; and 8:8, "No man has power over the wind to contain it" (cf. 9:11).

Several proverbs have been modified in Qohelet's language: "Whatever God does endures forever . . . God has made it so, in order that men fear him" (3:14). "Whatever exists has already been determined" (6:10). "Who can tell man what will happen under the sun after he is gone?" (6:12). "Far off and deep, very deep, is that which exists—who can find it?" (7:24). (Cf. also 8:7 and 11:5; there are several that may have been altered by Qohelet.)

Foolishness and Wisdom

"Then I set my mind to know wisdom, to know madness and folly" (1:17). "And I saw that wisdom is better than folly, just as light exceeds darkness" (2:13). "The wise man has eyes in his head, but the fool walks in darkness" (2:14). (Cf. also 2:16; 7:5; 9:17; 10:2, 12–14.)

The fool is characterized in 7:6, "As the crackling of thorns under the pot, so is the laughter of fools" (cf. also 10:13, 14), and Qohelet formulates in 2:16, "Just like the fool, the wise man must die too" (cf. also 6:8; 7:4, 16).

Proverbs of Antithesis Involving
the Righteous and the Wicked

In 9:2 we read, "All share a common fate—the righteous and the wicked." Yet Qohelet counters an absolute doctrine of retribution in the form of a discussion found in 8:10–14: "I have seen how the wicked . . . while the righteous. . . . This, too, is meaningless . . . yet because the wicked . . . still lives a long time."[80a] In accordance with his style, there are not parallels in Qohelet to the large number of proverbs of antithesis in the book of Proverbs. In this particular instance, Qohelet is representing the attitude of Job over against that of Job's companions. What is at work is a conscious polemic against a rigid doctrine of retribution.[81]

Extolling Wisdom

Sayings that extol the abstract notion of wisdom do not surface with Qohelet. Rather, he affirms a more functional notion of wisdom. This he presupposes when he understands himself as a wise man: "And I saw that wisdom is better than folly" (2:13; cf. also 1:16; 7:23; 8:1). He can thus borrow proverbs from an earlier era of wisdom that correspond to his functional understanding of wisdom—for example, "The wise man has eyes in his head, but the fool walks in darkness" (2:14a), and the awareness that a poor wise man saved a city by his wisdom (9:13–15; cf. also 7:11ff.; 7:19; 8:1; 9:18).

A sense of critical reservation, however, tempers Qohelet's extolling of wisdom: "For where there is much wisdom there is much sorrow; whoever increases in knowledge increases in sorrow" (1:18).

Such skeptical reservations about the possibilities of wisdom pervade Qohelet's work. However, he uses prose and not proverbs to communicate this.

Exhortations

Qohelet, just as with the earlier wisdom, catches the sense and the value of exhortations by his use of them. "Do not be quickly provoked to anger, for anger resides in the bosom of fools" (7:9). "Cast your bread upon the waters, for after many days you will find it" (11:1).[81a] (Cf. also 5:3–6; 7:21; 10:4ff.; 11:6; 12:1–8.)

Any of these proverbs could just as well be found in Proverbs 10—29.

In contrast to these, however, are two groups of exhortations that are typical of the Preacher and that only he could have composed: "Test it with pleasure to find out what is good!" (2:1). "In the day of prosperity be happy, and in the day of adversity, remember: God has made the one as well as the other" (7:14). (Cf. also 9:7–10 and 11:8–10, although these are closer to encouragements than exhortations.)

The same applies to a group of warnings that have to do with one's relationship to God: "Guard your steps when you go to the house of God. To approach and listen is better than to offer the sacrifice of fools" (4:17). "Do not be rash with your mouth . . . in uttering anything before God" (5:1). (Cf. also 7:10, 17; 9:10.) In these texts, the Preacher has made use of the form of a proverb, in order to communicate his critical reservation in the face of religious speech. We are reminded that it might not be genuine.

The exhortations of instructional wisdom are fully absent from Qohelet. The form of commendation is used several times: 4:2; 6:3; and others. Several royal proverbs resemble those found in Proverbs: 4:13–16; 8:2–4; 10:4ff., 16ff.; 10:20.

A part of that which the Preacher borrowed from the earlier wisdom consists of sayings from Proverbs 10—29. This excludes the didactic poems of chapters 1—9, the complex of antithetical proverbs concerning the righteous and wicked, as well as the exhortations relative to instructional wisdom. The material he extracts and further utilizes is deliberately restricted to functional wisdom.[82] The reason for this is the understanding that undergirds his notion of wisdom as a whole: human perception is incapable of comprehending what exists and what transpires; human wisdom is limited in every domain. It is this fundamental limitation to which human mortality ultimately points.

III. PROVERBS IN THE HISTORICAL
AND PROPHETIC BOOKS

O. Eissfeldt (*Der Maschal im Alten Testament,* 1913) found in the historical and prophetic books twenty-three sayings that he considered to be popular proverbs, in order to demonstrate that these were already present in the early texts of the Old Testament. This thesis was disputed by H. J. Hermisson (1968) (with only a few exceptions), who assumed the authors of these sayings merely to be sages in schools or in the court. Through C. R. Fontaine (1982), the discussion was taken up anew. Fontaine posits that the real *Sitz im Leben* of the proverbs was their customary usage in the life of the people and offers support for this by pointing to five texts in the historical books.[83] He maintains that the proverbs encountered here are in every respect entirely appropriate to the situation being described and also that the proverbs actually possess a very specific function in these situations. A proverb, for example, can serve as a settlement of a dispute. We thus find support for the notion that the proverbs had their true function in oral usage and that they were a living reality in this early period among the people. In terms of form, they concur with the sayings compiled in Proverbs in their distinguishing between indicative and imperative sayings, and they correspond to the same categories as far as their content. By far, most are proverbs of human observation and experience: "As the man is, so is his strength" (Judg. 8:21; cf. Ezek. 16:44). "What does straw have in common with grain?" (Jer. 23:28). "From the wicked come wicked deeds" (1 Sam. 24:14). "The fathers have eaten sour grapes" (Jer. 31:29). "They sow the wind and reap the whirlwind" (Hos. 8:7). " . . . the one who takes off his armor" (1 Kings 20:11). (See also Judg. 8:2; Isa. 37:3; 1 Sam. 16:7; 10:12; Jer. 17:11; 13:12, 23; 17:9; 31:29. For further discussion, see R. B. Y. Scott [1961] and W. McKane, *Commentary,* pp. 22–30.)

All of these proverbs correspond to groups of sayings that are found in the book of Proverbs. They confirm that there were, in fact, proverbs in the early part of Israel's history.[84]

IV. WISDOM SAYINGS IN THE PSALMS

In the book of Psalms are found three categories of proverbs and proverbial motifs that are comparable to those of Proverbs. Four texts in the collection of the *ma'alōt* psalms are expansions of individual proverbs into short poems: "If Yahweh does not build the house . . . " (127:1–2; a Yahweh saying). "Behold, sons are a gift of Yahweh" (127:3–5; a commendation). "Blessed is everyone who . . . " (128:1–4; a commendation similar to Psalm 1). "Behold, how good and pleasant . . . " (133:1–3; a blessing; cf. here an African saying: "Unity must reign between the brothers and sisters of a mother"; see Appendix).

That all of the above belong to the collection of Psalms 120—134 leads one to assume that they first received their form in which they were passed on by their insertion into the songs of pilgrimage and consequently were assimilated into the *Sitz im Leben* of this genre. Psalm 127:1ff. resembles Prov. 10:22 (cf. Sir. 11:10). Verse 1 has a close parallel in a Sumerian saying to the gods (W. von Soden and A. Falkenstein [1953], pp. 66ff.: "Nisaba, where you do not establish it, a person builds no house nor city . . . ").

All four of the above texts are expansions of proverbs that reach back to the early period of Israelite wisdom. They were transmitted orally until they were employed in expanded form in the collection of the songs of pilgrimage in Psalms 120—134. Our understanding of this Yahweh saying, a blessing, and two commendations is thereby greatly enriched.

Psalms 1 and 119 belong to a later period, in which the Psalter at one time did not include Psalms 120—150. Utilizing an inclusio, Psalm 1 develops the antithesis of the fate of the righteous and the wicked by way of a comparison. A proverb of antithesis was doubtless accessible to the writer of the psalm. We encounter the two-sided comparison elsewhere quite frequently. This is a typical example of how a proverb can be expanded into a poem. The comparison is presented in the form of a commendation. Psalm 119:76, as part of the acrostic, can be described as a devotional that honors the Torah. The link between the psalm and torah, just as with the link between wisdom and torah, is indicative of the postexilic era. In Psalm 119, a connection to wisdom arises only in the theme of comparing the righteous and the wicked.[85]

This motif of antithesis is also related to the individual laments. It will suffice to note Psalm 14 (= 53) as an example of an entire psalm. We could also mention Psalm 37 in this regard—a psalm that is wholly governed by this theme. Here it is instructive to compare the free verse of Paul Gerhardt's hymn "Befiehl du deine Wege." The very same exhortation to piety runs throughout the song, although the contrast between the righteous and the wicked is absent.

Psalm 49, a lament about perishing, is introduced in vv. 2–5 by a summons to listen, in the same way as it is employed in the later wisdom of Proverbs 1— 9: "Listen . . . , my mouth will speak words of wisdom."[86]

V. WISDOM IN THE BOOK OF JOB

Three complexes in the book of Job approximate wisdom. The shorter wisdom saying is found only in chapter 28, where it is expanded into a poem. The heart of the poem is a multiple-verse unit that consists of a question (v. 12 = 20) and answer in the form of a riddle (v. 23): "Where is wisdom to be found and where is the place of understanding? It is hidden from the eyes of every living thing . . . God understands the way to it and he alone knows its dwelling place."

The answer is expressed positively in vv. 24–27 and negatively in vv. 1–11, a parable with its resolution found in vv. 15–19: even the highest merits cannot be compared to her; God alone, the Creator, knows her location. This chapter follows on the heels of Job's companions and, in terms of its content, is a polemical poem: it is not Job's friends who have at their disposal wisdom; rather, it is God alone. Facilitated by the language and mode of thought expressed in earlier wisdom, the objectified wisdom that is extolled in Proverbs 1—9 is rejected. Wisdom is not disposable in the manner that the companions through their dogmatic, rigid speeches presume.

In the discursive portion of the book of Job, the friends portray the teaching concerning the deeds and fate of the righteous and wicked as it appears in Proverbs 10ff. Here the teaching is developed extensively up to the very verdict at the end: Job must qualify as a wicked man, given this teaching. In chapter 21, Job counters with an argument based on his experience: "Where, in fact, is evidence of this, as you presume?" Here the wisdom of experience opposes dogmatic rigidity.

The Elihu speeches in chapters 32—37 are a later addition to the book of Job. They constitute the discourse of a teacher of wisdom from a circle of sages, in whose presence he is dealing with the ruin of Job. The matter is introduced in 34:2, as in Proverbs 1—9, with the summons to listen: "Hear my words, you wise men. . . ."[87] Elihu condemns Job's speech as blasphemous. At the conclusion, Job is warned and exhorted to repentance. Elihu is speaking before a forum that is decreeing valid criteria for wisdom. In secure possession of this standard, Elihu rises up as a judge over Job. He is a stereotypical representative of an objectified and, therefore, readily accessible wisdom.

The portions of the text of Job that allude to wisdom do not justify our classifying the book of Job as wisdom literature. The speeches of the three companions, all of which develop a dogmatic version of retribution teaching, "have not spoken correctly about God." The author of the book of Job rejects this doctrine as applicable here.

In the Elihu speeches that follow, this doctrine of retribution is intensified even more. Chapter 28, in contrast, appears in the form of a poem, the core of which is a proverb. Polemical in nature, this material is intended to assert, against Job's friends, the inaccessibility of wisdom.

The self-evident nature of wisdom is juxtaposed poetically by the author with the unfathomability of human suffering. In terms of structure, this poem corresponds to that of a lament, in which suffering is given voice. The three persons integral to the dramatized lament correspond to its three objects: God, self, and the enemy. The lament is placed over against a reverential awe in the presence of the hidden God, expressed through praise.

VI. SUMMARY

Proverbs are to be found in many places outside of the Proverbs 10—31 collection. In the historical and prophetic books, they appear in the original form in which they were passed down and are employed in the context of narrative situations. This is especially true of proverbial statements. Without exception, all of these sayings belong to the era of early wisdom, of which the sole form was the short proverb. Neither didactic poems nor instructional proverbs surface in the historical or prophetic books.

Proverbs 1—9, didactic poetic material that is typical of the later wisdom, offers additional traces of the afterlife of the short proverb, which nevertheless surface only individually and in association with other forms. Evidence would suggest that didactic poems followed proverbial sayings and that they presuppose the latter.

Qohelet resembles the early proverbial wisdom much more closely than Proverbs 1—9. The Preacher borrows from tradition many individual sayings that he expands in part or wholly transforms. The didactic wisdom, however, is fully absent. Qohelet also has a conception of wisdom that is in harmony with the earlier functional mode, and he carries on a polemic against any mind-set that would be predisposed to presume upon wisdom. Moreover, the righteous–wicked antithesis does not occur in the Preacher's sayings.

By comparison, both of these elements occur in the Psalms. A continuation of early proverbial wisdom surfaces in the form of four poems in the psalms of pilgrimage, in addition to the contrast of the righteous and the wicked specific to later wisdom. Note, for example, the introduction of the Forty-ninth Psalm, which is couched in the language of a didactic poem.

In the book of Job we find clear evidence of the continuation of early proverbial wisdom—initially in the core of the poem found in chapter 28 and also in the author's polemic against a dogmatic antithesis of the righteous and the wicked that is so indicative of later wisdom.

The combined witness of these sources confirms that a later wisdom expressing itself through didactic poetry and other forms is to be distinguished from an earlier wisdom that is characterized by proverbial sayings. Each represents a separate line of tradition. The later wisdom manifests itself in Proverbs 1—9 and is reflected in the speeches of Job's companions, in the Elihu speeches, and as a motif in certain psalms. The early proverbial wisdom is carried on in individual sayings scattered throughout Proverbs 1—9 and in Qohelet, where the Preacher polemicizes against her. The early wisdom occurs further in the expanded form of short poems in the psalms of pilgrimage and in traces still detectable in Jesus Sirach. As evidenced by the early Jewish wisdom and the stock of wisdom sayings in the Synoptic Gospels, the oral development and transmission of proverbs continued into the postcanonical era.

5. THE CHANGE FROM PROVERBIAL WISDOM TO DIDACTIC POETRY

The difference between two categories of proverbs, one of which exhibits a functional mode of wisdom and the other of which is abstract, reveals a transformation in the understanding of the sage and about wisdom itself. In the one portion of sayings, wisdom is understood in the sense of empowering toward something concrete that the sage says or does. This is illustrated in the way the wisdom of Solomon is portrayed or in the Joseph narrative (esp. Genesis 41).

In the other portion of proverbs, this emphasis ceases. The sayings, accordingly, speak of being wise and depict wisdom as an entity in and of itself, abstract and objectified. As such, it can be learned. For this reason, it holds a special place in the realm of instruction; wisdom had become a teaching.

This transformation subsequently led to a modification in speech form. The short saying was no longer sufficient for the teaching mode; hence the more detailed didactic poem took the place of the proverb. We find this exhibited in Proverbs 1—9 and in other Near Eastern wisdom literature.

A history of the emergence of proverbs cannot be reconstructed. What we do find in its place, however, is a conspicuous transformation, namely, a change in the sense of the word "wise," as is so clearly demonstrated in the proverbs of antithesis involving the foolish and the wise as well as in the characterizations of the wise. We may best account for the transformation from short saying to didactic poem and from oral to written in this way. But the distance between the abstract concept of wisdom in Proverbs 1—9 and the more functional mode can be seen in another way as well: in order to explain the use of the word ḥākām in chapters 1—9, it will not suffice merely to examine the statements in which the word appears; in chapters 10—29, the word appears in individual, self-contained statements as well. In 1—9 it occurs in wider contexts; it constitutes the theme of the prologue, in addition to most of the didactic poems. Only on the surface would it appear as if the term ḥākām were the link between parts 1—9 and 10—31. In reality, a fundamental distinction is to be made.

6. A FORM-CRITICAL
SKETCH OF WISDOM

The earliest proverbial form is the short, self-contained, single-verse saying (esp. in Proverbs 10—31). These sayings originated orally among the people and were passed on in the same way. Here we find displayed the roots of Israel's wisdom. They appear here as a separate entity, as well as in texts of the historical and prophetic books that depict various situations. Two basic formulations have been passed down through separate channels: indicative sayings (statements) and imperative sayings (exhortations, notably Proverbs 22—24).

To the early phase of wisdom also belong some sayings outside of Proverbs 10—31. These are scattered throughout chapters 1—9, Qohelet, Job, and the Psalms. Oral development and transmission of proverbs with this simple form continued after the formal closing of the collection.

The compiling of sayings proceeded in various stages. Initially, smaller collections emerged (partly distinguishable by their inscriptions). These were then added to larger ones. They received their final shape in a book of proverbs contextualized by means of the literary device of parallelism. In this way, they assumed a form very similar to that of a poem. They became literary proverbs.

The collection of sayings in Proverbs 10—31 was combined with another, originally independent collection that emerged later. This compilation contained longer didactic speeches or didactic poems; hence, Proverbs 1—9. These were composed in schools by teachers, teachers of wisdom. They originated in written form and served a pedagogical aim, similar to the Near Eastern wisdom writings with which they have many points of connection. It was particularly the exhortations that were expanded in this fashion. The teacher addressed his students and summoned them to receive wisdom. Here the wisdom is inherently abstract and objectivized.

To the later phase also belong instructional exhortations, proverbs extolling wisdom, and the complex of proverbs about the righteous and the wicked (see esp. chaps. 10—15).

In a transitional stage, short sayings were extended in different ways; this included short poems (others becoming didactic poems), perhaps for the purpose of concluding short compilations. Yet these short poems—followed, in time, by longer ones—are amplifications of individual sayings and belong to the same category. A transition is also apparent in that proverbs of the later wisdom retain the basic form of the individual saying.[88]

The wisdom writings outside of the book of Proverbs belong to the postdevelopmental stage of proverbs. They are identified by their relationship to other forms and motifs and can be characterized as hybrids, with all manner of modification. Aside from its contextualization in wisdom discourse, the standard proverb occurs still in numerous later wisdom writings.

7. WISDOM PROVERBS
AS WORDS OF JESUS

Logia in the Synoptic Gospels
and Their Relationship to the
Sayings of the Book of Proverbs

How is the likeness of certain Gospel sayings and Proverbs to be explained? We cannot thoroughly examine this question here. For the purposes of offering some comment, the work of three theologians shall be presented.

I. RUDOLF BULTMANN[89]

Bultmann's thesis that many sayings in the Synoptics have been taken from "Jewish wisdom" still remains undisputed. The subheading "Jesus as a Teacher of Wisdom" could be misleading. Specifically, didactic wisdom (esp. the didactic poetry of Proverbs 1—9) plays no role in Bultmann's investigation, inasmuch as he is concerned only with proverbial wisdom. The subtitle could give the impression that the sayings were composed by sages (= teachers). Yet Bultmann notes again and again that these were popular proverbs.

On p. 113, Bultmann formulates his findings thus: "These examples demonstrate the necessity of understanding the synoptic sayings in the context of 'Jewish wisdom' and, as a consequence, reckoning with the fact that at least in part they were drawn from it."

In this regard, it is significant that Bultmann is here speaking of "logia" that correspond to individual sayings and not the didactic poetry of Proverbs 1—9, since no trace of the latter has been left behind in the Gospels.[90]

An important distinction between these two is that didactic poems (or dissertations), much like their Near Eastern, Egyptian, and Mesopotamian prototypes, were developed and passed on in schools of wisdom, whereas the proverbs from an early phase were oral in their emergence and transmission. Bultmann, following his teacher H. Gunkel, presumes the oral development of individual sayings. Even if collections already existed (which were unlikely for Jesus to have known), the oral tradition of proverbs continued at the same time. Bultmann's (1921) presuming an oral as well as written phase of transmission makes it possible for him to make a more precise identification ("Form und Geschichte der Logien," pp. 84ff.). His reasoning is as follows: "The basic form of the Old Testament and Jewish *māšāl* can be clearly recognized in the Logia"; hence, the arrangement according to indicative (significatory) and imperative (hortatory) sayings, in addition to amplifications and modifications differentiated according to their oral or literary stage. These are identified with more precision by Bultmann than by the majority of commentators. Proverbial statements, for example, are distinguished by Bultmann according to personal or material orientation, according to ways in which a saying may be extended, and according to the manner in which themes can be recast (e.g., the adaptation of secular sayings for religious purposes). All of this applies to the sayings of Proverbs as well as to the logia of the Gospel narratives.

Bultmann is correct to note that the question of authenticity can be answered only in a discriminating manner. For the most part, he goes only so far as to raise the possibility. Our own assessment of individual sayings aside, we may conclude: A significant portion of Jesus' preaching resembles Israel's proverbial wisdom, not only in form but in content as well. When Bultmann continues, "Still more precarious is the question of which of Jesus' sayings he could have adapted himself" (p. 109), I would contend that the matter can be expressed differently: It was unnecessary for Jesus to adapt himself to these sayings, since he was familiar with them from early on, inasmuch as he grew up with them. They were a living reality as popular proverbs in circles of common people with whom Jesus associated. Before his public appearance, they were his possession intellectually and remained so throughout the period of his ministry. Much of this entered into his preaching—some of it stemming from his own understanding of people, yet some of it also stemming from reference to God as framed by proverbial wisdom.

With regard to the much-discussed question of the so-called authenticity of Jesus sayings, I personally reject this term. Moreover, whether Jesus personally spoke them or whether they were later ascribed to him, a further question needs to be posed: What are the implications of the assertion that Jesus did not formulate many sayings in the Synoptic tradition that appear in proverbial form? In other words, can it be maintained that he assumed them in his preaching due to their correspondence, just as he had heard them and retained them from his youth?

If one concurs with this notion, the result is a task that heretofore has scarcely been recognized in terms of its importance: namely, a comprehensive and detailed examination of the relationship between Jesus' preaching and the early proverbial wisdom of Israel.

In any case, we can concur with Bultmann that the sayings in the Gospels as well as those of Proverbs had an oral phase of development before they acquired a literary phase.

II. MAX KÜCHLER[91]

In his 1979 work *Frühjüdische Weisheitstraditionen* (pp. 157–75), Küchler explores the "question of form and genre": "The wisdom-logia are among the oldest and most important literary forms that wisdom's struggle to compose and order reality produced. It presupposes insight into how things are; insight which comes only from long observation of experience. Insight, accuracy and aptness of expression assume their sharpest form in the wisdom-logia. Insightfulness, weightiness and beauty all characterize the wisdom-logia" (pp. 157ff.).

Küchler follows Bultmann in his identification of hortatory and interrogatory (*Fragewort*) proverbs as basic genres. He defines them as follows: "The proverb is a multifaceted saying shaped to relate to the world we experience. Fundamentally it seeks to ascertain the truth of an individual experience precisely through allowing the object of inquiry to acquire, even in its uniqueness, a certain generality and to develop an almost didactic tendency" (p. 161). Küchler places the didactic proverb between the standard proverb and the exhortation (p. 162); it is to be distinguished from the exhortation by its indicative mood and from the proverb in that it implies an exhortation. His understanding of exhortation follows that of D. Zeller (*Die weisheitlichen Mahnsprüche bei den Synoptikern*, 1977): "The less categorical emphasis differentiates the word of exhortation from the law and the prohibition. Its individual focus differentiates it from the teaching of the Law" (p. 163).

In an appendix at the close of his book, Küchler titles a section "Jesuanische Weisheit" (pp. 572–86) and concludes this section with a list of "wisdom sayings of Jesus according to the synoptics" (pp. 587–92). He arranges the *jesuanische Weisheit* according to "Jesus as early Christian wisdom teacher" and "Jesus as the ultimate expression of wisdom." Thus the *jesuanische* group is to be seen as a "didactic or learning community" (pp. 574–76). The Jesus of the Synoptics utilizes many arguments in his disputations that elucidate everyday experience by means of correspondences. He is also able to formulate precepts, the contours and definition of which can only be attributed to generations of experience. We find 108 of such wisdom sayings, with 196 occurrences of parallels (p. 579).

One difficulty with this thesis is that Küchler designates these texts as "weisheitliche Logien," insofar as, for him, the proverbs were *eo ipso* composed by sages and Jesus was an "early Christian wisdom teacher." Yet, when Küchler formulates, "He (Jesus) can also formulate rules, which gain their wisdom-like character only from generations of experience," this sounds more like deliberate composition than popular wisdom. Here it is necessary to distinguish clearly between proverbial wisdom as popular wisdom and teaching of the sages.

That there is no clear distinction between the two is reflected also in the selection of the proverbs that Küchler considers "jesuanisch." In 18 of these 108 texts, it is questionable to me whether they should be called "proverbs" at all. For example, announcements of the future such as are found in Mark 13:13, "Whoever stands firm to the end will be saved," are not proverbs. On the other hand, a number of statements that Küchler does not cite are unquestionably proverbs, such as "He causes his sun to shine on the evil and the good and sends rain on the righteous and on the unrighteous."[92]

Although one cannot lay down with precision the exact number of proverbs in the Synoptics, an important distinction needs to be made: all of these sayings that occur in the Synoptics as words of Jesus belong to early wisdom, in which wisdom takes the form of a short saying. There is no trace of the kind of didactic poetry found in Proverbs 1—9, nor are there sayings about instructional wisdom or the motif of extolling wisdom's virtue. It can thus be concluded that Jesus knew these sayings as a result of oral tradition—at least, the majority of them. This basic distinction Küchler does not make. In that some of these statements are composed using the literary device of parallelism—for example, Matt. 7:6, "Do not give to dogs what is sacred and do not throw your pearls before pigs," or Matt. 10:24 and 10:16, among others—it is indeed possible that he at the same time knew of short collections of proverbs that had not been gathered into the book of Proverbs. At any rate, whatever sayings are attributed to Jesus in the Synoptics belong to common popular wisdom.[93]

When we inquire into the relationship of proverbs occurring in the Gospel narratives to those of Proverbs 1—29; 31, we must address the matters of form and content. The correspondence in form is immediately clear: it is the form of short, self-contained proverbs, classified according to indicative and imperative sayings. We find scarcely any difference here regarding the actual realm of the proverbs: with few exceptions, the same situation is being reflected in which they are spoken, the same arenas of life, and the same type of characters tend to appear.

We also find agreement among the sayings in terms of their categorical classification. Proverbial statements are a clear majority, and most are observation and experience—notably human observation. In terms of content, this is the most important parallel. One may conclude that it is precisely this sort of observation and human experience that has been passed down through the centuries among the people in the form of proverbs, and Jesus assimilates this to a large extent in his preaching. These formulations are more important to him than theological, cultic, or other traditions. His understanding of people is molded by that which comes to expression in proverbs. Such constitutes one of the most important phenomena linking the Old Testament with the New Testament.[94]

III. W. A. BEARDSLEE[95]

Beardslee distinguishes between a practical and a speculative wisdom (a distinction that to a certain extent corresponds to my differentiation between functional and abstract wisdom). The practical variety is much more closely akin to the Gospels; the speculative is scarcely to be found. Against Bultmann, Beardslee correctly observes that the proverbs do not express general truths; rather, they concern actual, specific situations in people's daily life: "The proverb implies a story,"[96] that is, something that happens. Such is mirrored also when themes from Old Testament proverbs find their parallel in the parables of Jesus—for example, one's place at the table, the friend at midnight, the unfruitful fig tree. The proverbs possess an inherently apposite character, inasmuch as they constitute at any given time an appropriate word. In this way, they presuppose a "common body of human experiences,"[97] generally deemed valid. They point to a theme that is common to all people. At the same time, much in contrast to a speculative notion of wisdom, the proverbs very concretely refer the listener to his present reality.

IV. SUMMARY

Through allusion to the three aforementioned works, I have been able to draw attention to only a significant group of sayings from the words of Jesus as recorded in the Gospels. This has resulted in the awareness that we are restricted to the proverbial wisdom of early Israel. It is this notion of wisdom and not the later abstract or speculative didactic wisdom that occurs in the Gospel narratives. Jesus is not presented as a teacher of abstract, didactic wisdom (as, for example, in Proverbs 1—9); rather, he is one who has received the proverbial wisdom of the fathers. His understanding of people is thus shaped, just as is much of what he says about God in his preaching. This heritage links the New Testament with the Old Testament.

What this implies theologically in terms of our overall premise deserves some consideration. It will certainly mean not only that many statements which heretofore have been held as "original" words of Jesus are proverbs that long already were spoken and heard among his people but also that they retained their fundamental (oral) character in Jesus' preaching. They represent the expression of a particular understanding of people and a way of speaking of God that grew out of what was relevant to the corporate life of the people. In addition to this, these sayings find their meaning in the context of a particular situation. They are misinterpreted when we attempt to draw from them general and timeless rules, laws, or verifications. We can understand them properly only when we consider or inquire into the particular nature of the situation in which they were spoken.

V. A SKETCH OF A GROUPING
OF PROVERBS IN THE GOSPELS

People, body and spirit, health and sickness, eating and drinking: "The eye is the light of the body" (Matt. 6:22). "Out of the abundance of the heart the mouth speaks" (Matt. 12:34). "Can the blind lead the blind?" (Matt. 15:14). (Cf. also Mark 2:17, 19, 21ff.; 7:27; 9:50.)

Life and death, the limits of being human: "What does it profit a person to gain the whole world . . . ?" (Mark 8:36). "Wherever there is a carcass, there the vultures will gather" (Matt. 24:28). "Who of you can add to his life a single cubit?" (Matt. 6:27). (Cf. also Matt. 10:28–29; 8:20; 5:36.)

Proper and improper behavior: "Every good tree brings forth good fruit" (Matt. 7:17). "Whoever draws the sword, dies by the sword" (Matt. 26:52). "No one can serve two masters" (Matt. 6:24). (Cf. also Matt. 12:35; Mark 4:21; 7:15; 14:38; Luke 16:10.)

Work: "The worker is worthy of his rations" (Matt. 10:10). "The harvest is great, the laborers are few" (Matt. 9:37).

Rank: "A student is not greater than his master, neither is a servant over his lord" (Matt. 10:24). "Many who are first will be last" (Matt. 20:16 = Mark 10:31). (Cf. also Matt. 22:14; 23:12; Mark 6:4; Luke 22:27.)

Possessions, poor and rich, little and much: "To the one who has will be given . . . " (Matt. 25:29). (Cf. also Mark 4:25; Luke 7:41–42; 12:15; 10:42; 12:48.)

Hidden and open: "A city that sits on a hill . . . " (Matt. 5:14–15). (Cf. also Mark 4:21–22; Matt. 10:26.)

Might and power: "No one can enter a strong man's house . . . " (Mark 3:27). (Cf. also Mark 3:23; 9:40.)

God's operation: "God allows the sun to shine on the evil and on the good . . . " (Matt. 5:45). " . . . not one of them falls to the ground apart from the will of your Father" (Matt. 10:29–30; cf. Matt. 6:26). "All things are possible with God" (Mark 10:27). (Cf. also Mark 12:17, 27; 10:9; Luke 16:15.)

Characterization: " . . . a hard man, who harvests where he . . . and gathers where he . . . " (Matt. 25:24).

Comparison: " . . . for he says, 'The old is better'" (Luke 5:39). (Cf. also Luke 23:31.)

Imperative: Some of the words of exhortation are to be distinguished from the general exhortations that are specific to the circle of Jesus' friends and disciples.

General exhortations: "Judge not, so that you are not judged" (Matt. 7:1). "Be wise as snakes and harmless as doves" (Matt. 10:16). "With the measure you use, the same will be measured to you" (Mark 4:24). (Cf. also Matt. 7:4; 12:37; Mark 7:12–13; 9:35; 10:9; 12:17; Luke 4:23; 14:8–10, 12–14.)

In Matt. 5:39–45, the Master is addressing his disciples (" . . . but I tell you . . . "). In this case, the person speaking is addressing a small gathering, where we find a succession of corresponding imperatives with similar content. These, however, no longer constitute proverbs, by which everyone is addressed.

8. GOD AND HUMANITY IN
EARLY PROVERBIAL WISDOM

I. THE UNDERSTANDING OF HUMANITY
IN PROVERBIAL WISDOM

There is no book in the Old Testament that reflects such a thorough yet
diverse understanding about people in ancient Israel as the book of Proverbs.
Here, once more, we are keeping in mind the distinction between early proverbial wisdom and the later development of wisdom expressed in the didactic
poems of chapters 1—9, where the interest in people recedes notably.

The proverbs speak of the person in the same way that the creation narrative
of Genesis 2—3 speaks of creation, in variety and comprehensiveness. Accordingly, we can segregate the various spheres addressed by the proverbs as they
relate to human understanding: the fashion of the human being, his surroundings, his sustenance, work (the divine mandate), and community.

1. The Human Being; the Creature

The Fashion of the Human, Formed from the Earth

For his very existence the human remains dependent on the earth, from
which he is formed and to which he again returns. The potentiality of his life,
with attendant limitations, is a given at the time of his creation. His body, his
members, his mind facilitate his living on earth, and at the same time they limit
it: "Everything has its time, being born and dying . . . " (Qoh. 3:2). The proverbs of human observation speak with amazement and, at times, reverence of
the body, its members and its comprehension: "The hearing ear and the seeing
eye—Yahweh has made them both" (Prov. 20:12). "The spirit of man is Yahweh's lamp; it searches out his innermost being" (20:27). "Light is sweet, and
it is pleasant to the eyes to see the sun" (Qoh. 11:7).

Every part of the body, every one of its senses, surfaces in the proverbs. In terms of this fascination, the proverbs resemble the psalms that speak of the person as a creation; they possess the same understanding of humans as Psalms 8 and 139.

The Human as a Thinking and Acting Being

The basic arrangement of the proverbs is into categories of statements and exhortations. In the main, statements articulate observations and experiences; exhortations tend to mirror behavior. Both thought and conduct alike are a part of being human; the one promotes the other. For this reason, we have to do here with empirical thought. It is focused on reality, to which the person in his life journey is resigned. The early form of wisdom is not abstract or the least bit speculative; rather, it conforms to what is real. It is precisely for this reason that the understanding of wisdom as a "quest for a system" is highly improbable. Wisdom accompanies the person as an inherent means by which to order his life's path; it is functional in nature. With it, the person is able to set about doing something with his individual life; he can also do something in the context of community, to which he belongs. But inasmuch as wisdom is no set possession, rather a potential, there often exist in the life of the community those who are wise and those who are foolish. Foolish behavior and wise behavior stand in contrast one to the other, a reality about which the proverbs have much to say.

The proverbial statements in which human observations and experience are preserved and passed on ascribe to a person a particular gift with which he reflects, meditates, judges, and assesses. Hence, he possesses a limited autonomy in his thinking. (A separate proverb group deals with this demarcation.) For this task the human requires no didactic wisdom. He does not need to be instructed in order to observe a bird in its flight and formulate his thinking in this regard. Independence of thought plays an important role in the proverbs. For example, in the "better than" proverbs, substantiation is never offered for the truth of the comparison; the person being addressed is simply to judge for himself. To the extent that this capacity to think independently is present at creation, it is universal. It is not restricted to Israel, nor is it confined to a particular group of sages.

The Human in His Temporality

Human nature is understood within the limitations of its temporality, that is, from birth until death. The proverbs know nothing of a timeless "human existence." Thus, appropriate speech is that which is spoken at the proper time.

Seen in this light, wisdom is something that can accrue, and each phase of one's life is equally important in its positioning on the continuum between birth and death. Human temporality also manifests itself in the fact that a great many of the proverbial statements stand in juxtaposition. The movement back and forth between joy and sorrow is integral to the observations and experiences monitored in the proverbs. It is not possible to free the one or the other element from temporal reality, as illustrated by the reflective poem of the Preacher in Qohelet 3. The human is never pictured as living in a constant mode of existence. He is always moving in a realm suspended between two poles: birth and dying.

2. The Human Being as a Creature among Creatures; the Environment

We also find here a direct correspondence to Genesis 1—3. The human is placed by the Creator in the garden and coexists with trees, plants of the field, flowers, and animals. The garden is his world. This is communicated most clearly by the comparisons, which are an integral part of the proverbs. The garden is the realm in which the human makes his observations and experiences. The abundant variety in the comparisons is evidence of how a person and his environment belong together. In the comparisons, what has been created—the creature—joins in communicating the overall message of the proverbs. The human is a part of the whole to which his thought life and sense world are linked. He discovers things that correspond to him, since everything that he observes and ponders belongs to the whole. Here again, we see the difference between early and late wisdom: such comparisons occur only with the use of the functional type of proverbial wisdom, not with its abstract counterpart.

3. The Fruit of the Garden; Provisions

The Creator freely gives his creatures the fruit of the garden so that they have ample nourishment. Without the blessing of the Creator there would be no life. "The blessing of Yahweh alone brings abundance" (Prov. 10:22), and as a gift of that blessing, provision is received by human beings. Hence, nourishment, food and drink, plays an important role in the proverbs, just as it does in the sayings of other peoples. Provision is not merely something that is peripheral; rather, it is valued as a gift of the Creator, without which there would be no life. The proverbs speak of being hungry and being satisfied, by which, in some cases, it is an issue of life and death. This is taken seriously enough that the admonition to give food to the hungry and drink to the thirsty is constantly recurring; and conversely, namely, that the lust for eating and drinking can be characterized in unworthy terms. There is a connection between the high view of the meal in various other parts of the Bible and that in the proverbs that deal with eating and drinking, hunger and thirst. Even when one's behavior at mealtime is the subject of proverbial sayings, concern is also thereby being expressed regarding provision as a gift of the Creator.

4. Work and Its Yield

Work is grounded in the mandate of the Creator. Although this is not stated expressly in the proverbs, it is assumed. In this regard, the juxtaposition of the diligent and the idle plays an important role. The many related sayings underscore two aspects. On the one hand, they indicate that idleness, which indeed is natural and not in and of itself fatal, nonetheless can lead to a ruined life and the downfall of a family. On the other hand, this allusion to idleness offers occasion for humorous caricature. It is precisely this seeming contradiction between two opposing aspects that is manifest by the wisdom of these proverbs. Each side is valid, and the human being reflects both aspects; he is in need of hearing about both. If there were no humorous caricatures and only serious exhortations toward diligence, then a person would be mistaken as to his true nature; such serious admonition would only become burdensome. For this reason, the exhortations are also expressed through a number of appealing poems that deal with guarding one's possessions.

Several diverse aspects of the juxtaposition of the rich and the poor also come into consideration, of which the relationship one to the other must be properly recognized. The general experience that the idle person grows poorer and the diligent person acquires opportunities is not enough. Poverty was not always the result of sloth; neither is wealth always the consequence of diligence. One must live with certain realities; there are poor as well as rich: "Rich and poor meet together; Yahweh has made them all" (22:2). There is no attempt made in the proverbs to formulate or appraise this relationship in pure principle. This real and existing relationship, as well as one's reaction to it, is left open. The limitations of wealth are pointed out, in addition to the questionable nature of its accumulation. An exhortation is directed at the rich, that they share with the poor man and help him; the poor man is God's creation as well. Moreover, death awaits both rich and poor. The poor are told that, in some circumstances, it is better to have fewer possessions than to have wealth; the rich person can be blackmailed his whole life long.

5. The Human Being in Community

What has been said thus far is also applicable to people in community, since the proverbs in their early phase had foremost a social function.

In this regard, we are concerned with a cultivation of corporate life as opposed to a purely functional society in which there has been a shift from social relationship to a culture of commodities (where the individual person, i.e., the consumer, is fundamentally passive). The proverbs for this reason had significant meaning, because in them the experiences of the fathers in corporate life were granted a hearing in the present generation. In the case of the proverbs of characterization, the concern is a critical understanding of people that promoted the reconciliation of communal life. In the contrast of the wise and the foolish, criteria are established that speak for themselves, inasmuch as they grew out of experience. The wise person is the one who is conscious of accountability, who restrains himself, and who holds his tongue, while the fool is the one who is unrestrained, who cannot control himself, who does not consider his words and yet believes anything that someone else might say. This contrast has to do with promoting or damaging the community.

A part of corporate life obviously is the protection of the lowly, the weak, those without rights. Integral to this duty are works of mercy. Here we find agreement between the proverbs of ancient Israel and those of Egypt, Mesopotamia, Africa, and the Orient. Exhortation is sufficient in the light of such needs; commands are unnecessary, for one cannot be forced to respond. What we find in all of these sayings is something entirely natural and obvious: a community in which that does not occur is a community in deep trouble.

6. Discourse

An essential part of community is discourse. In the Old Testament the "word" is primarily something that happens and not what is merely articulated, and the basic function of speech is the address. The value of speech in the proverbs is measured according to what it delivers. Accordingly, the proverbs concern good speech and detrimental speech, what is beneficial and what is harmful. The proverbs are formulated not with a view of expressing abstract thoughts (here one can distinguish between an aphorism and a proverb), rather with a view of affecting something. Thus we find emphasized in the proverbs the difference between a word spoken at the proper time and one that is inappropriate. Particular speech is linked to the situation in which it is spoken; speech thereby receives its significance and meaning. This applies to good as well as abusive speech: "An appropriate answer is like a kiss on the lips"

(24:26); "There is one whose reckless words are like thrusts of a sword" (12:18). It is not incidental that Genesis 2—3 also speaks of the contrast of good and evil speech. Good speech can be beautiful speech as well. In some respects the proverbs resemble poetry in their compositional form and, in fact, not necessarily because of the literary device of parallelism. In their composition, the comparisons already suggest this. Good and appropriate speech should be attractive, so that ones likes to hear it and can easily retain it. Humor and wit thus are an integral part of the linguistic setting. In language that is abstract and didactic, in comparison, humor is absent.

II. THE WORK OF GOD IN EARLY WISDOM

R. N. Whybray (1979) counts 375 units from Prov. 10:1–22:16. Of these, fifty-five are Yahweh sayings. Proverbs 15:33–16:9 constitutes the core of these, with nine Yahweh sayings and an interruption only in 16:8. Additionally, we find five royal proverbs in 10:12–15. Of the remaining Yahweh sayings in 10:1–22:16, there are twenty-five that serve to interpret an adjoining word. This arrangement serves the purpose of providing theological explanation for secular proverbs. We must concur with Whybray that proverbs that are related due to their subject matter have been placed together by compilers or redactors, as elsewhere in the Old Testament. Also possible is the intention of the compiler to place a group of Yahweh sayings in the middle of the larger collection of 10:1–22:16. Such compiling, at any rate, is a redactive procedure; it mirrors the compiler's intention. It has nothing to do with the original development of individual proverbs; nothing alters the fact that, to begin with, each saying is an independent unit in and of itself. This is confirmed when we consider each individual Yahweh saying on its own merit. All of these are extremely diverse and, within the general grouping of Yahweh sayings, belong to different categories. When we inquire into contextual linkage, we must examine what each individual proverb says about God. Such gives rise to five categories: (1) Yahweh as Creator of human beings; (2) the operation of Yahweh as the limitation of human potential; (3) Yahweh's chastising intervention; (4) Yahweh's dealing with the righteous and the wicked; and (5) the fear of Yahweh.

1. Yahweh as the Creator of Humanity

P. Doll has demonstrated in *Menschenschöpfung und Weltschöpfung in der alttestamentlichen Weisheit* (1985, pp. 9–28) that Proverbs speaks of human creation in the sayings of the older wisdom (chaps. 10—29), whereas the didactic poetry of chapters 1—9 speaks only of creation of the world (chaps. 3 and 8). He assumes in this regard the *traditionsgeschichtlich* distinction between material and human creation that C. Westermann and R. Albertz (among others) demonstrated in Genesis 1—11 and the Psalms. All three text realms indicate that human creation belongs to an older line of tradition and that material creation is reflective of a younger tradition. This distinction corresponds to the *religionsgeschichtlich* assumption that human creation is spoken of particularly in primitive, nonliterary cultures and that material creation appears predominantly in more advanced cultures (notably in Egypt). (Support for this has been supplied in my commentary on Genesis.) The meaning of this for the present study is that the earlier wisdom speaks only of the Creator of human beings and, specifically, of the Creator's significance to humans. It is the later wisdom embodied in didactic poetry that initially takes up the traditions of the creation of the world. These were borrowed from the Psalms theme of extolling the Creator, inasmuch as it served the composer's purpose of elevating the significance of wisdom. Lauding wisdom is one of the most important motifs of the didactic poems. A further distinction consists in the fact that what the proverbs say about the human Creator is normally accompanied by some type of substantiation. In contrast, the discourse on material creation in chapters 3 and 8 elevates wisdom's significance intrinsically.

The Social-Critical Function of Yahweh as Creator of Humanity

"The one mocking the poor reproaches his maker" (17:5). "The one oppressing the poor reproaches his maker, but the one who is kind to the needy honors Yahweh" (14:31). "Do we not all have one Father? Did not God create us all?" (Mal. 2:10a). "Did not he who formed me in the womb make him?" (Job 31:15). " . . . who does not favor the rich over the poor, since they are all the work of his hands?" (Job 34:19). "The rich and the poor meet together; Yahweh is maker of them all" (Prov. 22:2). "The poor man and the oppressor meet together; Yahweh gives light to the eyes of both" (29:13). (Malachi and Job are adaptations of proverbs.)

These sayings are properly understood only in the light of the function that they had in their earlier oral stage (thus P. Doll, pp. 16ff.). "Auch wenn Prov 22, 2 einen einfachen Zusammenhang konstatiert, so kann es in einer Situation, in der dem Adressaten eben dieses verborgen ist und ihm gesagt werden muss, von lebenswichtiger Bedeutung sein" (Doll, p. 18). The proverbs are handed down along with their setting in only a slightly adapted form in Mal. 2:10 and Job 31:15; 34:19. They confirm the application of the proverbs in oral usage. (Above, I have listed another possibility offered by Doll as to setting.)

Sayings about the operation of the human Creator can also be associated with another category—simple observations about people: "The hearing ear and the seeing eye—Yahweh has made them both" (20:12). "The spirit of man is Yahweh's lamp; it searches all his innermost being" (20:27). "As in water face reflects face, so the heart of man reflects man" (27:19). "Light is sweet, and it is pleasant to the eyes to see the sun" (Qoh. 11:7). It is the Creator who has so wonderfully created the human being. One's awe-filled consideration of the handiwork of the human body with its organs and senses has the repercussion of praise for the Creator: "Praise the Lord, who has skillfully and delicately made you. . . ." These sayings resemble Psalm 139. Each of these works expresses joy of living and joy over the human body.

2. God and His Work as the Limitation of Human Possibilities

"To man belong the plans of the heart, but from Yahweh proceeds the reply of the tongue" (16:1). "A man's heart plans his way, but Yahweh directs his steps" (16:9). "Many are the plans in the heart of a man, but it is Yahweh's purpose that will be established" (19:21; cf. Amenemope, "Words that men say are one thing, but what God does is another thing" [see Appendix]). "The horse is made ready for the day of battle, but victory belongs to Yahweh" (21:31). "As a stream of water the heart of the king is in the hand of Yahweh; he directs it wherever he pleases" (21:1). "A man's steps are directed by Yahweh; how then can a man understand his way?" (20:24; cf. this Sumerian saying, "Man cannot understand the will of God, nor can the path of God be discerned" [see Appendix]). "There is no wisdom, no insight, no plan that can prevail against Yahweh" (21:30). "Death and destruction lie open before Yahweh; how much more the hearts of man!" (15:11; cf. the Egyptian Onchsheshonqy, "God sees into the heart" [see Appendix]). Two further sayings, defined by the phrase "but Yahweh," express that these limitations at times belie the belief that one is on the right path: "All of a man's ways are justified in his own eyes, but Yahweh weighs the desires" (16:2). "All of man's ways are right in his own eye, but Yahweh weighs the hearts" (21:2).

In terms of form, these are mostly proverbs of antithesis. The words "but Yahweh" are juxtaposed with a situation or an intention on the part of the human being. This "but" points to the limits that are placed on a person. It is the work of the Creator that defines the limits of human potential. Created by God, the human finds his limitations manifest in his mortality and his fallibility.

We are dealing here with a universal awareness—something that occurs in all of humankind, from nonliterary peoples on down to advanced cultures (e.g., in Egypt, the eye of Horus) of the contemporary era. These are not sayings that are specific to Israelite wisdom; rather, Israel shares in knowledge suited to all of mankind, namely, that human potential is limited. Even here we find a correspondence in earliest history: the tower of Babel.

Each of these proverbs was spoken in a particular situation in which it was necessary to address someone who was prone to forget or disregard these boundaries. It is precisely for this reason that these sayings were passed on: a serious danger lay before the individual as a consequence of this disregard. We encounter this peril, to illustrate, in the message of the prophet Isaiah, specifically in his pronouncement of the collapse of the mighty. Again and again throughout history we encounter this disregard or failure to recognize human limitations. Merely knowing about such limitations does not suffice. They must be enunciated at the right moment to the one who fails to acknowledge them.

The more powerful a person becomes, the more he can attain; and the more he would appear to approximate the Creator with regard to his own abilities, the more blind and foolish he becomes in terms of overestimating himself. At this point, speaking of God as the limitation of all human potential becomes critical for humankind: "Death and destruction lie open before Yahweh; how much more the hearts of men!" (15:11).

The proverb has the ability to communicate this reality because Yahweh is the Creator of the human just as he is the Creator of all things. In this way, the two groups of sayings that refer to Yahweh are united: Yahweh is Creator of humankind and he is the limitation of human understanding. Furthermore, Prov. 15:11 has a point of contact with Psalm 139, a psalm about the Creator of mankind: "Lord, you have searched me and known me . . . " And just as in Genesis 1—11, human capability and human limitation are presented alongside each other.

That one's understanding of the world, of one's own person, and of "the plans in the heart of man" has its limits is indisputable; precisely for this reason, a statement such as "man thinks, God directs" can come across as banal. Yet, this is only because this ossified statement of brute fact has lost the function that it once possessed in ancient Israel, that is, as a word pertinent to a situation in which it is necessary and in which it can affect something. This applies as well to statements that are incontestable merely as "truths." They retain their force where this general validity is not seen.

3. God Chastises and Forgives in Mercy

The notion that God punishes evil deeds and rewards the good is integral to the operation of the gods as is generally found in human religions. It is such a consistent feature of divine nature that, all other variables aside, it finds a virtually unanimous consensus. Thus, it constitutes an essential element in the

Old Testament narratives of the events of primitive history dealing with guilt and punishment (C. Westermann, *Genesis 1* [1985]).

"The eyes of Yahweh keep watch over knowledge; thus he frustrates the words of the faithless" (22:12). "When the ways of a man please Yahweh, he makes even his enemies be at peace with him" (16:7). "If your enemy falls, do not gloat . . . Yahweh will see it and be displeased . . . " (24:17–18; cf. also 22:22–23; 23:10–11).

With certain conditions, the preceding group of sayings belongs to the category of abominations before Yahweh. Here a cultic regulation is adapted to form an intensified expression of disapproval.

"Abomination" is a cultic term; every idolatry is an abomination to Yahweh. The term is then expanded: abomination comes to encompass everything that displeases Yahweh—for example, dealing in false weights and measures (11:1; 20:10, 23); then, even further, "those of a perverse heart" (11:20), "lying lips" (12:22), "wicked thoughts" (15:26), and "every proud heart" (16:5).

When something in cultic practice was designated as an "abomination," it was done so through simple pronouncement, as is the case with the characterizations—for example, "Lying lips are an abomination to Yahweh" (12:22a). This kind of statement, however, is also particularly well suited for the construction of a saying using parallelism; thus 12:22b, "but those acting faithfully are his pleasure" (also 11:20; 15:26; 16:5). That a single-verse depiction is the basis for all of these statements makes it abundantly clear that the antithesis resulting from expansion by means of parallelism is a secondary development. The form, consequently, is able to serve the antithesis of the righteous and the wicked, as in 15:9: "An abomination to Yahweh is the way of the wicked, but he loves the one who eagerly pursues righteousness."

None of these sayings, however, speaks about Yahweh's dealings or his speaking per se.

4. Proverbs of Antithesis: God's Dealing with the Righteous and the Wicked

This group is part of the complex of antithetical proverbs dealing with the righteous and the wicked, that is, a secondary stratum in chapters 10—31. The contrast between the two here is due to the operation of God, resulting in an intensification of the contrast. The effect, at any rate, is an absolute antithesis: "Yahweh does not let the righteous go hungry; but he thwarts the craving of the wicked" (10:3). "Yahweh tears down the house of the proud, but he preserves the widow's boundaries" (15:25). "Yahweh is far from the wicked, but the prayer of the righteous he hears" (15:29). "A refuge for the virtuous is the power of Yahweh, but it is ruin to those who do evil" (10:29).

The antithesis of the righteous and the wicked surfaces with profound acuteness in the proverbs that are inclusive of the operation of God and one's relationship to God. At the same time that the power of Yahweh is a refuge for the righteous, it is ruin for the wicked (10:29). The hunger of the righteous is appeased, yet the craving (!) of the wicked is frustrated (10:3). The prayer of the righteous is heard by Yahweh, but he remains distant to the wicked (15:29). Of the fear of God only good is spoken; while wicked people do not understand what is right, those who fear God understand it fully (28:5). Whoever abides in the fear of Yahweh will be blessed; whoever hardens his heart falls upon trouble (28:14).

With these contrasts, an assertion stands as a matter of fact: the one group does only good, the other only bad. Ever present is a theoretical antithesis; concrete features and situations do not appear here. A fixed teaching is developed by all of these sayings. What is said about God is, from the outset, bound up with this teaching: God is not capable of anything other than compensating the righteous and the wicked accordingly. Even the form of these antithetical sayings is that of exclusion. In the following two proverbs, the sense of each saying is shaped by antithesis: "The fear of Yahweh prolongs life, but the years of the wicked are cut short" (10:27); and "Yahweh is far from the wicked, but the prayer of the righteous he hears" (15:29). That God would be merciful to a wicked person, a sinner, does not surface here. The mercy of God is absolutely reserved for the righteous. It is a rigid teaching that is represented in these proverbs of antithesis; it constitutes a part of the early wisdom.

5. The Fear of Yahweh

Several different groups of proverbs speak of the fear of Yahweh. A few of these occur in the proverbs of antithesis involving the righteous and the wicked (10:27; 28:5; 14:2; 29:25), but most of them are independent of these. The majority of allusions to the fear of Yahweh concern a proper and necessary attitude toward him. The translation of these, for the most part, can be righteousness, since "fear" is to be understood in the sense of reverence: "In the fear of Yahweh is strong confidence; and for his children it will be a refuge" (14:26). "The fear of Yahweh is a fountain of life to turn one from the snares of death" (14:27). "By loyalty and faithfulness sin is atoned for, and by the fear of Yahweh one avoids evil" (16:6). "The fear of Yahweh leads to life, and the one having it rests satisfied and is not visited by evil" (19:23). "The reward for humility and the fear of Yahweh is wealth and honor and life" (22:4). "Do not let your heart envy sinners, but always be zealous for the fear of Yahweh"

(23:17). "Blessed is the man who always fears Yahweh, but the one hardening his heart falls upon trouble" (28:14).

"Righteousness is a fountain of life" (14:27), a strong confidence (14:26), a refuge (14:26). It leads toward life (19:23), and one is thereby secured (19:23). Blessed is the one who abides in it (28:14). By means of righteousness, one is kept far from evil (16:6). It rewards one with honor and life (22:4); one should seek to preserve it (23:17–18); and we are admonished toward it (24:21–22).

Trust is very closely related to the fear of God; at times both are synonymous (16:20; 29:25). Blessed is the man who trusts in Yahweh (16:20); he is abundantly rewarded (28:25) and his own are protected (29:25), for Yahweh is a shield (30:5–6). The power of Yahweh is a refuge for the righteous (10:29). The name of Yahweh is a strong tower; it is there that the righteous person finds safety (18:10).

The semantic range of "trust," as well as its cognates, belongs without exception to the confession of confidence found in the Psalms. Virtually all of the statements of this proverb group could just as easily appear in a psalm of trust. The "fear of Yahweh," in contrast, does not have its roots in the Psalms. Rather, it is a concept typical of pious wisdom from a later era; it links righteousness to wisdom: "A wise man fears and turns away from evil, but a fool is arrogant and careless" (14:16). "The fear of Yahweh is instruction in wisdom, and humility goes before honor" (15:33). " . . . so that your trust might be in Yahweh, I declare them to you this day, even to you" (22:19).

The connection between the fear of Yahweh and wisdom is subsequently much more strongly developed in Proverbs 1—9. There is present here a notable phenomenon relative to the history of proverbs. In the later era, after the exile, wisdom and righteousness become more clearly associated. Whereas in the proverbs of an earlier era secular parlance takes precedence, in the later period righteousness is a primary proverbial theme. The expression most typical of righteousness in this vein is "fear of Yahweh." Righteousness takes on the form of a wisdom saying; "the fear of Yahweh is the beginning of wisdom" (1:7). In place of "fear of Yahweh," the expression "trust in Yahweh" can be used; in this way, the language of confessing confidence is achieved. The language of the Psalms thereby passes over into the language of pious wisdom.

Summary

What is said about God in Proverbs 10—31 is distinguished in a conspicuous and rather remarkable manner from what the Old Testament otherwise says about him. An event occurring between God and his people Israel—a history of "God with his people" and everything which that might entail—is not given here. None of the important dates of this history is mentioned—

neither the flight from Egypt nor the revelation at Sinai nor the covenant; neither the migration into the land nor the law. Very little is spoken of worship to
God, while priests and the sanctuary are never mentioned. Perhaps even more
important is that God never speaks in the proverbs. There appears nothing
verbal that might be labeled God's speech, nor is any word cited that Yahweh
might have spoken. In addition, no person is ever mentioned who would have
mediated the word of God. The fact that God is alluded to here differently than
in the rest of the Old Testament is quite conspicuous. Furthermore, nothing is
ever spoken to God (a prayer appears only in a later supplement, 30:7–9).
Prayers are not mentioned or cited, nor any cry to God. The reason for this can
only be that the proverbs employ a language of the workaday world, the context of which is to be found only in people relating to one another. The word of
God and speech that is directed toward God have their own sphere of language.

This accords with the tendency in proverbs that a particular group mentions
God only as Creator. More precisely, this grouping corresponds to what is said
of God in the account of primitive history. God is spoken of as Creator who, as
such, is Lord of his creation. To this category belong proverbs that speak of
God's work as the boundary of human potential. These sayings communicate
in a universal sense the limitations placed on humans. Similar to the early
historical account of Genesis 1—11 are those proverbs in which God chastises
human wickedness, the effect of which is to restrain a person in accordance
with human limitations. Such concurs with the Genesis 1—11 narratives that
emphasize guilt and punishment. Hence, the sayings of Proverbs 10—31 referring to God testify to the fact that speaking about God and his universal operation must have been far more extensive in ancient Israel than has been assumed
in traditional interpretation of salvation history. These sayings, due to the oral
phase of their transmission, had a wide dissemination.

It stands to reason, then, that in our consideration of proverbial sayings
reflecting early wisdom that correspond to what we find in Genesis 1—11,
there is surely some sort of connection. It thus becomes apparent that the proverbs as such have a universal character. Proverbs can surface anywhere among
humankind, just like accounts of creation or the flood. Human creation, as we
have seen, is meant to show forth the full range of references to human existence—his environment, provision, work, community, speech. These aspects,
common to all people, are the subject of abundant and diverse proverbs. Allusion in the proverbs to God the Creator of human beings, who has conde-
scended to his creation in its existential form, is framed in this restricted
existential type of language.

This means, however, that the proverbs alluding to God are no "theological"
formulations in the sense in which "theology" and "theological" are normally
used. They have no specifically theological function in an explicitly theological

context. Rather, they speak of God in such a manner as would any person without stepping outside of everyday, secular discourse.

Here, there exists a certain correspondence to the phenomenon of "religionsinternen Pluralismus" that R. Albertz discovered in the religious history of Israel. His observation was that among the smaller groups of the pre-monarchy, everyday language did not conform to that of the official religion (R. Albertz, *Persönliche Frömmigkeit und offizielle Religion*, Stuttgart, 1976). In the context of wisdom as well, God is spoken of differently than in the official religion.

EXCURSUS 6
Wisdom and Theology

A theology in the normal sense cannot be inferred from the proverbs, since "theology" is not their focus. Where they do speak of God, it is no specifically theological discourse. Only that which the proverbs say about God in their own way can be contrasted with that which is said of God in the other books of the Old Testament. The proverbs allude to a God who, in contrast to all humans, is God. This universal God who relates to his creation governs everything spoken of him by the proverbs. This state of affairs should serve as a caution against ascribing a comprehensive meaning to the references to God issuing out of theological reflection. To the contrary, speaking about the Creator in ancient Israel must have had greater importance than we are accustomed to assume. The common people, in any case, spoke in this way about God, as reflected in the proverbs, and not, for example, as the Deuteronomic theologian spoke of him.

Above and beyond this, we can draw a conclusion for Christian theology in the West. A theology that expresses itself primarily in abstract concepts necessarily creates a distance between itself and the language of the common people relative to their reference to God. At the same time, it loses its universal character, which is an integral part of speaking about God in the proverbs. This should be a warning concerning the later, abstract wisdom, which changes into this kind of speculation in its speaking about God.

CONCLUSION

I. THE SIGNIFICANCE OF THE
UNIVERSAL ASPECTS OF THE PROVERBS

The proverbs, which as such do not yet admit of a division between religious and secular, were, in the course of a long history of tradition, partly assimilated into the sphere of religion. They constitute components of religious texts and/ or collections or books as found in the Old Testament, in Islam, or in the Christian church. Hence, they became constituents of "sacred scripture" as we find it in the canon of the Koran or the Bible. One manifestation of the universal character of proverbial wisdom is that one can observe a far-reaching agreement among the exhortations and warnings. For example, proverbs found all over the world contain warnings against people who are unable to govern themselves. Furthermore, in all of these warnings we find the admonition to help the weak, the poor, the suffering, the hungry, those without rights, and to stand by them. That is a fact that must be acknowledged from the start.

The question is whether or not a common understanding of commendable behavior or broadly condemned unwholesome behavior lies at the root of these many common sayings—that is to say, a general "knowledge of good and evil." If our awareness of this state of affairs is for the most part lost, then conscious recognition of the possibility that this "common knowledge" has more in common than not possesses considerable significance for drawing humanity closer together. This view is also expressed by W. A. Beardslee (1970, p. 127): The proverbs suggest a "common body of knowledge," the validity of which is generally acknowledged.

There is also something common in the manner in which the proverbs speak about God. Absent in these sayings is that which is specifically theological and cultic, that is, precisely that which distinguishes and divides the religions of humanity from one another. What is said about God is simply that

132

which touches the everyday lives of those who speak of him, that which is seemingly necessary to lead one's life. When the exhortation is given to help the weak who are in need, it is stated correspondingly that God will reward the one helping the weak or that God is on the side of those suffering. As Creator, God is portrayed as the one who establishes the limits of human capability. The manner in which God is depicted, both as the human and material Creator and as the one who determines the limitations placed on humans, is common to most religions. This is not a phenomenon that separates religions; rather, it unifies them.

When we view two elements together—first, a notion of "common sense" in the realm of human behavior that is communicated in the proverbs, and second, a depiction of God as is found in the primitive history of Genesis 1— 11, a narrative description common to and not exclusive of most religions— then proverbial wisdom retains a certain significance that, in terms of its effects, is accessible to all people. The notion of humanity as a whole is indeed an ingredient of the proverbs of Israel in their universal function. Thus L. Naré (1986; see the Appendix): "Biblical wisdom seems to have been built on the ground of a common human wisdom."

II. HUMANITY COMES OF AGE

A peculiarity of the proverbs that up to the present has received little attention is the consistent tendency to allow those being addressed the freedom of self-observation and self-perception, of self-assessment and freedom to decide, inasmuch as one's own interests are thereby taken into account. This is evidenced particularly in the substantiations that frequently proceed along the following lines: the essence of this exhortation has in mind your own best interests!

This peculiarity is founded on the reasoning that both statements and exhortations/warnings never are decreed from above. The person uttering the proverb never appeals to a position of authority. Rather, he stands on the same level as the one listening; he addresses the listener as a fellow human being who has come of age.

It is different, however, with the exhortations that are found in the instructional context. These presume a reflection on the part of the one teaching and are predicated on the notion that the one learning will be furthered as a result. A distinguishing mark of the instructional proverbs is that they exhibit this "pedagogic" orientation quite clearly.

For this reason, I cannot concur with G. von Rad when he identifies and classifies the wisdom of Israel collectively as "didactic wisdom"—a type of wisdom in which the one speaking is *eo ipso* the one teaching and the one listening is *eo ipso* the one being taught. I am even less prone to agree with such an equation of teaching and wisdom—an equation indeed presumed in many commentaries—for the simple reason that the subject per se in the texts of Proverbs 1—9 and 22—24 is unmistakably specified. These are matter-of-factly didactic texts; they constitute didactic wisdom.

Elsewhere in the texts of Proverbs, those sayings that cannot be categorized as instructional wisdom exhibit the freedom of the individual to generate a response and are formulated in two ways. These two forms—the indicative and the imperative—encompass the entire balance of texts.

Prior to my undertaking this investigation, I was never fully cognizant of this distinction. Only as I discovered that this distinction in fact defined all of the collections of proverbs known to me among Israelite, Near Eastern, and even nonliterary people did this occur to me. Hence, it follows that not only the short sayings but also the double-verse arrangements in indicative and imperative form are part of the universal character of the proverb. In this way, a human being is shown to be understood as a thinking and acting agent. This human understanding, in turn, is integral to one's self-perception as a created being. As a thinking and acting agent, one is a human come of age. Hence, the proverbs serve as a necessary corrective to the modern notion expressed most forcefully and effectively by Descartes, "Cogito, ergo sum." On the contrary, only thinking and acting together (that is, work!) constitute being human.

Several times during the course of the present study, the question of the relationship of the imperative proverbs to commandments was intimated. Laws first surface in a later stage of cultural development; they presume institutions whereby they can be "put into effect." The double-verse formulation of laws communicates a correlation of the legislative and executive domains. It is different, however, in the case of the commandments. Their form concurs in part with that of the words of exhortation (to illustrate, see the samples from among the Batak sayings in the Appendix). Another distinction is that in commandments, God is the one who is decreeing.

General exhortations, aside from their didactic function, are not authoritarian. They are spoken and heard in all spheres of corporate life. The fact that they were handed down orally indicates that they were generally known from childhood on in nonliterary cultures. Possessing a social function, they served as a tranquilizing factor in community life and were generally acknowledged as having this function. They represented nothing that constituted a threat. The laws, on the other hand, were limited in ancient Israel in terms of their significance. They were comprised of a written corpus accessible only to a relative few and thus generated only an institutional force (consider, for example, the twofold construction of law: case and consequence). Even when the laws were already in existence, the imperatives retained their regulative significance. The apostle Paul's description of mankind feeling threatened before God and longing for a release from the law to which they were indentured was, in any case, not applicable to preexilic Israel. The Gospels confirm the role of proverbs, inasmuch as a considerable number of sayings that parallel the imperative sayings of Proverbs are handed down as words of Jesus.

III. WISDOM, SCIENCE, AND PHILOSOPHY

1. Time and Place

Wisdom has existed as long as there have been people. For this reason, it is associated in the Old Testament and otherwise with creation and, more specifically, human creation. The human being is made in such a way that he can distinguish between good and bad. Wisdom thus cannot be confined to a particular location; everywhere that people are found there also exists the potential for speaking and acting wisely. Wisdom expressed in the form of a proverb exists everywhere on earth.

Science and philosophy, in contrast, presuppose a developmental process. They have been cultivated in a relatively late stage of human history in more advanced cultures and have been qualified by particular assumptions while dividing into distinct realms.

The "oral literature" of proverbial wisdom experienced its prime in nonliterary cultures, and with the literary compilation of the proverbs began its aftermath. Science and philosophy presuppose not merely the invention of writing but, above and beyond this, an elevated level of civilization. This also entails a notable social differentiation. With few exceptions, science and philosophy are driven by a very specialized, well-off, and educated sector in public affairs. Wisdom and oral sayings, in contrast, were living among the people as a whole; every member of the community participated.

The blossoming of science and philosophy resulted in a gradual receding of wisdom in its peculiar form of wisdom saying, as well as a loss of meaning. As the discourse of the lowly and the language of humble folk, it grew to be displaced by literary discourse, by philosophy and science. This, in turn, resulted in our forgetting the fact that the universal significance of wisdom, for which it was suited, had grown out of the experience and reflection of many generations.

Both philosophy and the sciences in time inherited worldwide significance and acclaim. What was lacking, however, was the restraint that had been a by-product of the mature wisdom of successive generations and a society that had prior been undifferentiated.

For this reason, neither science nor philosophy is able to replace wisdom.

2. Science and Wisdom

We live in an age of scientific expansion. Its refinement was important and has had enormous consequences. It has become the most dominant factor in the life of people living together throughout the world. The attendant unhampered and ever-increasing preeminence of science has menacing implications for humanity and the earth. As a result of its inclination toward differentiation, it has lost the view of the whole. Wisdom, in contrast, possessed a view of the whole. It embodied the totality of human existence as well as the surrounding human habitat.

The ever-increasing expansion of the sciences cannot continue. There exists in the present, however, no channel that would suggest the limits of science or that is in a position to affect a countermovement in holistic thought.

There is no one who would possess the authority to declare that science is not wisdom and that science is incapable of producing wisdom. For wisdom cannot be manufactured; it must grow. No one is there to say that the distinction between wisdom and foolishness cuts across all scientific disciplines and that it is critical for humanity to recognize folly as folly, insofar as it is perpetrated in the sciences; or to say that much existing differentiation is entirely senseless and only serves to further obscure the whole, that the realm of specialists is ambivalent because each area of specialization is capable of deception or folly. To everyone who seriously considers this, it becomes abundantly clear that with the ever-increasing degree of specialization in the sciences, humanity as a whole becomes increasingly ignorant. The overestimation of the sciences and the underestimation of wisdom are capable of doing considerable damage. Behind this scientific overestimation stands an overestimation of the capabilities of the human mind. Opposing this is the critical appraisal of human potential inherent to wisdom, where opportunity is afforded to address human limits. This reference point to human limitation is one of the reasons why the early wisdom of Israel was preserved in the canon.

3. Wisdom and Philosophy

Philosophy is closer to early wisdom than is the later, independently evolving science, in that from the beginning it consisted of reflection on the nature of the world and the whole of human existence. This was particularly so due to the central importance of the notion of being in Greek philosophy. Yet Greek philosophy is different from wisdom, inasmuch as that which exists is to a large extent spiritualized and the material realm is esteemed less in comparison. This sort of dualism is not possible in wisdom, since both material and spiritual dimensions are equally a part of creation and thus given equal worth. This basic philosophical premise has had and continues to have the consequence of restricting the philosophical enterprise to a relatively small part of society, in which there develops an esoteric language that is unintelligible to a farmer or a tradesman. The meaning of such would remain inaccessible even where attempts might be made to forcefully hammer home "philosophy" in a people.

There is thus a stark contrast between philosophy and wisdom. A philosophy that is comprehensible only to a small band of intellectual elite is and cannot be wisdom. The value of wisdom that is expressed through proverbs consists in the fact that it is accessible to every person among a particular people, that it necessarily is able to bridge all social and educational differences. It consistently touches every sphere of life; it has its roots in the life of a people and transmits across generations the experiences of the fathers to their descendants. Wisdom possesses deeper roots than philosophy, in which one particular system replaces another or where one "ism" and elitist language displace another.

In the present state of human affairs, in which primary concerns are the survival of humanity and the planet, it is indeed feasible to ask whether it is again possible for philosophy and wisdom to converge—a type of philosophy that finds its way back to an understanding of creation as a whole, informs discourse that can be understood by all, and does not isolate itself in some elitist fashion.

The question of the relationship of wisdom to philosophy has yet another aspect that can only be hinted at here.

In the later wisdom writings, especially in the Wisdom of Solomon, wisdom is integrated in the language and thought world of Greek philosophy. The result is a syncretistic literary product. In earlier history of the church, the influence of Greek thought grew stronger to the point where Aristotelian philosophy was incorporated into Christian theology. At that time the lines were drawn, pointing in the direction of scholasticism, which doubtless produced amazing accomplishments but in terms of systematic theology was alien to the Bible. In this brand of scholastic-systematic philosophy, the simple language of the Bible as well as that of Israel's early wisdom came to be silenced. In this regard, even the Reformation did not produce any fundamental shift. It remains to be asked whether or not in an ecumenically minded church the early wisdom that possesses a universal character should be heard once more.

IV. ECCLESIASTES 3:1–11 (LUTHER'S TRANSLATION): HUMANITY IN ITS TEMPORALITY

"For everything there is a time, and a season for everything under heaven: a time to be born and a time to die, a time to plant and a time to uproot, a time to kill and a time to heal, a time to tear down and a time to build, a time to weep and a time to laugh, a time to mourn and a time to dance, a time to scatter stones and a time to gather stones together, a time to embrace and a time to restrain from embracing, a time to seek and a time to destroy, a time to keep and a time to cast off, a time to tear and a time to sew together, a time to be silent and a time to speak, a time to love and a time to hate, a time for war and a time for peace.

"What gain does the worker have from his toil? I have seen the toil that God has placed upon the sons of man to occupy him. He has made everything beautiful in its time. He has also placed eternity in human hearts, yet they cannot fathom what God has done from the beginning to the end."

The text is structured in such a way that the summary statement found in v. 1 is developed in a unique series of polarities in vv. 2–8. Up to this point, Qohelet speaks the language of the proverbs. Every one of these statements in its present or similar form could appear in the book of Proverbs. In vv. 9–11, he affixes to these individual statements a consideration articulated in his own language. Yet this reflection, too, rests on one of the sayings of the group that speaks of human limitation and the operation of God. This entire section is intended to stimulate the readers to ponder Qohelet's individual statements appearing in vv. 1–8. Qohelet 3:1–11 as a whole is a poem with literary origins.

Qohelet comprehends the temporality of human existence in terms of polarity, in the same way as the proverbs: being born has its time and dying has its time. Belonging to the realm of temporality is human existence, which stems from birth and stretches to the point of death. Life is suspended in a balance between and determined by both poles: living with a certain life expectancy, wanting to be alive, having a joy in living or longing for a satisfying life, as well as anticipating approaching death with a conscious or unconscious apprehension. Because being born and dying both have their appointed time, human existence resembles a bow; it ascends as a result of birth and descends at the time of death. This is the biblical understanding of human existence. It stands in contrast to the notion that conceives of life as a straight line, whereby ascent and descent play no role and a human is viewed as the same in every instance. Accordingly, the latter view grasps and defines human existence in terms of timeless conception.

Human temporality is displayed through the juxtapositions of vv. 2–8. To human existence belong both laughing and crying, as expressed by the individual sayings, yet in such a way that they cannot be misunderstood; the same can be said of planting and uprooting, building and tearing down, killing and healing, embracing and restraint from embracing, tearing and mending, being silent and speaking. All are held in tension.

In the concluding reflection found in vv. 9–11, Qohelet speaks of God and his work: "He has made everything beautiful in its time." By speaking of God in this way, he indicates the limits of being human, similar to the individual sayings. Only God the Creator has the perspective on the whole and holds it in his hands—from beginning to end.

APPENDIX

I. COMPARISONS WITH PROVERBIAL SAYINGS FROM OTHER TIMES AND PLACES

This sort of comparison has hitherto barely been undertaken, inasmuch as Israel's wisdom, following the discovery of Near Eastern and Egyptian wisdom literature, has been exclusively compared to and derived from the latter.

In my investigation of the proverbs, I encountered a remarkable state of affairs that had been significant to my interpretation of Genesis 1—11. I discovered correspondences and features common to various texts of the Old Testament that suggest an early stage of oral development and transmission, in addition to texts that were outside the circle of Near Eastern cultures in yet nonliterary societies—texts such as the creation and Flood narratives. These are not confined to the periphery of particular isolated cultures; rather, they are to be observed in different locations in all of humanity. The proverbs are one of the linguistic forms that are held in common among mankind.

There exist obvious correspondences between the sayings of Proverbs 10—31 and proverbs of diverse peoples. Among the most notable are the basic, self-contained short sayings; sayings arranged according to their indicative or imperative form; equivalent groups of proverbs found in numerous unrelated places, and comparisons. In an essay written in 1971,[98] I noted agreements between sayings in Proverbs and a collection of proverbs of the Ewe people in Africa.[99] These instances of correspondence and similarity are evidence of the existence of a linguistic phenomenon common to humanity.[100]

The purpose of the inventory that follows is confined to calling attention to proverbs outside of the Near Eastern context, and indeed, only examples. It is hoped that a collaboration between scholars in various disciplines would be forthcoming. The universal character of the proverb, particularly in our own time, is so important that any cooperation of this type would be worthwhile.

II. AFRICAN PROVERBS[101]

In reading the chapter on proverbs found in the work of Ruth Finnegan, *Oral Literature in Africa* (1970), one initially has the impression of peering into another, distant world—one that nevertheless seems to be somewhat familiar. It strikes the reader as foreign to the extent that he is struck by a lifestyle of community in which the proverbs appear to be a common component of collective life, without which community would be unthinkable. Corporate life as a whole is infused and imbibed as a result of the proverbs, and every aspect of community shares in this. The proverbs possess abundant and quite diverse functions that make them requisite for life in the community. They are employed in a plethora of situations; it is not possible to imagine being without them.

This also strikes the reader as foreign, since we no longer know this function of proverbial sayings in the corporate life of a group. For us they are simply a relic; they merely exist in compilations or in occasional citations. In this context they are at times decorative, at times even animated, but they are never really employed. We can live without them. If they are recognized, they are categorized as "common" literature. Their value, however, should not be assessed according to categories that correspond to our own notion of proverbial sayings. This notwithstanding, these sayings do seem somewhat familiar to us, inasmuch as they remind us largely of the biblical book of Proverbs.

Since the work of J. Fichtner, Israel's wisdom has been viewed as a particular extension of ancient Near Eastern wisdom—a form of wisdom adaptable in literary form and among those peoples that had already possessed a literary culture for centuries or even millennia. Hence, the direction of this study, with its focus on the question of a possible earlier phase in which proverbs had an oral development and function in the life of the people while they were being handed on orally, really has been excluded from most scholarly treatment from the start. In truth, the issue of a possible early stage of oral transmission has not even entered most investigations of Proverbs relative to Israel's wisdom. Even as recent a work as H. D. Preuss's 1987 book *Einführung in die alttestamentliche Weisheitsliteratur* is governed from beginning to end by such an understanding; the matter of an early phase of oral transmission of proverbs in Israel is not considered once, and proverbial wisdom among nonliterary peoples is not even mentioned, in spite of a number of existing studies that point in this direction.

Thus, when one reads the chapter on proverbs in Ruth Finnegan's book *Oral Literature in Africa*, one is initially surprised to encounter again and again features and themes that concur with the sayings in the book of Proverbs. This is assuming, of course, the premise that it is unproductive and futile to search for lexical agreement between individual sayings or statements (notwithstanding the correspondences that are present). Rather, the best line of approach is to inquire into common categories of particular topics, structures, motifs, and forms.

The Significance of the Proverbs

The proverbs have a great significance for virtually all of the African people. Here we observe commonalities cutting across the boundaries of various people-groups. In cases where sayings of a particular people diverge notably from those of others, the reason has to do with their lifestyle.

The significance of proverbs is first recognized when we no longer consider them merely in their appearing in lists of compilations, each isolated in the context of written sayings, but rather when they are viewed as a form of expression of a "literature" that is still being passed on orally. This form possesses its meaning in the context of human community; it is comprehensive and at the same time literary and social in character; thus, "A counselor who understands proverbs soon sets matters right" or "The Chagas have four big possessions: land, cattle, water, and proverbs." Finnegan summarizes, "Proverbs are essential to life and language, without them the language would be but a skeleton without flesh, a body without soul. Proverbs are something of the soul of the people."[102]

The Function of Proverbs in Their Usage

Without an awareness of their function and the setting in which they were employed, proverbs cannot be properly understood. "There is no proverb without a setting." Here we find the chief point of deviation from the sayings in the book of Proverbs. In that the sayings of the latter without exception have been passed down apart from the situation in which they were employed, it is possible to explain each only in its relationship to the text; hence, we do not inquire into possible situations in which they were employed. Here the African proverbs can benefit our interpretation of the sayings in Proverbs, to the extent that their usage is essential to their meaning and, at the very least, makes it possible for us to inquire into a preliterary stage.

The proverb retains its social significance as a result of the speaker presenting the one being addressed with the option of bettering his own situation. In this vein, the indirect and merely suggestive mode of speech inherent to the proverb is important. It permits a tactful means by which to influence the one being addressed.

The use of analogy in the realm of disputation or legal cases is helpful in the resolution of conflicts; an agreement can be brought about through a broader perspective that preserves a bit of a distance. In the legal realm, the use of such is of universal significance. By means of this kind of wider perspective, one is able to give advice or offer a warning: "Your mouth will turn into a knife" (similar to Proverbs) or "We do not like the pride of a hen's eggs" (since the eggs in a nest are all the same). Such can serve as a warning to a talebearer. At the same time, an intention clothed in the form of a hint is also able to serve a polemical purpose.

Another function is the art of cultured communication, cultivated discourse. Proverbs constitute the primary part of oral literature. Speech can sparkle through the use of striking sayings. In each case of usage, what matters is not so much the timeless sense of the proverb as the appropriateness of meaning embodied in the saying for a new situation.

Two Diverse Functions of Instruction

In commentary on Proverbs up to now, it has frequently been assumed that training and instruction are the only function of proverbs or that wisdom in its entirety is "didactic wisdom" (thus G. von Rad, among others). This is very improbable, however. African parallels illustrate that instruction is one of many functions in proverbs and that two different functions, moreover, are to be distinguished. Proverbs are able to serve the purpose of a deliberate and more institutional instruction, as seen, for example, in situations where they play a special role in certain rites of initiation. Apart from this, however, they possess a latent function in the sense of a noncalculated practice of principles of communal life and thus serve as a socializing mechanism in everyday life for members of a given society.

In addition, proverbs are able to mirror something approaching the "philosophy" of a people, inasmuch as they gather the observations and experiences of a people and exhibit them before the world: "Proverbs represent the soul of a people." This resonates with the "observations about people" category found in the proverbial statements of the book of Proverbs.

As a general rule, proverbs are common property of a people as a whole, at times reserved in part for "older folks." Whoever formulated the proverb initially is almost never known. A saying becomes a proverb, then, at the point of broad acceptance. When we on occasion recognize a saying as the dictum of a famous person, then this dictum becomes common property of a people's language.

Form

The fundamental distinction between indicative and imperative sayings is well known. The form of a saying is determined wholly by its function in oral usage. Proverbs are known everywhere to be short, pithy sayings in fixed form, and virtually everywhere there exist features of a more elevated, "poetic" language, such as rhythm, assonance, and so forth. Figurative language is also found to be universal—for example, comparison, metaphor, allusive or suggestive language—as is a fixed, consistent structure—for example, "It is like . . . " or "He said . . . " The simplest structure is that of an object with an attendant observation or two statements forming an antithesis: "The body went, the heart did not go." Another form might be two sentences that "balance" each other, which could qualify as a precursor to *parallelismus memborum*. In yet another form we find sentences that consist only of a negation ("x doesn't do something," therefore "no x does something"; "If . . . , then . . . "; or "Better . . . than . . . "), not unlike Proverbs. Other formal devices are hyperbole, the question, contrast, contradiction, and abbreviation.

With few exceptions, we find agreement or similarity here with the formal devices utilized in the book of Proverbs.

Content

A proverb can possess a literal as well as figurative sense, which is important in terms of flexible usage. One must not restrict it to one particular sense. In this regard the proverb resembles the riddle: One must determine how the spoken word fits the situation in which it is being uttered.

Humor consistently plays a part in the formulation of the proverbs. This is also the case in Proverbs 10—31, whereas in the proverbs about instructional wisdom and in the Proverbs 1—9 depiction of wisdom, humor is not to be found.

The proverbs are unusually effective due to the high ratio of comparisons employed—for example, "A chief is like a dust-heap, where everyone comes with his rubbish and deposits it." The world of everyday living, people, animals, plants, and weather combine in communicating to the audience in these sayings. The proverbs are able to relate to every imaginable situation by an endless variety of caricatures and metaphors. Occasionally, a proverb resembles a narrative when, as a result of the use of a brief and often suggestive illustration, a scene is portrayed.

The other side of this diversity is that the proverbs rarely contain conceptual abstractions.

As is the case in Proverbs, emphasis in diverse realms is given to human observation and experience—man and woman, work and harvest, poor and rich, idle and diligent, that is, human behavior in all its possibilities; but also the habits of animals (normally in the form of a comparison), the exercise of authority, service, hospitality, and much more. It is not uncommon for the proverbs to touch on popular stories, but only in their stereotypes. For this reason, they are difficult to recognize.

The characterization of particular types of people in the life of the community plays a central role in the proverbs, similar to the book of Proverbs. Often, due to the facility of the speaker, a well-known proverb is applied to an unexpected situation.

Selected Individual Proverbs
(see R. Finnegan, pp. 389–425)

Experience and human observations. "Much silence has a mighty noise" (p. 396). "He ate food and it killed him" (p. 397). "The heart of a man is a sea" (p. 404). "It is patience which gets you out of the net" (p. 408).

Proverbs about animals. "One fly catches for another" (p. 397). "No polecat ever smelled its own stink" (p. 397). "The strength of a crocodile is in the water" (p. 397). "No one teaches a leopard's cub how to spring" (p. 405). "Authority is the tail of a water rat" (it falls off easily; p. 419). "A butterfly that flies among the thorns will tear its wings" (p. 419).

The surrounding world. "There is no grinding stone that got the better of a miller" (p. 397). "Even the Niger has an island" (p. 405). "The earth does not get thicker" (p. 335). "When it rains, the roof always drips the same way" (p. 420).

Characterization of the fool, the idle, the incorrigible, the talker. "Mr. 'I don't know' took cover from the rain in the pond" (fool; p. 402). "He even milks the cows that are heavy with calf" (p. 398). "He has the kindness of a witch" (p. 398). "He has no chest" (he can keep no secret; p. 399). "The child who refuses to run an errand says he does not know the way" (p. 410). "We do not like the pride of a hen's eggs" (eggs are equal; p. 410). "When a fool is told a proverb, the meaning of it has to be explained to him" (p. 415).

Characterization of behavior. "He works as long as he is still fresh" (p. 399). "The body went—the heart did not go" (p. 400). "Hurry! Hurry! has no blessing" (p. 400). "A woman quick to love means a woman who does not love" (pp. 402–3).

Proverbs of evaluation, "better than . . . ." "It is better to be hated by a prince than by the people."

Antitheses. "Ordinary people are as common as grass; good people, however, are as precious as one's eye" (p. 402).

Power, ruling, wealth. "A chief is like a dust-heap where everyone comes with his rubbish and deposits it" (p. 396). "Even the Niger has an island" (every power has its limits; p. 396). "Authority is the tail of a water rat" (it falls off easily; p. 405). "A counselor who understands proverbs soon sets matters right" (p. 409). "Wealth is dew" (p. 396).

Instruction. "The sons of a king do not need to be taught about power" (p. 405). "No one teaches a leopard's cub how to spring" (p. 405).

Man and woman. "When you marry a beautiful woman, you marry problems" (p. 419). "Two wives are two pots full of poison" (p. 405).

Indirect exhortation/warning. "Your mouth will turn into a knife and cut off your lips" (p. 410). "There is no grinding stone that got the better of the miller" (p. 397).

Royal Proverbs

For a summary of royal proverbs, the reader is encouraged to consult F. W. Golka, "Die Königs- und Hofsprüche und der Ursprung der israelitischen Weisheit," *VT* 36, 1 (1986):13–36. In this essay Golka counters the thesis represented by many commentators that royal proverbs in the book of Proverbs all arose in the royal court; thus, especially, H. J. Hermisson in *Studien zur israelitischen Spruchweisheit* (1968, p. 71): "With regard to the royal proverbs we quickly realize that they can in no way be considered popular material." Golka, on the contrary, in the first part of his essay maintains that "with a probability approaching absolute certainty, these [royal proverbs] originated among the people" (p. 34), not unlike what we find in the book of Proverbs. Evidence for this is convincing.[103]

The Relationship of the Sayings in the Book of Proverbs to the African Proverbs

Parallels in form. The parallels in form are so considerable that one scarcely needs to name one. Form corresponds to function in the proverbs, that is, to their oral development and oral transmission as they come to be employed. This concurrence alone makes it certain that proverbs having the same form in the Old Testament also had an early phase of oral development and transmission. The few examples we do find in the Old Testament[104] receive their significance as a result of comparison with proverbs of nonliterary cultures, from which we can speculate as to the specific situations in which they were employed.

There are also formal similarities with regard to detail that can be noted. In African as well as Israelite proverbs there are indicative sayings, imperative sayings, proverbial statements, and exhortations/warnings. However, whereas the proverbial statements far outnumber imperatives in both African proverbs and older compilations found in Proverbs 10—29, imperative sayings predominate in the later wisdom of Proverbs 1—9 and in Oriental wisdom literature—so thoroughly, in fact, that at times they tend to overpower the proverbial statements. This can be explained by comparing them to their African counterpart: proverbs that are still oral have multiple functions, which promotes the declarative type of saying. In the later wisdom, teaching and instruction become the most important or perhaps the sole function; hence the preponderance of imperatives. African proverbs have in common with those of Israel an elevated, "poetic" language (this is common, in fact, to many other peoples), in addition to literary devices that achieve this effect—meter, word placement, assonance, a balance of both verse halves (an early form of parallelism), and the brief, terse form that is sparing with words. The late wisdom, in contrast, is wordy, discursive, and fond of repetition, illustrated abundantly by Proverbs 1—9.

Integral to proverbial form and content are graphic language, comparisons, and an abundance of metaphors. In this way African proverbs correspond to their Israelite counterpart, as well as in their use of direct speech, exaggeration, contrasts, and contradictions.

Parallels in content. What is initially striking about both proverb groups is their exceeding richness; in both, the entire surrounding world comes to expression. The different categories of proverbs agree virtually without exception: for example, animals; the earth and the environment; the characterizations of types of people such as the fool, the idle, or the wicked; the characterization of particular actions or types of behavior; instruction; man and woman; power; authorities; wealth. A significant difference is that in Africa, proverbs quite frequently appear in the context of jurisprudence, whereas in Israel (as is the custom throughout the Near East), jurisprudence had its own language.

One particular point of emphasis in both proverb groups is that of human observation and experience. In both, one encounters reference to the poor and the rich, the foolish, the idle and the diligent, ruling and serving, work and harvest, man and woman. It is characteristic of both to distinguish between an indirect education by means of living together in the community and a deliberate, institutional form of instruction. The awareness that observations and experience, which are formative in a person's life, must be preserved and passed on is a fundamental premise on which all tradition rests; this occurs in the simplest form: a short saying. This affords us the insight that the process of a saying originating and being passed on is, in fact, a thoroughly human process.

III. HORTATORY WORDS OF TOBATAK OF SUMATRA

In a 1967 dissertation at Mainz, A. A. Sitompul compared the exhortations of Proverbs with those of the Batak people.[105] The author had access to extant literary sources in addition to transmitters of the oral tradition of proverbs who are still living today. The significance of this for our study of the Proverbs of the Old Testament is that here, as well as among many nonliterary peoples, the oral transmission of proverbs is capable of being continued for years—even centuries—after written compilations already exist. Such a phenomenon is also evident elsewhere, notably in Asia and Africa. The author examined a major group of Batak sayings—words of exhortation and warnings. He alludes to and cites examples from one other chief group, declarative sayings, only occasionally (see, e.g., p. 56). In the Batak proverbs as well as in the book of Proverbs, both major groupings—proverbial statements and imperatives (exhortations and warnings)—are to be found.

Yet another feature can be observed: the Batak sayings give impressive support for the notion that, as a species, the proverb reached its zenith in terms of significance during the preliterary history of a given people. A good portion of the preliterary "literature" consists of these sayings, thus demonstrating multiple popular functions in several areas: "Die Lebensordnung im Bereich der Batak ... deint dem Schutz und der Festigung des Sippenverbandes von Generation zu Generation ... Heil oder Unheil der Sippengemeinschaft sind abhängig von der Verwirklichung der gegebenen Lebensordnung durch alle Sippenglieder." When the life of proverbs is reduced merely to collections, then we can really speak only of their aftermath. This is affirmed by the very literary nature of transmission, by which the proverbs are loosed from their context and set together successively in the book of Proverbs, without any (apparent) connection. The *Sitz im Leben* of the imperatives in the Batak sayings (words of exhortation and warnings) is much more clearly recognizable than in Proverbs. In the former, the training of children is elucidated—for example, proverb 32 (p. 26), "Be careful that you do not stumble, take heed that you do not fall in a pit!" (a saying that can be carried over to adults as well). This teaching, however, can be applied to the instruction of those growing up, young married couples, even parents. It becomes apparent through these sayings that the imperative proverbs had their origin in instruction. In many instances, they are introduced by a summons to listen, just as in Proverbs 1—9; 22—24.

Several Examples of Words
of Exhortation and Warning

There are Batak proverbs that parallel those found in Egypt and in the book of Proverbs: "A stone memorial may not be moved, the gadu-gadu [a dam situated between rice fields] may not be displaced" (proverb 12 [p. 20]). Here, as is often the case, we find a parallelism of two exhortations that go together. The points of correspondence issue out of similar living conditions. Agriculture requires such admonitions.

Other examples can be cited that are characteristic of the Batak people. They are applicable in all realms of living (see p. 16): Proverb 1: "Do not touch the hind foot of a horse!" (literal and figurative). Proverb 2: "Do not play with burning coals!" (literal and figurative). Proverb 3: "Do not foul the source of your fountain!" Proverb 4: "Do not give children a horse's head!" Proverb 5: "Do not show a fool flowers!" (cf. the warning about instructing a fool). Proverb 7: "One should not use force and supplant justice." Proverb 8: "Do not sit down to think wicked thoughts; do not stand up to speak malicious words!" Proverb 9: "Do not strike the one who treats you with respect!" Proverb 15: "One must not depend on thickness of leg and the strength of one's arm!" Proverb 33: "Do not walk erect, so that you are not leveled!" (Pride comes before the fall). Proverb 35: "One must use Pela leaves as well as Palia leaves; unity must prevail between brothers and sisters of a mother in order to have blessing and a long life" (cf. "Behold, how good and lovely it is . . . ," Ps. 133:1). Proverb 39: "Do not have a damaged fence, so that no one can thereby sneak in. Say nothing that is exaggerated so that you are not remembered for it later." Proverb 40: "When the king sends someone out, one must not be disobedient. If one does not obey him, one will fall upon calamity." Proverb 41: "Do not play with a knife, for a knife brings much shame when it has no good use" (an exhortation aimed at children, yet valid for adults in a figurative sense).

Frequently, a word of exhortation is identical to a command: "You may not fight," "You may not steal," "You should not lie," "You must not kill." Even in grammatically apodictic form, these correspond to the commandments of the Decalogue (cf. here E. Gerstenberger [1969]).

The sense and meaning of comparisons in the Batak sayings are often clearer than those of the book of Proverbs. Here the association of image to fact, that is, the illustrative function inherent to comparison, is clear. The comparisons juxtapose an occurrence among people and an occurrence in their surrounding world. The deduction "thus it is" finds its confirmation in the world around them (most often in plant and animal life).

The similarity of these admonitions to those found in Proverbs cannot be overlooked.

IV. FORM AND SCOPE OF SUMERIAN PROVERBS

Keeping in mind that only a relatively small number of Sumerian sayings are being illustrated, we may make the following observations. In this regard, I am drawing from the collection found in H. H. Schmid, *Wesen und Geschichte der Weisheit* (1966, pp. 226–29), where original sources are listed. The forms of these are, for the most part, the same as what constitutes the main part of Proverbs 10—31. Compiled as such, they are not found elsewhere in Mesopotamian wisdom literature. Inasmuch as the Sumerian collection of proverbs is considered to be the oldest Mesopotamian specimen, the parallels relative to the early portions of the book of Proverbs are indicative of a fairly early era even for parts of Proverbs 10—29; 31. Alongside these parallels, too, are many differences; the sayings exhibit peculiarities.

Proverbial Statements

Proverbial statements frequently resemble narrative description; some would appear to be small excerpts. They describe what exists or what is happening. They are not expressly shaped or molded as proverbs, so that standing outside of the context they might not be recognizable. The same is true of many African proverbs. An explicit parallelism is not evident. It can be concluded, therefore, that these indicative sayings belong to an early phase of civilization predating those sayings in the book of Proverbs.

Human Observation and Experience

"That which is mine has made other things unknown." "One does not speak about what has been found; one speaks only about what has been lost." "It is a matter of short duration."

These proverbs are typical. We are not told what is of short duration stemming from the situation in which this was uttered. Sayings such as these can only have originated and been passed on orally.

"A poor man is always concerned about what he will eat." This proverb corresponds to the category of human observations: specifically, being filled and being hungry. It can have different functions—for example, "A hungry man even breaks into a house built with bricks."

"Tell a lie, then tell the truth, and people will call it a lie" (cf. "Whoever lies once will not be believed"). "If you love, you carry a yoke!" "Fruit that ripens too soon brings trouble" (literally and figuratively, similar to African proverbs).

All of the above are general human observations and experiences that resemble or are equivalent to the proverbs of other peoples. They retain their pungency foremost through their application.

Human Experience of the Work of God

"Destruction comes from his own god; he knows no deliverer. If it is his god, his very own god, who is behind the destruction, he cannot call out to him as deliverer; his lot is hopeless."

"Gird yourself; your god is your help!" This frequently occurring saying, the subtlety of which lies in the close link between the declarative and the imperative, implies the warning "Help yourself, then God will help you!"

"When you struggle, God is yours; when you do not struggle, God is not yours" (i.e., he is not on your side).

"It is not wealth that supports you, it is God!" (a general religious statement reflecting the work of God that, quite naturally, belongs to everyday life, which could just as well be found in the book of Proverbs).

"Whether you are small or big, it is your God who will help you" (a peculiar saying about the hidden work of God as the boundary of human ability, which could just as well appear in Qohelet or Proverbs).

"The purpose of God cannot be understood, the way of God cannot be perceived."

Comparisons

"The boat sat in the water at an angle; this resulted in the chests going overboard." That is, the person whose wants are too strong must reckon with loss.

"Possessions are sparrows in flight that find no place to settle." This comparison illustrates the fleeting nature of riches. Observing a creature serves the purpose of underscoring the peculiar character of possessions. The bird can settle here or there; one never knows exactly where. A beautiful, well thought-out comparison to the animal kingdom. The same proverb is found in Amenemope, where the illustration uses a goose.

"Goods that are damaged no longer generate interest." This saying can have direct as well as comparative application. What is damaged loses its value, even in joint human associations.

"He behaved as a blind man." This is a comparison that takes on the form of a report and/or an excerpt from a report. Such could be a reprimand or reproof, but it also could be dressed as a warning. This comparison, too, retains its primary function from the situation in which it was initially spoken.

"Fruit that ripens too soon brings trouble." This comparison suggests prematurity on the part of a person or a person's behavior.

"A boat with an honorable goal sails downstream with the wind; Uru has chosen a reliable place of docking for it. A boat with a deceitful purpose sails downstream with the wind; Uru will cause it to shipwreck on the shore." Here we have a proverb of antithesis not dissimilar to those in Proverbs. It contrasts the action and lot of the righteous and the wicked.

Characterization

In their expressing observation and experience, the Sumerian proverbs correspond to the same groups found in the book of Proverbs—comparison, antithesis, characterization.

"The one who walks in righteousness brings forth life."

"You do not return what you've borrowed!" This characterization is dressed as a reproof that is raised against the one being depicted.

"You have not been lax in the face of the present evil." Here someone is being characterized who was actively opposing evil. It carries the function of commendation as well as exhortation.

"Food, that's the thing! Drink, that's the thing!" This typical proverb characterizes someone who is preoccupied with eating and drinking. The description consists of the person actually being cited.

Imperative Proverbs; Exhortations and Warnings

Exhortations and warnings take the form of an imperative or a vetitive, and they can also be implicit in statements.

"He acquired all manner of things; he must be very careful to watch [over] them." This statement implies an admonition or warning. It intends that the one addressed draw the conclusions for himself.

"Pleasure is in the fish, fatigue is in the road."

"Whoever drinks much beer must drink water; whoever eats too much will not sleep."

"If you set out and seize your friend's field, the enemy will come back to rob your own." This is a simple warning about plunder or theft.

We might encounter a proverb in question form: "Who will listen to the explanation that you will give?" This intends to say that one should not even attempt first to explain one's action, for the deed speaks more strongly than one's explanation.

Following are imperative or vetitive sayings that are partially substantiated by suggested consequences:

"Do nothing wicked, then you will not experience lasting calamity."

"Commit no crime, then you will not be consumed by fear."

"Slander no one, and sorrow will not touch your heart."

"Do not chop off anything; later it will bear fruit!" (a saying that relates to the description of a barren fig tree, suggesting that a number of narratives in the Synoptic Gospels have their origin in a proverb).

"A shepherd should not try to be a farmer" (cf. "Cobbler, remain at your work!").

"We all die, so let us revel!"; "We will live a long time, so let us save up!" (an example of two contradictory admonitions also occurs in Prov. 26:4, 5). The above are characteristic of proverbial exhortations, which are dependent on a situation and certain conditions. The very fact that admonitions contradict one another would lead one to the conclusion that the proverbs developed and were passed down orally.

The Scope of the Sumerian Proverbs

The person; one's body and parts of the body. Hunger and thirst, eating and drinking, water and bread, baking a cake, beer, provision, consumption and saving, sleeping and waking, clothing, disposition, love, responsibility, suffering, truth and deceit, honesty and dishonesty, strength and weakness, praise and reproof, sickness, blindness, austerity, justification of behavior, friend and enemy.

House and household. Fire and coal, squandering and saving, losing and finding, work and pleasure, effort, exertion, working and rewards for work, farming, tilling a field, fruitfulness, grain, herdsman and cattle, the foreman, the servant, ship and river, plants and animals.

Commerce and goods. Methods of dealing, honesty and dishonesty, lending money, paying money back, wealth, possessions, preserving and losing, poor and rich, mine and yours.

Wicked conduct. Theft, plunder of someone's land, fraud, crime and consequences, the curse, wickedness, evil, a city visited by calamity.

The working of God. God may work for or against the person. He may delight in him or oppose him. He builds up and destroys. He comes to one's aid when someone exerts himself. God, not riches, promotes a person. The purpose of God is understood by no one.

It is the simple life of the farmer that is mirrored in these proverbs. Because of the very limited selection of Sumerian sayings available, a comparison to Proverbs 10—31 is possible in only a limited way. Yet, in this small sampling, correspondence is astounding and far-reaching. What is most clearly reflected in this selection is that many subjects, as in Proverbs, do not surface—for example, politics and power, battle and soldiers (with one noteworthy difference: mention of the king and one's relationship to him is absent in the Sumerian proverbs). Also absent are the cult as an institution, higher culture and art, large-scale building, fortresses, civil servants and administration.

To that extent, the Sumerian proverbs resemble those of the book of Proverbs more than the later Mesopotamian or Egyptian wisdom but also the sayings of primitive, nonliterate people.

H. Cazelles ("Les nouvelles études sur Sumer et Mari," in M. Gilbert, *La Sagesse de l'Ancien Testament* [1979], pp. 17–27) makes reference to pp. 20ff. of R. Marzal, *Gleanings from the Wisdom of Mari* (Coll. Studia Rohl 2; Rome, 1976), especially pp. 15–45. Of the texts reproduced, seven of these could be considered proverbs. Three examples follow: "La chienne qui en allant ici et là ne donne naissance qu'à des avortons"; "Le feu consume le roseau et ses compagnons pretent attention"; "C'est sous la paille que l'eau coule."

While the sayings noted here concern proverbial wisdom, the tablets of Abu Salabikh (ca. 2500 B.C.) contain the oldest didactic speeches (see B. Alster, "La Sagesse de Shuruppak," in *Inscriptions from Tel Abu Salabikh: A Sumerian Proverb Collection* [1974]; *Studies in Sumerian Proverbs* [1975]). One of the tablets begins, "Début de l'enseignement fait par le prince, le fils royal . . . à son fils: Amende toi à tes yeux. . . . Mon fils, que je te donne des instructions, fais-y attention. . . . Ne néglige pas mes instructions, ne transgresse pas le parole, que je te dis . . . "

The proverbs from Mari that H. Cazelles (pp. 20ff.) cites correspond in form to those of Proverbs 10—31. All are proverbial statements, and all belong to the category of human experience. They are, however, single-verse. They employ comparisons, they summon the hearer to personal reflection, and they are located in the life of the community.

In contrast to these proverbs, the tablets of Shuruppak contain didactic speeches that parallel Egyptian teachings, with the primary motif of the teacher summoning the students to listen. This finds exact agreement in the juxtaposition of proverbs and instructions in Proverbs 10—31 and 1—9, as well as in the fact that all the proverbs are declarative in nature, with a notable preponderance of imperative sayings found in the teaching portions.

One further parallel is that the proverbs are assimilated into the didactic speeches, much the same as in Egyptian didactic speeches; in this way, proverbs serve the purpose of instruction. This parallel confirms that even in Sumer the proverbs and didactic speeches each had independent traditions. They are only linked together inasmuch as proverbs eventually were assimilated into didactic material (for examples, see C. Kayatz [1968], p. 58). It is important, then, when we speak of wisdom texts, to distinguish between these two types.

V. THE TEACHING OF AMENEMOPE

Introduction and Conclusion

"The beginning of the rule of life: the instruction for prosperity." This book purports to be a teaching, instruction—that is, rules for courtiers in their association with nobility, so that they might be able to give oral and written account of themselves and so that the instruction might be spoken highly of by people. In the book's conclusion, it is added that the thirty chapters of the work should delight and instruct the reader with a view of making the ignorant knowledgeable, so that the reader, in time, will be able to be a teacher. Here we find very clear definition: the book is instruction; it purposes to mediate knowledge.

Simultaneously, it is also stated that the instruction of Amenemope does not intend to be a book of wisdom in the philosophical sense. When we compare it to Qohelet, one thing becomes clear: the definition of instruction given by Amenemope does not fit Qohelet at all. The latter is a wisdom book. Qohelet wishes to record insights that he (and those before him) has gleaned and thereby pass them on. He desires to expose them to the judgment of others; in this way, Qohelet is closely linked to philosophical works. The Preacher, however, is not attempting to pass on knowledge to students who are learning. Qohelet is a book of wisdom, a philosophical book; Amenemope is a textbook, as stated in the introduction and conclusion.

Form

The teaching of Amenemope is developed in thirty chapters, from its introduction to the conclusion (on the number thirty, a subject not taken up here, see Prov. 22:20), that exhibit only a partial unity.

The first chapter is essentially a summons to hear: "Give ear, hear what is being said, give of yourself to understand it . . . " Here we find confirmation that the teaching which follows, just as in the didactic poems of Proverbs 1—9, is wholly defined by the repeated summons to listen.

This summons finds its substantiation in the promise of success: "Then you will find that it leads to success." This is consonant with the character of the teaching found in Proverbs 1—9.

The actual teaching begins with the second chapter. From this point on to the end, it consists principally of imperatives (repeatedly expanded exhortations and warnings) that are listed successively without any connection. This parallels Prov. 22:17–24:31, where imperatives predominate. It is true that exhortations occur in Proverbs 1—9, yet these are mostly of a different type.

Moreover, the form of the longer poems is different. The most obvious parallel here is Proverbs 22—24 with its admonitions. It is here that most of the correspondences to individual proverbs are concentrated.

The stated purpose of the book of Amenemope is also more clearly defined in this section—the transmission of knowledge. The book's primary concern is what one must do, how one must conduct himself. All else that is said in the thirty chapters recedes into the background. Instruction thus is aimed at behavior. The reason given would seem to support this: instruction should lead to success (just as advertised today by various teaching institutions!).

We may therefore make some conclusion about those being addressed. Throughout the world, imperatives for guidance are normally directed at young people, at those growing up, who are being challenged to learn. (This is certainly not the case with the book of Qohelet, which is addressed to adults.)

In that the texts of Amenemope are strung together successively without any connection, they correspond to other collections of proverbs that exhibit a similar tendency. In this way, Amenemope is distinguished from the longer didactic poems or didactic speeches, as well as from thematically linked wisdom writings; Amenemope is more akin to the older tradition.

Individual Selected Exhortations/Warnings

Admonitions toward protecting the weak and disadvantaged. Chapter 2: "Beware of depriving the poor and banishing the weak!" Chapter 25: "Do not deride the blind and mock a cripple; do not make more difficult the lot of the lame!" "Do not scoff at a man who is in God's hand!" Chapter 28: "Do not take advantage of a widow by singling her out in the field!" "Do not pass by the alien with the pot, rather give him double!" "God loves the one who regards the lowly more than the one who honors the distinguished."

Warning against displacing the boundaries of a field. Chapter 6: "Do not remove the landmark from the border of fields and do not shift the measuring line from its proper location. Do not be greedy for a field and do not infringe on the borders of a widow."

Warning against contentiousness. Chapter 3: "Begin no quarrel with a loudmouth and do not attack him with words; hesitate in answering an adversary . . . God will call him to account." Chapter 9: "Do not be a companion of the hot-tempered man and do not look for conversation with him!" Chapter 22: "Do not agitate your opponent . . . , do not be in a hurry to approach him; place yourself in the arms of God and your silence will be his ruin."

Warning against oppression. Chapter 20: "Do not belittle a person in court and do not force uprightness aside! Take no bribe from the powerful, do not oppress one who is weak!" Chapter 13: "Offer no false testimony and do not forge with your feather!"

Loquacity. Chapter 9: "The speech of one whose heart is hurt is more impulsive than wind and rain; it is like a ferryman who weaves words: he comes and goes with strife!" Chapter 2: "You hot-tempered one, what is with you? He cries out and his voice reaches to heaven!" Chapter 4: "The truly restrained holds himself back." Chapter 21: "Do not empty your heart out in front of the whole world and do not damage your esteem; do not allow your talk to pass everywhere among people. Better is a man whose account remains with himself than one who damages it by talk." Chapter 5: "Stay with one who is reserved and you will find life."

Warning against duplicity. Chapter 10: "Do not separate your heart from your tongue and all of your plans will have success." "God despises the falsification of words; an abomination to him is the one who is sick in the heart." Chapter 7: "Do not set your heart on riches!" "If you acquire riches through plunder, they will not last overnight . . . , or they have wings like a goose and fly away!" Chapter 11: "Do not covet the belongings of the dependent and do not hunger after his bread; the belongings of a dependent get stuck in the throat and are an emetic."

Table etiquette, conduct before one's superiors. Chapter 23: "Do not eat bread in the presence of an official and do not be the first to eat!" "Look at the bowl that is set before you and allow it to satisfy your needs!" Chapter 9: "Keep your tongue wholesome in answering your superior and be careful not to agitate him!"

The operation of God. Chapter 25: "Do not despise a blind person. . . . The human being is mud and straw, God is his architect. He destroys and he erects daily, he causes a thousand lowly ones to be his beloved and a thousand people to have authority during the hour of a human's existence. How he rejoices when he reaches the west, when he achieves happiness in the hand of God!"

Summary. The exhortations of Amenemope are akin to those in Proverbs 22—24. Many find exact parallels in Proverbs—for example, warnings against displacing landmarks; admonitions to protect the weak; the warnings against duplicity, oppressing the weak in court, false witness, and many more. The respective texts corresponding to the book of Proverbs are cited in Beyerlin (1978). Apart from table etiquette, literary dependence is not to be presupposed. Some of these exhortations—for example, the warning against moving boundary markers—are also found in Sumerian, African, and Asian proverbs. They are reflective of a common level of culture with attendant constitutive parts. The universal dissemination of this sort of hortatory speech is demonstrated here quite clearly.

Quite naturally, there exist dissimilarities in addition to these parallels. One is that we perceive a greater social distinction in Proverbs 22—24; superiors and subordinates are mentioned frequently. Another difference is the rather emphatic contrast of the hot-tempered to the peaceful (see here A. Alt [1951]).

An important difference in form is that the admonitions in Amenemope are expanded. It is seldom that a single-verse or double-verse saying stands independently. From this we may conclude that the collection of Amenemope is further removed from its original oral form than Proverbs 22—24, where the individual proverbs for the most part stand independently. Relatively short substantiations occur in both collections, showing no essential difference in this regard; on occasion they are absent altogether. The magnification of the summons to listen is precisely as we find it in Proverbs 1—9, at times, word for word; here we may assume some form of dependence. In several chapters, the exhortations are strung together successively with little or no expansion (e.g., chaps. 13; 20; 21; and 23). In the sixth chapter, the admonition not to move the borderstone runs through the entire chapter, with amplifications in between; frequently, we encounter as an amplification a portrait of the wicked man and his deeds, as in Proverbs—for example, chapters 2; 5; and 6, where ten verses are devoted to this, and chapter 11, which mentions consequences of coveting the belongings of subordinates. Additionally, here the hot-tempered person is depicted extensively. In the seventh chapter, the exhortation "Do not set your heart on riches" is substantiated by ten lines of how riches can vanish; they disappear overnight and are not there in the morning. The earth has devoured them, "they have dug a hole for themselves," they have made themselves wings like those of geese and have flown away (a depiction that is precisely the same in a Sumerian proverb). Here the description is humorous.

The expansion of the exhortations into brief portraits corresponds exactly to those of the short poems found in Proverbs. Both are indicative of the transition from oral to written tradition in the proverbs.

There are here more frequent allusions to God in the substantiations than is the case with the book of Proverbs: "Place yourself in the arms of God, then your silence will be the ruin of your adversary"; "God loves those who take care of the weak, false words are repugnant to him"; "this is an abomination to your God" resemble Proverbs.

Other Forms Appearing with Exhortations

A frequently occurring form is the comparative proverb, "better . . . than . . . " Several times a chapter concludes with such: Chapter 6: "Better is poverty from the hand of God than riches that are stockpiled" (cf. Prov. 17:1; 15:16). "Better are pieces of bread if your heart is excellent than riches with trouble" (cf. Proverbs here). Chapter 13: "Better to be praised as philanthropic than to have wealth in the storehouse." Chapter 21: "Better is a man whose advice remains to himself than one who does damage by talk."

The degree of correspondence between comparative sayings here and those in Proverbs is truly remarkable. It penetrates deeply into the realm of human understanding. Comparative proverbs occur in Egypt, Mesopotamia, Israel, and central Africa.

Proverbs of Antithesis

Chapter 4: "The hot-tempered person is like a tree that is ingrown . . . " "The quiet person is like a tree that grows in the sunlight" (cf. Psalm 1).

Contrast of God to Humans

Chapter 18: "The words that a person says are one thing; it is another thing what God does." "The tongue of a person is the rudder of a ship, and yet the Almighty is the pilot." Chapter 20: "God gives you *ma'at* when he wills." Chapter 21: "Do not say . . . , for truly you do not know the plans of God!" Chapter 25: "Do not deride the blind . . . "

From the group of proverbial statements here, only a few comparative and antithetical proverbs are adduced. Declarative and imperative sayings are also to be distinguished here, as in Proverbs 22—24 and in the sayings of other people (e.g., Batak sayings).

Also, as with the book of Proverbs, the relatively few comparisons in Amenemope are gathered almost exclusively among the declarative statements.

Allusion to God appears in two connections: as the substantiation for an exhortation, especially regarding the protection of the weak (notice, too, in Proverbs that God has also created them), and in the proverbs of antithesis, which juxtapose human and divine capacity. The sayings of the book of Proverbs point to human limitations and the knowledge of God.

VI. THE INSTRUCTION OF ONCHSHESHONQY[106]

The special significance of the teaching of Onchsheshonqy, though a relatively late writing, consists in its reflecting an early stage of development, as held by its initial translator, S. R. Glanwille. This material mirrors a less developed stage of proverbial collections. In contrast to other Egyptian wisdom literature, no principle of arrangement is here recognizable. In some respects, the compilation found in Proverbs reflects a more fully evolved developmental stage than the Onchsheshonqy collection.

Of particular interest is the narrative describing the setting. Accordingly, the author has written from prison, where he had landed as a result of political intrigue in the court over a purported plot against the pharaoh. There he wrote this as instruction for his son, piece by piece until his death, as the individual proverbs came to mind. This narrative is easily deciphered. It serves to equate itself with other Egyptian wisdom literature by being attributed to an officer in pharaoh's court. What is striking about the account is the author's claim to have written on individual clay fragments, just as the sayings came to mind. Such is a reasonable explanation for the primitive form in which we find the proverbs, strung together in a series without any connection (as in Proverbs 10—31). Occasionally, small clusters of sayings occur that fit together according to content or style. The compilation is linked to the genre of instruction by means of the court official who sits in prison and writes for the instruction of his son. Two things issue out of this narrative setting. First, the redactors of this collection were aware of its early origins and of the transition from oral to literary tradition. Second, they desired to preserve the collection in its original form (in contrast to the later wisdom writings). This would explain the notable affinity between the Onchsheshonqy collection (dating in the fifth century B.C.) and the Old Testament Proverbs. With respect to transmission, they belong roughly to the same period of history.

The collection of Onchsheshonqy (since 1896 in the British Museum) is quite voluminous. It contains twenty-seven and one-half columns of some 550 proverbs and is almost entirely preserved. The sayings are predominantly single-verse, with some double-verse. Their basic structure is that of indicative and imperative sayings. Regarding form, they reflect a less-developed construction in terms of detail. The transition from being individual sayings to their assimilation into more discursive literary contexts has not yet occurred here, as is the case in the later Egyptian wisdom writings.

The proverbs from this collection mirror a rural background, natural life in the country. It is not the world of court officials or writers in their schools; the court and attendant officials surface only in the setting narrative. The work of the farmer stands in the foreground as illustrated in the proverbs about daytime and the seasons: "Whoever does not gather wood in the summer will not be warm in the winter." When mention of the sons does occur, it comes in association with their agricultural responsibilities. Animals, both domesticated and wild, occur frequently in these sayings, as well as in the comparisons. In this way these proverbs resemble their African counterpart; also in their allusion to different kinds of grain. This proximity to rural life has already been noted by the translator S. R. Glanwille.

The categories of proverbs are reminiscent of those found in the book of Proverbs. The tendency toward separation of mere statements and words of exhortation can be seen in that both at times are mixed together but on occasion stand separately, so that a column may consist solely of statements or words of exhortation.

Comparative sayings ("better than . . . "). These occur only in the form exhibited in the book of Proverbs. They also repeatedly display the same orientation: that is, the tendency toward acquiescing to the lowly—for example, "It is better to live in your small house than . . . "

Indicative sayings, statements. "A blessing exists for . . . " (followed by a series of five sayings). "A blessing for a province is a ruler who exercises uprightness." "A blessing for a household is a wise woman."

Human observations. "A person's disposition is reflected in his face." "A thief steals in the night; during the day he is caught." "One sows, another reaps." "If you show kindness to one hundred people and only one thanks you, then some of your effort is not in vain."

Proverbs of antithesis. "A small man who acts arrogantly is greatly despised; a big man who acts modestly is respected." "The hiss of a snake means more than the braying of a donkey."

Comparisons. "A good woman of sterling character is like bread that arrives at a time of hunger" (over fifty proverbs contain the woman as a theme).

Exhortations concerning young and old, father and mother. "Do not say 'young man' to someone who is grown up!" "Serve your father and your mother so that it might go well with you!" "Render to your father and your mother respect!" "Do not despise an old man in your heart!" "Serve a wise person so that he might serve you!" "Render to the king respect and conduct yourself in his presence in a way that is proper."

Exhortations to discretion. "Do not speak hastily so that you don't stir up a scandal!" "Do not generate any excessive expenses before you have erected a storehouse!" "Better being silent than having a hasty tongue!" "Do not say the first thing that immediately comes to mind!"

Exhortations to specific behavior. "Do not be afraid to do what you are authorized to do!" "Speak the truth to everyone!" "When your enemy entreats you, don't hide!" "Don't be annoyed by a fool!" "Allow your good deed to reach the one who needs it!"

One's relationship to the deity. "Serve your God, so that he might protect you!" "Offer sacrifice and libations to God; let the fear of God be great in your heart!" "Do not pray to God and then disregard what he says!" "Lay that which preoccupies you in God's hands!" "Do a good deed and cast it in the river; when it dries up, you will find it again!"

Statements. "Every good deed is from the hand of God." "Everyone shares in the fate of God." "Nothing occurs that God has not decreed." "The directions of God are different from the thoughts of people." "When a woman lives in peace with a man, that is the will of God." "God looks into the heart."

Summary

Viewing Egyptian wisdom literature as a whole, the collection of Onchsheshonqy illustrates that the original form of the word of wisdom was the single-verse saying. The proverbs are arranged according to indicative and imperative sayings. Moreover, the compilation exhibits many proverbs that have parallels in other collections.

The proverbs speak of a person as a human without fragmenting him. It is a human frame of reference that defines these sayings and that is expressed through both the declarative and the hortatory statements. Most of these could be found in Proverbs 10—31, even to the point of loving one's enemy, and the categories of sayings are the same as in the Old Testament proverbs. These sayings even speak about God in the same fashion, without any peculiarities; the proverbs of ancient Israel also tell us that God looks into the human heart and that God's manner of guidance is different from human thoughts.[107]

VII. CONCLUSION

For the sake of comparison, we have drawn on three texts from Sumer, two from Egypt, proverbs from Africa, as well as Batak sayings from Sumatra.

Form

The earliest form of this entire extant body of collections is the series of successive individual proverbs. The earliest form of textual unit is the short proverb; it is normally single-verse and rarely double-verse. Originally the sole form of wisdom saying, it has universal significance.

The sayings examined in all the compared texts have two basic forms: indicative and imperative sayings, statements and exhortations. Our comparison to the five extrabiblical proverb collections representative of wisdom literature yields the following conclusion: in the case of the proverbs that are early in terms of their transmission history, declarative statements predominate, while imperative sayings are more numerous in the older writings, notably in Amenemope and Proverbs 1—9.

One observation resulting from this synopsis is that a phase of oral development and oral transmission (reflecting real-life usage) preceded the phase of compilation and literary tradition everywhere. Such is the case with nonliterary societies in Africa, Sumatra, and so forth. And it is still clearly recognizable in the Sumerian proverbs, in the Egyptian collection of Onchsheshonqy, in the book of Proverbs, and even in traces of Amenemope (thus A. Alt [1951]). None of these texts developed literarily from the beginning. It is quite apparent that several of the texts still have traces of their oral beginnings, for example, the Onchsheshonqy collection. Others, such as Amenemope, are further removed. Nonetheless, these texts show that where smaller or larger collections had already emerged, an oral transmission continued, as illustrated by Qohelet.

Our comparative study, to the extent that the proverbs encompass the preliterary as well as the literary phase, yields a further observation: the proverbs enjoyed their greatest significance for the community in the preliterary period; the phase of their compilation, on the other hand, exhibits a tertiary character. In terms of the history of the genre, the most critical stage for the proverb was the transition from the preliterary to literary phase. Those texts that were deliberately linked together, extending beyond the short saying (esp. the didactic poem), belong initially to the literary stage and for this reason *eo ipso* are to be seen as later.[108]

As touching the declarative sayings, one further particularity in the history of their tranmission is to be noted. In the African and Sumerian proverbs, the proverbial statement often as such does not possess a fixed form. Not infrequently it resembles a simple statement, not unlike a description. Then, in a later stage, it takes on a fixed, more defined form.

Content

During the oral stage, content is determined by the function of the proverb in its usage. It originally had foremost a social function. In the literary phase, this function is divorced from the saying, since the proverb has lost its original context.

The comparisons are to be relevant because of their abundance. In African proverbs, this is particularly the case for the animal comparisons, which simultaneously say something about the human being.

The proverbs also have the function of entertaining. They represent the art of cultivated discourse, in which humor plays a very real part. Wisdom is related to wit.

The categories, particular style, and subject matter of proverbs are astonishingly similar to one another, conditioned by the similarities in mode of living and cultural milieu. Comparative proverbs, proverbs of value judgment ("better than . . . "), and proverbs of observation and experience exist among all groups, since critical assessment is part and parcel of living together with others.

Imperative sayings are to be found among all the groups, yet the exhortations can be extremely diverse. All groups make a distinction between general exhortations and those that have a specifically didactic character, as illustrated in the introduction of the teaching of Amenemope and Proverbs 1—9.

A striking manner of speaking about God is also worthy of note. Mention of God occurs only in the sense of how he affects a human's everyday life. Anything specifically theological is absent. Allusion to God is very human in character.

VIII. EPILOGUE

Only after concluding this work did I receive a copy of L. Naré, *Proverbes salomoniens et proverbes mossi,* a comparison of the sayings in the book of Proverbs and those of the Masai people of West Africa—proverbs written in the author's language. This examination confirms the notable proximity of a portion of Proverbs to the sayings of an African people in a preliterary phase. In his conclusion (pp. 303–6), the author writes: "In form and content there are ample parallels; this is especially the case in form as compared to content. In both sets of proverbs the sayings are the immediate natural reflex of a social milieu, which for both is agriculture. Similar themes occur repeatedly: chastising the sluggard and the liar, the boisterous woman, the tyrannical king (chieftain). In both we find the observation of natural and human phenomena, both of which are expressed in similar ways. Profound sayings are to be found in both; both 'condemn evil in all its forms and encourage the good; like the biblical proverbs they know God not only as the Creator of the universe, but also as the savior of the poor and the supreme guarantee of the moral order.'" The author draws a very noteworthy conclusion: "From this point of view, biblical wisdom seems to have been built on the ground of a common human wisdom."

ABBREVIATIONS

ANET	*Ancient Near Eastern Texts*, ed. J. B. Pritchard (1950; 1969 [3d ed.])
Bibl. Or.	*Bibliotheca orientalis*
Bibl. Stud.	Biblische Studien
BN	Biblische Notizen
BZAW	Beihefte zur *ZAW*
FS	Festschrift
HSAT	Heilige Schriften der Alten Testament
ICC	International Critical Commentary
JAOS	*Journal of the American Oriental Society*
JBL	*Journal of Biblical Literature*
JQuR	*Jewish Quarterly Review*
OBO	Orbis biblicus et orientalis
SAIW	*Studies in Ancient Israelite Wisdom*, ed. J. L. Crenshaw (1976)
SBL	Society of Biblical Literature
THAT	*Theologische Handbuch zum Alten Testament*
ThB	Theologische Bücherei
ThLZ	*Theologische Literaturzeitung*
ThR	*Theologische Rundschau*
VT	*Vetus Testamentum*
VTSup	Vetus Testamentum, Supplements
VuF	*Verkündigung und Forschung*
WMANT	Wissenschaftliche Monographien zum Alten und Neuen Testament
WO	*Die Welt des Orients*
ZAW	*Zeitschrift für die alttestamentliche Wissenschaft*

NOTES

1. This, or something similar, is maintained in the literature by many commentators. Here there is no dispute.
1a. Biblical references containing only chapter and verse designations are always from the biblical book of Proverbs.
2. For this reason, generally speaking, any effort to define wisdom comprehensively, as it relates to particular texts, is often not even attempted.
3. Hence the definition of Lord Russel: "The wisdom of many, the wit of one" (cited in J. M. Thompson, 1974).
4. That there existed a late stage for proverbs in advanced cultures is evidenced by the fact that it is usually included as a supplement to most larger works.
5. Accordingly, R. E. Murphy (1978) accurately points to the growth in literature from the time of W. Baumgartner's survey (1933–51) up to more recently. This is reflected in the survey of J. L. Crenshaw (1976). Wisdom and wisdom literature as categories have been used in this sense since the work of J. Meinhold in 1908. For further, more recent surveys of the literature, most of which deal with a portion of past work in this area, see E. Gerstenberger (1969), J. L. Crenshaw (1976), B. Gemser (1976), R. E. Murphy (1975; 1978), M. Gilbert (1979), C. R. Fontaine (1982), P. Doll (1985). Gemser and O. Kaiser (1984) emphasize in particular the significance of J. Fichtner's alternate view, as well as the earlier essay of W. Zimmerli (1933), for the later work of H. Gese and G. von Rad, in which "structure" or purpose (*Ordnung*) plays an important role for wisdom. Works that include a brief section on the history of research, with particular focus on the question of the origin of wisdom and its relationship to folk sayings, include F. W. Golka, C. R. Fontaine, and P. Doll. See also C. Westermann, *Forschungsgeschichte zur Weisheit, 1950–1990* (forthcoming).
6. I wish to thank Prof. Dr. Assmann for the valuable suggestions on the significance of the Egyptian *ma'at* (from a letter dated 10 July 1988).
7. Cf. André Jolles (1930), 155: "Jede Erfahrung wird jedesmal selbständig begriffen."
8. So esp. W. Zimmerli.

9. C. Westermann, *Ausgewählte Psalmen* (1984), 186ff.; G. von Rad (1970): ". . . das einfache Staunen über Tatsächliches und Gegensätzliches; in ihm ereignet sich Erkenntnis."

9a. Westermann's explanation of 20:5b is scarcely correct. The wise person is the one who understands that in order to realize his plans, which are hidden from others, they must be made visible by deeds and cannot remain forever hidden. The person of 5b is therefore one of the group referred to in 5a (also against Ringgren, *Commentary*).

10. Among primitive peoples, proverbs that speak of the animal kingdom are abundant; this applies as well to the early Sumerian proverbs (see the Appendix).

11. The text is uncertain. Another rendering is that of Rothstein: "Arglistig mehr als alles ist das Herz (und bösartig ist es); wer aber kennt es aus?"

11a. Westermann's interpretation of 27:17 is improbable. The contrast is not between hardness and softness but sharpness and bluntness. And that signifies the contrast between useful and unuseful. Thus we need for others to be "useful," one who helps to keep the community strong. The proverb has a social thrust. It originated in a small community. It is not referring to people's "behavior" (against Ringren, *Commentary*) but rather aims at the whole of life.

12. Paradoxes occur also in African proverbs (see the Appendix—e.g.: "There is a silence that has a powerful voice").

13. W. McKane (1979) translates this "Ruthless anger and floodwaters of rage, but who can stand before jealousy?"

14. This proverb has the form of a comparison, and it causes the listener reflectively to confront the proverb. This, too, is intended to demonstrate a polarity.

15. See Qohelet 3.

16. If we consider this correspondence alone, to which many others could be added, we can no longer entertain the verdict of H. D. Preuss (1987) that the book of Proverbs does not belong to the canon.

17. Such is the intent behind W. A. Beardslee's remark: "A proverb is a story" (1970, 65).

18. Many commentators have acknowledged that a proverb can be a story in the sense of being an independent, self-contained unit. When this is recognized, the frequent attempts at constructing a literary context out of the numerous proverbs placed together must be acknowledged as misguided.

19. When C. R. Fontaine and C. Westermann speak of the social function of proverbs, then 15:30, which links the observation with the effect of the proverb on the community, may serve as a prime example.

19a. Ringgren correctly explains: "What one acquires through deception can indeed appear pleasant at first. But no blessing rests upon it."

20. W. McKane (1979): "Speech is seen as an action, which has constructive and destructive possibilities."

21. See esp. W. Bühlmann, *Vom rechten Reden und Schweigen: Studien zu Prov 10—31,* OBO 12 (1976).

22. See above.

23. Here also the social function of the proverbs is clearly seen.

24. For a more detailed discussion, see C. Westermann, "Das Schoene im Alten Testament," ThB 73 (Munich: Kaiser, 1964), 119–37.

25. The case of a writer looking down on other vocations (esp. working with one's hands), such as is found in an Egyptian satire (*ANET* [1969], 432–34), is unknown in ancient Israel.

26. The proverbs about the idle and the diligent demonstrate that proverbs concern an entirely different dimension of life than laws—in Israel and elsewhere. If there are no legal proscriptions of idleness, the reason is that the contrast between idle and diligent is self-regulating in the realm of living. Excessive idleness is restricted first of all by its consequences and second by scorn, which "singles out the individual." This is sufficient.

27. Even the notion that these proverbs are concerned with a social order that is to govern the relationship of poor and rich together is fully absent here.

27a. The text "in his imagination" is uncertain. It can also mean "in his background" (see Ringgren, *Commentary*). Then 18:11 does not go beyond 10:15. Therefore, no great conclusions should be drawn from the expression "in his imagination"!

28. The notion that "he will reward him for what he has done" is folk wisdom and is preserved in the expression "God will pay back" or "for God's sake" down to the present.

28a. The popular proverb "Whoever gives, he takes" corresponds to 11:25!

29. When we speak of parallelism, we are referring only to these literary constructions and not to proverbs of antithesis, such as 22:2. In this case, the actual saying itself consists of an antithesis; it is double-verse because it expresses a contrast. To denote this as "antithetical parallelism" is inappropriate. Such a designation is accurate only in multiple-verse compositions, where a line is constructed by means of antithesis, such as in Psalm 1:6: "For Yahweh knows the way of the righteous, but the way of the wicked errs."

30. When H. D. Preuss (1987) writes, "Die Bildungsweisheit . . . gehört zu den Besitzenden . . . so wird immer wieder der Vorzug des Reichtums herausgestellt" (41), the proverb group concerning the poor and the rich is being misread. When it is said, in 18:23, "A poor man pleads for mercy, but a rich man answers harshly," is a moral judgment being made about the rich? The poor–rich proverb group is explained in a proper fashion by P. Doll (1985), 16–29.

31. When J. L. Crenshaw (1974) and W. H. Schmidt (1979) conjecture that proverbs arose within the family, no traces of such are existent. To be sure, one particular group of proverbs has its origins unquestionably within the family: the farewell exhortation of the parents to the children as they leave home (see the section on words of exhortation). This particular *Sitz im Leben* is also recognizable in a number of Batak sayings (see the Appendix).

32. Calling attention to the operation of God in the context of business and legal process, such as we encounter in the proverbs about the poor and the rich, coincides with the notion of God's work found in the Prophets. God stands on the side of the lowly and the disadvantaged.

33. This category of proverbs demonstrates clearly that the designation "intellectual tradition" by R. N. Whybray (1974) is inappropriate.

34. This group of proverbs conveys the political wisdom that the king is not to be esteemed in absolute terms; rather, he is acknowledged only in his function, in his justice working. The majesty and honor of kingship are never mentioned here.

34a. Proverbs 31:8 became especially important to Dietrich Bonhoeffer when the National Socialists, in 1933–34, silenced whole groups of people and gave new tasks to the church in Germany.

35. The king and kingship were ascribed significant worth, particularly in the expression "kingdom of God" in the later stages of the Old Testament and are strengthened in the New Testament. Mention of God as found in the proverbs is far removed from such reverence; the focus, rather, is on the king in a sober and restricting way, at times even critically.

36. J. M. Thompson (1974), 67: "There is a democratic spirit in the book of Proverbs."

37. It is indeed not incidental that such sayings lauding the messenger are found in early Sumerian proverbs.

38. So also G. von Rad (1970), 131–50.

39. Ibid.

40. Here see J. Blenkinsopp, *Wisdom and Law in the Old Testament* (1983).

41. Gemser's translation of 26:28 is probably better: "Falsche Zunge haβt ihren 'Besitzer' und glatter Mund bereitet Sturz." This saying allows one to speak of a cause-and-effect mentality.

42. No attempt is made in the characterizations to distance the offender or the malicious person from the community. This would be illusory. The characterizations describe things as they really are.

43. We see the particular wisdom of these proverbs involving the contentious in that they do not flatly exhort people simply to avoid conflict and be peaceful; rather, they make us aware of the human tendency. They remind us of the human proclivity toward strife and what instigates it.

44. This proverb summarizes Theodor Fontane's novel *Grete Minde*.

45. This is one of those proverbs that one must ponder in order to understand it. The second part encompasses two levels: as such, the pious person has kept himself, yet in a crucial situation, he is afraid to resist the person who is about to cause damage. The failing of such an individual is compared to fouling in the realm of natural creation and is depicted in a twofold manner. A spring offers life to the thirsty; yet when it really counts, the source is muddied. It is necessary to allow the individual proverbs to communicate.

46. "The legs of a man hanging limp" is not to disparage the handicapped; rather, it tells the fool what he has made of himself.

47. This proverb belongs to the group dealing with failure. This portrait concerns the culture of speech.

48. The narrative about Nabal and Abigail in 1 Samuel 25 assumes the proverb of antithesis.

49. The situation being mirrored in this proverb finds its setting in the city. That this is the case is expressly stated.

50. Wisdom and folly manifest themselves in economics as well. Saving and squandering are a part of this.

51. One aspect of wisdom is a discerning view of others. The simple-minded person is portrayed as foolish.

52. The despising of a deed or a person is not being censured here; rather, what is important is how one reacts [to a situation].

53. Here again we encounter the concern for the culture of discourse.

53a. Proverbs 25:28 belongs here as well: "Like a city with breached walls is the one who has no control over himself." The hot-tempered person himself beats a hole in the wall that protected him and harms himself. The saying does not go so far as to say that his lack of self-control endangers the community (against C. Westermann in "Weisheit und praktische Theologie," in *Pastoral-Theologie* [1990], 517).

54. This proverb is a variation on the statement "The fear of Yahweh is the beginning of wisdom."

55. This group of proverbs also illustrates that the expression "intellectual tradition" does not apply.

56. It is probable that an earlier collection had been extended by means of sayings of this type.

57. O. R. Johnson (1955) has demonstrated that the fundamental meaning of *māšāl* is comparison.

58. One can put this assertion to the test by contrasting the comparisons in the book of Ezekiel with those of Proverbs.

59. Here a frequent literary device of the proverbs is employed: the exaggeration. For a more thorough discussion, see W. A. Beardslee (1970). The bearing of coals is an act of contrition, a sign of remorse: the "enemy" confesses his guilt.

59a. The proverb in 16:32 originated in a time in which the one who conquered the city was hailed as war hero and victor. The proverb says that, contrary to customary opinion and the standards of later history writing, the patient one who controls himself is better than the celebrated war hero. Patience takes precedence over the glory of war!

60. The question of good and evil here does not lead to a teaching of fundamental values, as G. von Rad has observed on occasion. He notes: "Eine Quintessenz der Ethik Israel's findet sich nicht, sie ist prinzipienlos" (110). A proverb of value judgment takes into account the actual situation. In this sense, the once-for-all fixed principle shows its weakness to the extent that it is removed from the situation.

61. H. J. Hermisson (1968) designates 11:31; 15:11; and 19:10 as "Sprüche der Steigerung."

62. See G. Vanoni, "W. Richter zum 60. Geburtstag," BN 35 (1986), 102, for sources.

63. These are generally designated as numerical proverbs but are really poems, a further expansion of the proverb.

64. See H. W. Wolff, *Amos geistige Heimat* (1964), 24–30, where the numerical proverb as a whole is dealt with.

65. Here the proverbs reflect a similarity to Genesis 1—11. On the relationship of the human being to the animal kingdom in the creation narrative, see Gen. 2:19–20.

66. See also *Genesis I*, Biblischer Kommentar (1974), 8–23.

67. "The Use of *'ashre* in the Old Testament," ThB 55 (1974), 191–95.

68. These proverbs of antithesis involving the righteous and the wicked belong to the later wisdom. Their form is borrowed.

69. So also R. B. Y. Scott (1971), 161.

70. It is unnecessary here to go into the related discussion.

71. Hence, there can be no tolerance. It is certainly not accidental that G. von Rad does not cite a single one of these proverbs.

72. For further discussion, see W. McKane, *Commentary,* 400ff. Ringgren assumes that what is meant here is someone innocent who has been declared guilty.

73. Thus the suggestion of C. Kayatz (1968) that the Egyptian texts were already being borrowed in early Israel.

74. Notably Jesus Sirach.

75. So also W. McKane (1979), among others.

76. It is noteworthy in the exhortations that both the concept of a model as well as admonitions to outstanding performance are absent. These, rather, parallel Greek thought: "Always being the best and outstanding among others."

77. See the Instruction of Onchsheshonqy. W. McKane points to this in his commentary (1979).

78. When, in this instruction, esp. the teacher's exhortation, parental training is continued—whereby the teacher assumes parental authority—parental admonition is already presupposed. Tobit 4 shows evidence of this; we also find it in the hortatory sayings of Batak (see the Appendix). Such would therefore presuppose for the type of exhortation occurring in Proverbs 22—24 a prehistory of oral admonition that had as its subject the father and mother. To this extent, the suggestion of J. L. Crenshaw and W. H. Schmidt, i.e., that the proverbs, specifically words of exhortation, were rooted in the family.

79. The expansion of a proverb into a poem also occurs in words of ridicule—e.g., 1 Sam. 17:44 and Isa. 23:16.

79a. The prayer in 30:7–9 impresses with its humility and clarity. The petitioner knows how vulnerable to temptation he is and therefore asks God to protect him from both poverty and riches. He knows that riches can harden the human heart and deceive him into pride and spiritual self-sufficiency. Bitter poverty, on the other hand, can drive one to theft and therefore to the breaking of God's command. The petitioner cannot secure himself against these threats and asks God for enough earthly goods, but not too much.

80. The expression of the Preacher "I saw that . . . " would seem to confirm that proverbial observations constitute their own category in the book of Proverbs.

80a. Qohelet 8:12b–13 is a later, redactional expansion that contradicts Qohelet's theology.

81. Thus, the Preacher confirms that the proverbs of antithesis concerning the righteous and the wicked in the book of Proverbs are a secondary addition. The same applies to the absence of instructional wisdom with the Preacher.

81a. Qohelet 11:1 is probably not an admonition (against Westermann) but a word about how things in life slip away from us in an unforeseen and surprising way. Humanity does not have under its control the things of life! (Also against W. Zimmerli, *Commentary.*)

82. The wisdom of the Preacher bears a closer resemblance to the proverbial wisdom found in Proverbs 10—31 than to the didactic wisdom of Proverbs 1—9.

83. Judges 8:2, 21; 1 Sam. 16:7; 24:14; 1 Kings 20:11.

84. See the recension of C. R. Fontaine, cited by F. W. Golka in *Bibl. Or.* (1984): 162–64.

85. J. P. M. van der Ploeg, in "Le Psalm 119 et la sagesse" (1979), characterizes Psalm 119 as "un contique sur la tōrāh"; the psalm is sui generis.

86. J. Luyten, in "Psalm 73 and Wisdom" (1979), initially offers a helpful survey of current works done on the wisdom psalms. He then investigates formal wisdom devices in Psalm 73 (pp. 64–72). Following Pardue, he meticulously scrutinizes the elements comprising wisdom. He notes the resemblance to the book of Job yet does not classify the psalm as a "wisdom psalm": "Psalm 73 has a character of its own." The first-person speech is similar to the Preacher, but the psalm more closely resembles the book of Job. Psalm 73 is essentially the writer's reflection that presupposes the motif of the righteous and the wicked and their fate.

87. The summons to listen in 34:2 assumes the didactic poetry of Proverbs 1—9. In Job 34, a sage is addressing other sages, evidenced by a later phase of wisdom.

88. A transition can also be identified in the proverbs of instruction, those extolling wisdom, in individual proverbs about the foolish and the wise, and in certain comparative proverbs. In each of these cases, the subject is abstract wisdom.

89. R. Bultmann, *Die Geschichte der synoptischen Tradition* (1921, 1970 [4th ed.]), 73–113.

90. This is one of numerous examples showing the importance of distinguishing between proverbial wisdom and didactic wisdom.

91. M. Küchler, *Frühjüdische Weisheitstraditionen,* OBO (1979), 157–75.

92. This proverb belongs to the "God as Human Creator" group.

93. Thus, it is erroneous to want to interpret these sayings in the Synoptic Gospels as "christological" or "eschatological."

94. It is astonishing that, to my knowledge, attempts at a biblical theology in this regard have not been undertaken up to the present.

95. W. A. Beardslee, "Use of the Proverb in the Synoptic Gospels," *Interpretation* 24 (1970): 61–73.

96. Ibid., 65.

97. Ibid., 71.

98. C. Westermann, "Weisheit im Sprichwort," reproduced in *ThR* 55 (1974), 149–61.

99. More recently also F. W. Golka (1989), 149–65.

100. On proverbs in general, consult W. Mieder and A. Dundes, *The Wisdom of Many: Essays on the Proverb* (New York, 1981).

101. For guidance to literature that pertains to African proverbs, I am grateful to the library of the Basler Mission.

102. In *Dictionary of the Ewe Language,* written by my father, D. Westermann (1954), most of the texts that illustrate words are proverbs.

103. Examples of royal proverbs are given. See F. W. Golka (1989).

104. See C. R. Fontaine (1982).

105. A. A. Sitompul, "Weisheitliche Mahnsprüche und prophetische Mahnrede im Al-

ten Testament auf dem Hintergrund der Mahnungen im Leben der Tobabatak auf Sumatra" (Diss., University of Mainz, 1967). I am grateful to Prof. H. W. Wolff for bringing this dissertation to my attention.

106. So B. Gemser, "The Instruction of Onch-Sheshonqy and Biblical Wisdom Literature," VTSup 7 (1960): 102–28.

107. On Onchsheshonqy, see, more recently, H. Brunner, *Altägyptische Weisheit* (1988), 257ff.

108. For a different view, see C. Kayatz (1968).

A SELECT CHRONOLOGICAL
BIBLIOGRAPHY

1910–1940

1908   Meinhold, J. *Die Weisheit Israels in Spruch, Sage und Dichtung.*

1913   Eissfeldt, O. *Der Maschal im Alten Testament.* BZAW 24. Giessen: Töpelmann.

1921   Bultmann, R. *Die Geschichte der synoptischen Tradition.* 4th ed., 1970.

1923   Steuernagel, D. Die Sprüche. HSAT.

1930   Hempel, J. *Althebräische Literatur, Sprüche,* 44–55.

1930   Jolles, A. *Einfache Formen, Der Spruch.* 2d ed., 1956.

1933   Gunkel, H., and Begrich, J. *Einleitung in die Psalmen, Weisheitsdichtung.*

1933   Baumgartner, W. "Die israelitische Weisheits-Literatur." *ThR* 5: 259–300.

1933   Zimmerli, W. "Zur Struktur der alttestamentlichen Weisheit." *ZAW* 51: 177–204.

1933   Fichtner, J. *Die altorientalische Weisheit in ihrer israelitisch-jüdischen Ausprägung.*

1936   Schmidt, J. *Studien zur Stilistik der alttestamentlichen Spruchliteratur.*

1939–40   Gordis, R. "Quotations in Wisdom-Literature." *JQuR* 30: 123–47.

1950–1960

1950   Pritchard, J. B., ed. *Ancient Near Eastern Texts.* Princeton: Princeton University Press. 3d ed., 1969.

1951   Alt, A. "Die Weisheit Salomos." *ThLZ* 76: 133–44.

1953   Köhler, L. *Der hebräische Mensch.*

1955   In Noth, M., and Thomas, D. W., eds. *Wisdom in Israel and in the Ancient Near East.* Society for Old Testament Study in association with editorial board of *Vetus Testamentum:*

Alt, A. "Zur literarischen Analyse der Weisheit des Amenemope," 16–25.
de Boer, P. "The Counsellor," 42–71.
Johnson, A. R. "Māšāl," 162–69.
Lindblom, J. "Wisdom in the OT-Prophets," 192–204.

Mowinckel, S. "Psalms and Wisdom," 205–24.

Porteous, N. W. "Royal Wisdom," 247–61.

Scott, R. B. Y. "Solomon and the Beginning of Wisdom in Israel," 262–79.

1957 von Rad, G. *Theologie des Alten Testaments*. 2 vols. 6th ed., 1969.

1958 Gese, H. *Lehre und Wirklichkeit der Weisheit.*

1960–1970

1960 Gemser, B. "The Instruction of Onch-Sheshonqy and Biblical Wisdom Literature." VTSup. 7: 102–28.

1960 Humbert, P. "Le Substantif tō 'ēbā . . . dans l'AT." ZAW 72: 217–37.

1961 Scott, R. B. Y. "Folk Proverbs of the Ancient Near East." *Royal Society of Canada* 15: 47–56.

1962 Skladny, U. *Die ältesten Spruchsammlungen in Israel.*

1962 Murphy, R. E. "A Consideration of the Classification 'Wisdom Psalms.'" VTSup 9: 156–67.

1963 Zimmerli, W. "Ort und Grenze der Weisheit im Rahmen der alttestamentlichen Theologie." ThB 19, 300–315. Munich: Kaiser.

1964 Wolff, H. W. *Amos geistige Heimat*. WMANT 18. Neukirchen-Vluyn: Neukirchener Verlag.

1964 Westermann, C. *Grundformen prophetischer Rede*. 5th ed., 1978. Pp. 70–91.

1965 Gerstenberger, E. *Wesen und Herkunft des apodiktischen Rechts*. WMANT 20. Neukirchen-Vluyn: Neukirchener Verlag.

1965 Whybray, R. N. *Wisdom in Proverbs*. Studies in Biblical Theology 45. Naperville, Ill.: Allenson.

1965 Murphy, R. E. Die Weisheitsliteratur des Alten Testaments, Concil, 855–62.

1966 Schmid, H. H. *Wesen und Geschichte der Weisheit*. BZAW 101. Giessen: Töpelmann.

1968 Hermisson, H. J. *Studien zur israelitischen Spruchweisheit*. WMANT 28. Neukirchen-Vluyn: Neukirchener Verlag.

1968 Kayatz, C. *Studien zu Proverbien 1—9*. WMANT 22. Neukirchen-Vluyn: Neukirchener Verlag.

1969 Kayatz, C. *Einführung in die alttestamentliche Weisheit*. Bibl. Stud. 55. Neukirchen-Vluyn: Neukirchener Verlag.

1969 Gerstenberger, E. "Zur alttestamentlichen Weisheit." VuF: 28–45.

1969 Crenshaw, J. L. "Method in Determining Wisdom Influence upon 'Historical' Literature." *JBL* 88, 2: 129–42.

1970–1980

1970 von Rad, G. *Weisheit in Israel*. 3d ed., 1985.

1970 Beardslee, W. A. "Use of the Proverb in the Synoptic Gospels." *Interpretation* 24: 61–73.

1970   Finnegan, R. "Proverbs." In *Oral Literature in Africa,* 389–425. Oxford: Oxford University Press.

1971   Westermann, C. "Weisheit im Sprichwort." Reprinted in ThB 55, 149–61. Munich: Kaiser, 1974.

1971   Scott, R. B. Y. *The Way of Wisdom in the Old Testament.* New York: Macmillan.

1972   Lang, B. *Die weisheitliche Lehrrede.* Stuttgarter Bibelstudien 54.

1974   Crenshaw, J. L. "Wisdom." In *Old Testament Form-Criticism,* chap. 4.

1974   Whybray, R. N. *The Intellectual Tradition in the Old Testament.* BZAW 135. Berlin: de Gruyter.

1974   Thompson, J. M. *The Form and Function of Proverbs in Ancient Israel.*

1975   Murphy, R. E. "Wisdom and Yahwism." In FS McKenzie, 117–26.

1976   Bühlmann, W. *Vom rechten Reden und Schweigen, Prov 10—31.* OBO 12.

1976   In Crenshaw, J. L., ed. *Studies in Ancient Israelite Wisdom.* New York: Ktav:
        Crenshaw, J. L. "Prolegomenon," 1–35.
        Fohrer, G. "Sophia," 63–83.
        Würthwein, E. "Egyptian Wisdom and the OT," 113–33.
        Gemser, B. "The Instruction of Onch-Sheshonqy," 134–60.
        Gemser, B. "The Spiritual Structure of Biblical Aphoristic Wisdom," 134–60.
        Priest, J. F. "Where Is Wisdom to Be Placed?" 281–88.
        Crenshaw, J. L. "Popular Questioning of the Justice of God," 380–95.

1977   In FS W. Zimmerli.
        Keller, C. A. "Zum sog. Vergeltungsglauben im Proverbienbuch," 223–38.
        Rendtorff, R. "Geschichtliches und weisheitliches Denken im Alten Testament," 344–53.

1977   Müller, H. P. "Die weisheitliche Lehrerzählung im Alten Testament." *WO* 9: 77–98.

1978   In Gammie, J. G., ed. *Israelite Wisdom: Theological and Literary Essays in Honor of Samuel Terrien.*
        Murphy, R. E. "Wisdom Theses and Hypotheses," 35–42.
        Hermisson, H. J. "Observations on the Creation-Theology in Wisdom," 43–57.
        Humphreys, W. L. "The . . . Wise Courtier in the Proverbs," 177–90.

1978   Beyerlin, W., ed. *Near Eastern Religious Texts Relating to the Old Testament,* Old Testament Library. Philadelphia: Westminster.

1978   Mieder W., ed. *Ergebnisse der Sprichwortforschung.*

1979   In Gilbert, M., ed. *La Sagesse de l'Ancien Testament.* Louvain: Louvain University Press:
        Cazelles, H. "Les Nouvelles Études sur Sumer et Mari," 17–27.
        Brekelmans, C. "Wisdom Influence in Deuteronomy," 28–38.
        Luyten, J. "Psalm 73 and Wisdom," 55–81.
        van der Ploeg, J. P. M. "Le Psalm 119 et la sagesse," 82–87.
        Crenshaw, J. L. "Questions, dictons et épreuves impossibles," 96–111.
        Whybray, R. N. "Yahweh-Sayings . . . in Prov 10—22," 153–65.
        McKane, W. "Functions of Language and Objections of Discourse," 166–85.

           Lang, B. "Schule und Unterricht im alten Israel," 186–201.

           Marbök, J. "Sir 38f., der schriftgelehrte Weise," 293–316.

1979   Küchler, M. *Frühjüdische Weisheitstraditionen.* OBO.

1979   Schmidt, W. H. "Die Spruchweisheit." In *Einführung in das Alte Testament,* 320–26.

1980–1989

1981   Murphy, R. E. "Hebrew Wisdom." *JAOS* 101, 1: 21–34.

1981   Crenshaw, J. L. *Old Testament Wisdom: An Introduction.* Atlanta: John Knox Press.

1981   Williams, J. G. *Those Who Ponder Proverbs: Aphoristic Thinking and Biblical Literature.* Sheffield.

1982   Fontaine, C. R. *Traditional Sayings in the Old Testament.* Sheffield, England: Almond Press.

1983   Rendtorff, R. *Das Alte Testament. Eine Einführung,* 114–18.

1983   Blenkinsopp, J. *Wisdom and Law in the Old Testament.* Oxford: Oxford University Press.

1983   Golka, F. "Die israelitische Weisheitsschule oder . . . ," *VT* 33: 257–70.

1984   Kaiser, O. *Einleitung in das Alte Testament,* 366–82.

1984   Plöger, O. *Sprüche Salomos.* Book 7, Einleitung.

1985   Murphy, R. E. "Wisdom and Creation." *JBL* 104, 1: 3–11.

1985   Doll, P. *Menschenschöpfung und Weltschöpfung in der alttestamentlichen Weisheit.* Stuttgarter Bibelstudien 117.

1985–86   Westermann, C. *Genesis,* Continental Commentary. 3 vols. Minneapolis.

1986   Vanoni, G. Volkssprichwort und Jahweethos (zu Prov 15, 16). BN, 73–108. Munich.

1986   Golka, F. W. "Die Königs- und Hofsprüche und der Ursprung der israelitischen Weisheit." *VT* 36, 1:13–36.

1986   Kutsch, E. "Weisheitsspruch und Prophetenwort (zu Jes 9, 22f.)." In FS E. Kutsch, 198–215.

1986   Naré, L. *Proverbes salomoniens et proverbes mossi (zu Prov 25—29).*

1986   McKane, W. *Jeremiah: Chapters 1–25, Vol. 1,* ICC.

1987   Preuss, H. D. *Einführung in die alttestamentliche Weisheit.*

1987   Murphy, E. "Die Weisheit des Alten Testaments." *Word and World* 3.

1988   Hildebrandt, T. "Compositional Units in Proverbs 10—29." *JBL* 107, 2: 207–24.

1988   van Leeuwen, R. C. "Context and Meaning in Proverbs 25—27." SBL Diss. Series 96.

1989   Golka, F. W. "Die Flecken des Leoparden." In FS C. Westermann, 149–65.